MW00364195

Slavery and Rice Culture in Low Country Georgia, 1750–1860

SLAVERY AND RICE CULTURE IN LOW COUNTRY GEORGIA 1750–1860

Julia Floyd Smith

THE UNIVERSITY OF TENNESSEE PRESS
Knoxville

Manufactured in the United States of America.
Cloth: 1st printing, 1985; 2nd printing, 1987.
Paper: 1st printing, 1992.
The paper in this book meets the minimum requirements of the American National Standard for Permanence of Paper for Printed Library Materials.
∞ The binding materials have been chosen for strength and durability.

Library of Congress Cataloging in Publication Data

Smith, Julia Floyd, 1914—
Slavery and rice culture in low country Georgia. 1750—1860
Bibliography: p.
Includes index.
1. Slavery—Georgia—Condition of slaves. 2. Rice trade—Georgia—History. 3. Plantation life—Georgia—History. 4. Georgia—History—1775–1865. I. Title.
E445.G3S65 1985 975.8'00496073 84-27063
ISBN 0-87049-462-7 (cloth: alk. paper)
ISBN 0-87049-731-6 (pbk.: alk. paper)

To the memory of
my children, Bonnie and Harry,
and my mother, Julia Floyd

CONTENTS

Illustrations ix
Tables xi
Preface xiii
Introduction 3

PART ONE: PRODUCTION OF RICE

Chapter One Tidewater Culture in the Colonial Era 15
Chapter Two Expansion of Slavery and Profitability of Tidewater Plantations in the Nineteenth Century 30
Chapter Three The Labor of Low Country Slaves 45
Chapter Four Overseers and Drivers 64
Chapter Five The Factorage System and Plantation Supply 76

PART TWO: THE SLAVES

Chapter Six The Slave Trade, International and Domestic 93
Chapter Seven Care, Maintenance, and Health of Low Country Slaves 113

Chapter Eight Marching to Zion: The Religion of Slaves in Coastal Georgia 141
Chapter Nine Slave Culture on the Georgia Coast 166
Chapter Ten Slave Resistance, Free Negroes, and Racial Attitudes in Coastal Georgia 183
Conclusion 207
Appendix A. Agricultural and Population Statistics for Low Country Georgia 211
Appendix B. Noted Rice Planters of Coastal Georgia 219
Bibliography 227
Index COMPILED BY JULIUS ARIAIL 252

ILLUSTRATIONS

1.	Regional Map of Georgia	16
2.	Percentage of Slaves to Total Population, 1860	33
3.	Plantations Producing More than 100,000 Pounds of Rice Annually, 1850–1860	38
4.	Wild Heron, 3,400-acre Estate of Frances Henry McLeod	39
5.	A Rice Plantation in Operation on the Ogeechee River near Savannah, Georgia	47
6.	"Aunt Phebe," a Former Rice Plantation Slave in South Carolina	51
7.	A Sheaf of Rice	52
8.	An Outside Drainage Ditch Leading Away from Wild Heron's Rice Fields	53
9.	The Winnowing House	56
10.	Mansion Designed by William Jay in 1818 for Richard Richardson	79
11.	Side View and Balcony of the Richardson Mansion	80
12.	The Firm of Robert Habersham and Company on Factor's Walk	82
13.	A Rear View of the Old Factorage and Commerce Houses, Savannah, River Street	83
14.	Charles Spalding's Tabby Slave Houses at the Thickets	120
15.	Slave Houses on Henry McAlpin's Hermitage Plantation	123
16.	Former Slaves Who Continued to Live on Hermitage Plantation After the Civil War	124

17. "Aunt Lucy," Oldest of Former Slaves at Hermitage Plantation 125
18. Slave house Still Standing Near Owner's Residence on Grove Point Plantation 127
19. Interior of Slave House 128
20. Slave Houses made of Tabby on Saint Catherines Island 129
21. Tabby Slave House on James Hamilton Couper's Hamilton Plantation 131
22. Liverpool Hazzard, Former Slave of Pierce Butler 134
23. Ruins of the Slave Hospital near Thomas Butler King's Retreat Plantation, St. Simons Island 135
24. A Baptism at Pin Point near the Montgomery River on the Outskirts of Savannah 144
25. The Bryan Street African Baptist Church 147
26. The First African Baptist Church 150
27. Detail of the Left Front Interior of the First African Baptist Church 151
28. The Second African Baptist Church 152
29. St. Stephens Episcopal Church 155
30. A "Praise House" in Liberty County 160
31. Interior of the "Praise House" 161
32. A Former Slave of Coastal Georgia Making a Casting Net 169
33. Uncle Ed McIver, a Former Slave of McIntosh County 170
34. Matilda Beasley, the First Black in Georgia to Become a Catholic Nun 198
35. Lavinia Tompkins 201
36. Her Descendants, the Harris Family of Camden County 202

TABLES

Table 1. Slave Importation into Georgia from America and the West Indies, 1755–1765 94

Table 2. Slave Importation into Georgia from America, the West Indies, and Africa, 1766–1771 95

Table A-1. Agricultural Statistics for Lower Piedmont, the Coastal Strip, and the Whole State, 1860 212

Table A-2. Barrels of Rice Exported from Charleston and Savannah, 1755–1773 213

Table A-3. Quantities and Prices of Rice Shipped from the United States, 1712–1860 214

Table A-4. Population Figures by Counties in 1790. 216

Table A-5. Population Growth in the Rice Coast Counties from 1800 to 1860 217

Table A-6. Total Population Growth of Georgia from 1800 to 1860 218

PREFACE

This study examines the economy of rice culture and the nature of slavery within the confines of coastal Georgia. The limited amount of land available for rice production and the unusual demands of this industry encouraged specialization and a remarkable degree of efficiency among owners and slaves. Because the production of rice required a comparatively large labor force, tidewater plantations and labor-management needs were, in some respects, unlike the needs of plantation-slave units in other areas. The culture that developed along the rice coast was made possible by the exploitation and utilization of large forces of slave laborers. The presence of these Afro-Americans must be recognized, for without their contributions there would have been no tidewater society.

The contents of this volume have been drawn from county court records (deeds, wills, tax books, inventories, and appraisals of estates), unpublished census returns and other federal and state data, plantation account books, correspondence, and contemporary literature. These sources have proven to be of considerable worth in evaluating the profitability of production with the use of slave labor. Estate accounts offer a complete record of all transactions made to supply the plantation for any given year, as well as net returns to the owner after all expenses and commissions charged for marketing the crop were paid. Thus, not only the cost of maintaining the slave population is shown but also the financing involved in the factorage system. These sources have also been invaluable in analyzing conditions and treatment of slaves and in evaluating the significance of their contribution to the total culture of coastal Georgia.

A Senior Fellowship Award from National Endowment for the Humanities provided me with time to pursue this study. A travel grant from the Faculty Research Committee of Georgia Southern College covered a small portion of the expense of research. I gratefully acknowledge the assistance of both NEH and GSC. I am grateful to Eugene D. Genovese and Stanley L. Engerman for their careful reading of the entire manuscript and their helpful comments and suggestions. I also wish to express sincere appreciation to Catherlene R. Washington of Savannah, Georgia, without whose help as research assistant this project would have been prolonged. She pointed me to many African cultural elements retained by blacks today that I might not have noticed without her suggestions. For the use of manuscript collections, I am indebted to many people in Georgia. In particular, I wish to express thanks to Bessie Lewis of Pine Harbor, Georgia, who was most helpful and generous in supplying me with information of McIntosh County.

Thanks are due the staffs of the Georgia Historical Society, the Georgia State Department of Archives and History, the Duke University and University of North Carolina libraries, the Library of Congress, the National Archives, and the Departments of Agriculture and Commerce in Washington as well as clerks in county courthouses throughout coastal Georgia who were cheerful and helpful while material was being gathered from their record rooms. Two special individuals contributed to the creation of this volume and I express my sincere appreciation to them: Leonora Quarterman, Savannah artist who prepared many of the illustrations, and Mrs. Jack G. Haylow, who undertook the painstaking work of typing the final draft.

Slavery and Rice Culture in Low Country Georgia, 1750–1860

INTRODUCTION

The rice industry, with its technical specialization and wide-ranging social consequences, largely determined the cultural development of coastal Georgia. Afro-Americans largely determined the economic growth of the rice industry. Yet, with the exception of the edited works by Albert V. House and James M. Clifton, and the study done by Dale Evans Swan, the industry in general and the role of Afro-Americans in particular have not been studied.[1] The agricultural histories of Lewis C. Gray and Ulrich B. Phillips contain brief references to rice culture. Ralph B. Flanders, in his history of slavery in Georgia, concentrates on the cotton belt and merely makes use of Phillips's and Gray's references to the rice coast. James C. Bonner's history of agriculture in Georgia, a classic of its kind, devotes only passing attention to the rice coast. Thomas P. Govan, in calculating the profitability of rice culture and slavery, used the records, previously presented by Phillips, of two Georgia rice plantations and one on the South Carolina side of the Savannah River to estimate income from investment. Robert S. Starobin, in writing of industrial slavery in the Old South, in turn used Govan's figures to illustrate annual average rates of interest on capital investment. These few references virtually exhaust the scholarly literature on the subject, although we have many popular books about plantation life and slavery in coastal

1. Albert V. House, ed., *Planter Management and Capitalism in Antebellum Georgia: The Journal of Hugh Fraser Grant, Rice Grower* (New York: Columbia Univ. Press, 1954); James M. Clifton, ed. with an introduction, *Life and Labor on Argyle Island: Letters and Documents of a Savannah River Plantation, 1833–1867* (Savannah: Beehive Press, 1978); Dale Evans Swan, *The Structure and Profitability of the Antebellum Rice Industry, 1859* (Ph.D. diss., Univ. of North Carolina, 1972; New York: Arno Press, 1975).

Georgia.[2] Caroline Couper Lovell's *The Golden Isles of Georgia*, Burnette Vanstory's *Georgia's Land of the Golden Isles*, and Eugenia Price's more recent novels are representative of the popular literature.

Conversely, an impressive amount of literature has been written on rice culture in South Carolina. The most extensive published treatment of Carolina rice is the edited work of the papers of Governor Robert F.W. Allston, in which J.H. Easterby, in his editor's introduction, analyzes Allston's operations to determine annual income or interest earned on capital investment. The narratives of David Doar and Duncan Clinch Heyward, descendants of Carolina planters, are only two of a number of choice monographs that tell of the methods used in planting and producing rice, but these studies, like many older ones, ignore the subject of profitability and the role of Afro-Americans. The Carolina planters, in their letters and essays to the editors of contemporary journals, contributed accurate information on the techniques of rice planting. Agricultural reporters from the North also contributed information on rice plantations in Carolina and Georgia in their valuable travel reports.[3]

Before 1865 rice culture was confined to a coastal strip along the eastern seaboard, commonly called tidewater or low country—a relatively narrow belt that stretches from North Carolina to Florida. South Carolina and Georgia, which offered the great abundance of available swamp lands suitable for conversion into rice fields, accounted for about 90 percent of the rice produced in the United States. Producing this staple for a world market demanded attention to certain unique characteristics of rice culture and its labor-management needs. For successful maturation, rice required systematic irrigation at certain intervals during the period

2. Lewis C. Gray, *History of Agriculture in the Southern United States to 1860*, 2 vols. (Washington, D.C.: Carnegie Institute, 1933); Ulrich B. Phillips, *American Negro Slavery* (New York: D. Appleton, 1918); Ralph B. Flanders, *Plantation Slavery in Georgia* (Chapel Hill: Univ. of North Carolina Press, 1933); James C. Bonner, *A History of Georgia Agriculture, 1732–1860* (Athens: Univ. of Georgia Press, 1964); Thomas P. Govan, "Was Plantation Slavery Profitable?" *Journal of Southern History* 8 (Nov. 1942): 513–35; Robert S. Starobin, *Industrial Slavery in the Old South* (New York: Oxford Univ. Press, 1970).

3. J.H. Easterby, ed., *The South Carolina Rice Plantation as Revealed in the Papers of Robert F.W. Allston* (Chicago: Univ. of Chicago Press, 1945); David Doar, *Rice and Rice Planting in the South Carolina Low Country* (Charleston: Charleston Museum, 1936); Duncan Clinch Heyward, *Seed From Madagascar* (Chapel Hill: Univ. of North Carolina Press, 1937; rpt. Spartanburg: Reprint Company, 1972).

of growth, and a large labor force to cultivate, harvest, process, and prepare the crop for market. Rice lands had to be situated in low areas near or along fresh water rivers where these rivers may be affected by tides from the Atlantic Ocean so that their waters could provide a source for flooding and draining fields. An intricate system of hydraulics made possible the control of these waters for irrigation. The rice frontier in Georgia, unlike other agricultural frontiers, was restricted to an area of from ten to twenty miles wide; hence, the rice industry became highly specialized and extremely profitable for the majority of those who invested in its land, machinery, and slaves.

During the nineteenth century the rice magnates of coastal Georgia, like their forebears and relatives along the Carolina coast, constituted the elite of the planter aristocracy. Their cultural heritage and traditions had been nurtured by generations of slaveholders whose affluence and good breeding embellished their way of life. None among them had risen from the small-scale farmer or overseer class that gradually expanded holdings in land and slaves. With few exceptions, the rice planters inherited their status and property from older generations of Carolinians who migrated to the Georgia coast to develop the rice frontier.

Numerous estate accounts found among court records show that by contemporary standards this class was rich. Among the sixty or so planters whose rice production was 100,000 pounds or more annually and who owned seventy-five or more slaves, estate values ranged, slightly more or less, between $100,000 and $500,000. Ralph E. Elliott's rice plantation on the Ogeechee River was valued at $91,785 in 1854; of this amount, 135 slaves were valued at $62,185. Charles W. Rogers's plantation, also on the Ogeechee River, was valued at $117,627 in 1861; of this amount, 147 slaves were appraised at $69,595. James Potter's two rice plantations on the Savannah River were valued at $570,226 in 1861, with the 453 slaves on these two units appraised at $231,650.[4]

4. Inventories and Appraisements, Book K, 82–86, 164–65; Book M, N, 111–19, 134, 137, Probate Records, Chatham County; Swan, *Structure and Profitability of the Antebellum Rice Industry*, 87, 97, 110–11, 126. Swan has shown that the ten rice counties of Georgia and South Carolina contained some of the largest production units in the South, "with sometimes over half a million dollars of capital and a labor force exceeding 500 persons." He emphasizes the positive relationship between productivity and scale of operations. Small rice-producing units were less efficient and usually produced some Sea Island cotton as another cash crop. My findings verify such a conclusion.

All factors considered, cotton plantation values ranged slightly less. For example, among the 1,186 cotton planters in middle and southwest Georgia classified as large holders in 1860, estate values ranged between $60,000 and $150,000. These individuals owned fifty or more slaves, and cotton produced on their units amounted to 400 bales or more. John Carswell's cotton plantation in Burke County was valued at $60,000; of this amount, 58 slaves were appraised at $44,000. James W. Belvin's plantation in Houston County was valued at $120,000; of this amount, 99 slaves were appraised at $85,000. Alexander Pope's plantation in Wilkes County was valued at $135,000, with the 152 slaves appraised at $113,000.[5]

Much more numerous in Georgia and throughout the South were those cotton planters who owned about thirty slaves; production on their units ranged from ten to thirty bales. Richard Wheeler of Franklin County in north Georgia was fairly typical of this class. In 1860 Wheeler's 750-acre farm was valued at $6,000. The exact value of his twenty-four slaves is not known. On 270 acres of improved land, ten bales of cotton were produced. Production of food crops such as corn, peas, beans, sweet potatoes, wheat, oats, and fodder for livestock suggests that Wheeler's farm, like others, was self-sufficient. Unlike the majority who owned fewer than ten slaves in Franklin County and are classed as small holders, Wheeler was an average holder. Typical of the small holder was C.T. Turner of Terrill County in southwest Georgia. Turner owned a 630-acre farm and ten slaves; his yield in 1860 on 225 acres of improved land was sixteen bales of cotton.[6]

5. Joseph Karl Menn, *The Large Slaveholders of the Deep South, 1860* (Ph.D. diss., 2 vols., Univ. of Texas, 1964; Ann Arbor: Univ. Microfilms, 1972), 2:544–904. For references to the three planters mentioned above, see 563, 702, 898. Bales of short staple cotton contained 400 lbs. per bale. Menn's dissertation is based upon the unpublished census returns (1860) for Alabama, Georgia, Louisiana, and Mississippi. These four states of the Deep South contained most of the slaveholders owning fifty or more slaves whom Menn classifies as large cotton planters. In his listings for Georgia, Menn has included 128 planters of the rice coast counties who produced Sea Island cotton and/or rice. I have chosen not to identify these individuals as typical upland cotton planters, for they were not. About half of them were large rice planters and the others produced small amounts. Menn's total number of large cotton planters in Georgia in 1860 is 1,314; my total is 1,186.

6. Menn, ibid., 544–904; Franklee Gilbert Whartenby, *Land and Labor Productivity in United States Cotton Production, 1800–1840* (New York: Arno Press, 1977), 131–32. Whartenby states that a fairly typical cotton plantation used thirty workers and that the average cotton plantation was not as large as the average rice or sugar plantation; Stanley L. Engerman, "The Antebellum South: What Probably Was and What Should Have Been," in William N. Parker, ed., *Structure of the Cotton Economy of the Antebellum South* (Washington, D.C.: Agricultural His-

The size and management of plantations and the treatment of slaves varied throughout the South, and in essential respects so did the members of the planter class. The elite of the slaveholding society, those few planters who owned hundreds of slaves, tended to be absent from their estates, vacationing in the North, traveling abroad, or residing in the city, leaving the management of their slaves and plantations to the care of overseers. Along the rice coast of Carolina and Georgia, these elite planters tended to be local or part-time absentees. They preferred city life and maintained residences in Charleston or Savannah. They made regular visits to their plantations to observe conditions of their slaves and crops and to confer with overseers and drivers concerning plantation management.

Local absenteeism is not the same as Caribbean absenteeism, for most Caribbean planters, after accumulating sufficient wealth, returned to England to live in the style to which they had accustomed themselves, leaving the management of their estates to local attorneys and overseers.[7] The West Indian plantation was directed on behalf of an impersonal owner and there was no esprit de corps such as existed in the United States among local absentees and their bondmen; a common spirit of sympathy, enthusiasm, and devotion pervaded the plantation community and was displayed by owner and slaves. Local absentees lived near their plantations, knew their people, and had strong personal ties with them. They preferred city life to the unsophisticated confinement of the plantation and considered having a residence away from the plantation essential to their health, most especially during the summer months, as a protection against miasma, the environment believed to have been conducive to malarial fever. Their preference for city life is evidenced by the 90 percent increase of the

tory Society, 1970), 127–42. On 134, Engerman discusses the degree of self-sufficiency of farms and plantations and suggests that the plantation may have been a more efficient form of economic organization than the farm. In the same volume, Eugene D. Genovese, in "Commentary: A Historian's View," 143–47, states on 145 that slaves' garden plots and poultry may have contributed to plantation self-sufficiency.

7. Michael Craton, "Jamaican Slavery," Stanley L. Engerman and Eugene D. Genovese, eds., *Race and Slavery in the Western Hemisphere: Quantative Studies* (Princeton: Princeton Univ. Press, 1975), 262–63; Lowell Joseph Ragatz, *The Fall of the Planter Class in the British Caribbean, 1763–1833* (New York: American Historical Association, 1928; rpt. New York: Octagon Books, 1963); Elsa V. Goveia, *Slave Society in the British Leeward Islands at the End of the Eighteenth Century* (New Haven: Yale Univ. Press, 1965); Orlando Patterson, *The Sociology of Slavery: An Analysis of the Origins, Development, and Structure of Negro Slave Society in Jamaica* (Cranbury, N.J.: Associated Univ. Presses, 1969).

urban population in Georgia during the prosperous 1850s. This growth was especially evident in Savannah where by 1860 the white population for the first time outnumbered the black.[8] In Savannah an influx of immigrants from abroad, many of whom were Irish, helped to swell the urban population.

The hierarchy extended downward from the planter aristocracy through the middle class to the small-scale planter. The middle class planter resided on his plantation. He and his wife participated actively in its management, though he employed an overseer to direct the work of slaves and to punish them. The slave population on this kind of plantation was no less than thirty to forty and could be more than a hundred.[9] The owner of a small plantation, though hardly in the planter class, deserves to be classified as a planter, for he directed the labor of others and played the role defined here. He did not engage in field work and cannot be called a farmer, as farmers owned only a few slaves in a general district of small farms and worked side by side with their slaves in informal relationships.[10]

Because the size and management of plantations and the treatment of slaves varied, it is reasonable to ask if the conditions of slaves were better or worse on rice plantations than on other plantations in the Old South. By general standards, living conditions of rice coast slaves who worked under the task system were less confining than under such labor systems as the gang system used on cotton and sugar plantations and the factory system in which slaves worked a ten- to twelve-hour day. After completing the day's work, the slaves of coastal Georgia used their boats to fish and hunt; they sold their surplus produce and acquired small amounts of cash. Under the hiring system slaves also had opportunity to accumulate small amounts of cash. They had adequate care and maintenance as measured by contemporary standards—housing, clothing, diet, and medical attention. Within the slave plantation community they created and practiced their own forms of social activity; they preserved their religious beliefs and tradi-

8. *United States Census Returns*, 1850, 1860. Many of the townhouses in Savannah, built for these country squires, have been preserved through historic restoration and are reminders of the elegant lifestyle they enjoyed. The wealthy cotton planters of middle Georgia were also local absentees. They maintained townhouses in Augusta, Macon, and Milledgeville.

9. Julia Floyd Smith, *Slavery and Plantation Growth in Antebellum Florida, 1821–1860* (Gainesville: Univ. of Florida Press, 1973), 142–43, 147, 151.

10. Gray, *History of Agriculture*, 1:499–500.

tions, family concepts, African songs, stories, dances, and many other cultural expressions.

Among whites, attitudes toward their slaves varied. Out of affection, appreciation, or compassion a few provided manumission for favorite servants, but the majority looked upon their ownership in slaves as a matter of profit and loss. Slaves expressed affectionate and loyal feelings for owners, but the vast majority nonetheless longed to be free and cared little for the white overlords whose way of life caused their degradation.

The rice industry was unusual, for available land was limited and specialization demanded a greater capital outlay in labor and machinery than did other southern industries. The total land area suitable for rice culture extended along the coast from the Cape Fear River in North Carolina to the St. Johns River in Florida. According to the census returns for 1850 there were 551 rice plantations in operation and 125,000 slaves laboring on these units, an average of 226 slaves per unit. When we compare this average with averages for units producing cotton, hemp, sugar, and tobacco, the differences in labor-management needs become apparent: cotton plantations numbered 74,031 and there were 1,815,000 slaves on these units, an average of 24 slaves per unit; hemp plantations, 8,327, with 60,000, an average of 7; sugar plantations, 2,681, with 150,000, an average of 55; tobacco plantations, 15,745, with 350,000, an average of 22.

Agricultural statistics are a valuable source for locating the plantation belts in Georgia and for verifying the comparative wealth of rice planters and cotton planters. These statistics may also be used to compare labor demands and capital investment involved in producing rice as opposed to cotton. The cotton belt, located in the lower Piedmont and, after 1850, in several counties in southwest Georgia, was characterized by many small holdings of land and slaves. Cotton plantations greatly outnumbered rice plantations; however, they were smaller, contained fewer slaves per unit, and their total capital investment was lower. Rice plantations were specialized and required more equipment, machinery, and slaves per unit to cultivate and produce the grain for market. (See Appendix A, Table A-1 for agricultural statistics of the lower Piedmont [cotton belt], the coastal strip, and the whole state in 1860.)

Georgia rice fields were generally more fertile than those in South Carolina and produced an average of from fifty to fifty-five bushels per acre, as opposed to an average of from forty to forty-five in the Palmetto State. Rice fields in Georgia were rather constantly revitalized during periods of irrigation, as rich soil deposits from the interior were washed downstream by slow-moving fresh water rivers when these rivers became swollen by heavy rains, causing freshets. In South Carolina, extensive timbering in the interior of the state eroded the land and much of the topsoil was lost, with silt left to be washed and deposited on fields.[11]

The soil consistency that caused a decline in production of yields per acre on rice plantations in South Carolina is well illustrated when one compares figures for the two states. In Georgia for the year 1850 there were 71 rice planters whose units produced 100,000 pounds or more while total production (including those who produced smaller amounts) amounted to 38,950,691 pounds; in 1860, there were 68 planters whose units produced 100,000 pounds or more while total production of rice increased to 52,507,652 pounds. In South Carolina for the year 1850 there were 256 planters whose units produced comparable amounts while total production was 159,930,613; in 1860 those planters whose production was of the same dimensions decreased in numbers to 173 while total production of rice decreased to 119,100,528 pounds. Total production in the United States reflected this decline in a decrease from 215,313,497 pounds in 1850 to 187,167,032 by 1860, making the point clear that rice production peaked in 1850 and by 1860 had declined, though in Georgia production increased during these years by 13,556,961 pounds.[12]

The land area suitable for growing rice in Georgia was restricted to a narrow belt along the coast above the salt-water line where fresh water river tides were affected by tides from the Atlantic Ocean and were available for irrigating fields. Rice planters were thus able to expand operations only within certain limits, whereas the planters of middle Georgia continued to have available for their culture new lands to develop as the cotton frontier moved westward. The peculiar requirements for the growth of rice, a wet culture, demanded a larger labor force than was necessary for growing cotton, a dry culture. Variations in

11. Ibid., 2:731; House, *Planter Management*, 23–24; Willard Range, *A Century of Georgia Agriculture* (Athens: Univ. of Georgia Press, 1954), 15. Range writes that rice lands were "calling for the fabulous price of $150 to $300 per acre" by 1845.

12. Unpublished Census Returns, 1850, 1860; *United States Census Returns*, 1840, 1850, 1860.

demand meant that, with few exceptions, individual ownership in slaves was comparatively large among rice planters, though this group constituted only a small percentage of the total slaveholding planter class.

The plantation districts of low country Georgia were unlike those in the interior cotton belt. They were settled earlier, they were wealthier, they depended on crops that were unique and could not be grown elsewhere. The slaves lived on larger plantations, relatively isolated from whites, and worked under a different system of labor organization. These differences created white and black cultures that were in many ways distinct from those of the interior regions of the South. The purpose of this study is to examine the extent of these differences in culture and society of owners and slaves in low country Georgia.

PART ONE

Production of Rice

CHAPTER ONE

Tidewater Culture in the Colonial Era

The tidewater lands of coastal Georgia are bounded by the Savannah, Ogeechee, Altamaha, Satilla, and St. Marys rivers. The northern boundary is the Savannah River and the southern boundary, the St. Marys River, representing a total distance from north to south of 126 miles. These fresh-water rivers and their tributaries are affected by the rise and fall of salt-water tides from the Atlantic Ocean for a distance inland of from ten to twenty miles. This setting made possible the utilization of fresh-water tides for systematic irrigation, a necessary factor in the successful cultivation of rice. English settlements and Negro slavery in Georgia developed earlier along this coast, where a mild climate, moderately fertile soil, and accessible land attracted inhabitants. It was in this narrow belt that extensive plantations were developed in the colonial era; after the American Revolution they were enlarged and increased in numbers to constitute what became known as the rice coast.

Coastal Georgia, with its stretches of marsh lands, highlands, hammocks, swamp lands, and chain of sea islands, has a distinct and unique geographical beauty. It resembles, in many respects, the tidewater lands of the Carolina coast. The geography may be characterized as low, flat country consisting of oak lands, pine barrens, swamp lands, and marshes. Rivers and streams cut through the extensive stretches of salt marshes that separate the mainland from the islands. These waterways served as a network for transportation between the two. Tree growth indigenous to the mainland and the islands includes cabbage palmetto, cypress,

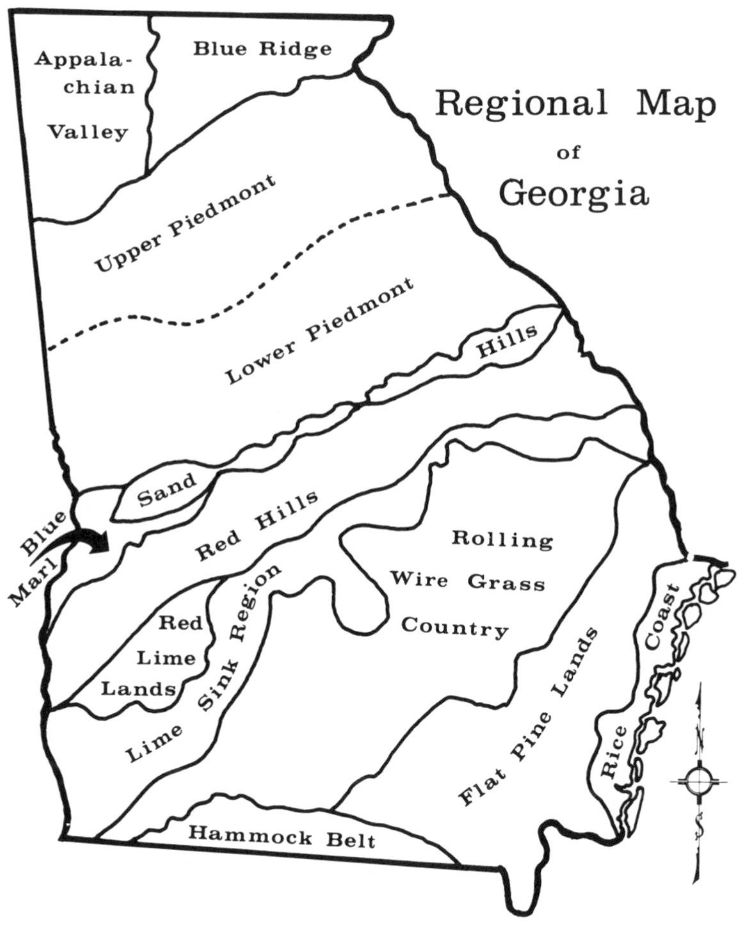

Figure 1. Regional Map of Georgia. (Drawing by Leonora Quarterman.)

laurel, live oak, myrtle, red maple, sweet gum, and several varieties of pines. The principal soil types are fine sand, fine sandy loam, coarse sandy loam, clay, clay loam, and swamp. The soil is impregnated with lime or a marly content, a factor contributing to its fertility.[1]

Prior to the creation of a plantation economy along the rice coast, Georgia did not flourish, ostensibly because of the colonization program initiated in 1733 by James Oglethorpe and the twenty other founding Trustees. The program of the Trustees was designed to promote the liberal ideals of seventeenth-century European thought, which reached maturity in the philosophy of John Locke to mean social law and the rights of man. Two distinct movements that reflected such thought in the eighteenth century were organized philanthropy and penal reform. The Trustees, desiring to promote such social reform in Georgia, placed restrictions upon Negro slavery and land grants as safeguards against the designs of those few who would obstruct the freedom of the many, and also to avoid the direct sponsorship of an imperial government, far more interested in a profitable mercantile economy than in the rights of man.[2]

An act of 1735, which prohibited the importation of "Black slaves or Negroes," expressed the wishes of the Trustees, who planned to settle the colony with free white laborers to be drawn from the lower classes of England and Europe as indentured servants; these laborers would produce the two staples, wine and silk for the independent landowners (freeholders). A colony of such settlers would establish white supremacy and reinforce the English claim against Spanish and Indian incursions.[3] The Trus-

1. Bonner, *History of Georgia Agriculture*, 102; Harry J. Carman, ed., *American Husbandry . . . .*, 2 vols. (London: J. Bew, 1775; rpt. New York: Columbia Univ. Press, 1939), 225–27; Patrick Tailfer et al., *A True and Historical Narrative of the Colony of Georgia, in America, From the First Settlement Thereof Until the Present Period . . . .* (Charleston, 1741), 75–76; Roland M. Harper, "Development of Agriculture in Lower Georgia from 1850 to 1880," *Georgia Historical Quarterly* 6 (June 1922): 107.

2. Milton S. Heath, *Constructive Liberalism: The Role of the State in Georgia to 1860* (Cambridge, Mass.: Harvard Univ. Press, 1945), 4–5, 45. Heath states that the Trustees followed an experimental policy of social welfare that was at odds with prevailing practices of commercial interests. They were fearful that "Georgia would sink into bondage to the merchant capitalists" if their benevolent program failed.

3. Allen D. Candler and Lucian Lamar Knight, eds., *Colonial Records of the State of Georgia*, 26 vols. (Atlanta, 1904–1916), 1:50–54, 4:275–76, 412–13 (cited hereafter as *Colonial Records);* Ruth Scarborough, *The Opposition to Slavery in Georgia Prior to 1860* (Nashville: George Peabody College for Teachers, 1933; rpt.

tees looked to the defenseless condition of South Carolina resulting from her large slave population in proportion to her white, with most of this population concentrated on tidewater rice plantations, as well as South Carolina's continuing fears from threats of slave insurrections and the problem of her runaway slaves. Georgia, to serve as a military frontier for South Carolina, would have to establish a colony of white settlers, most of whom, as small farmers, would develop the land and serve as a nucleus for military defense.[4]

Because of the sorriness of the indentured servants and the sparseness of their supply, the plan to substitute white for black labor failed. Many of those indentured fled into South Carolina and further northward to escape the laborious work of clearing and cultivating land for production. The freeholders, in turn, could not procure adequate labor through the indenture system; thus, the two staples, wine and silk, upon which the colony had to depend for its economic life were not produced, and the province languished. The unrealistic system of land tenure also stunted Georgia's growth. A restriction prohibited free title to the 500 acres that a freeholder might obtain; quit rents of four shillings per hundred acres (higher than in other provinces) had to be paid on the land. The act restricting rum and other spirituous liquors was not in tune with the times; violations were widespread and enforcement of the act failed. It was repealed in 1742.[5]

New York: Negro Universities Press, 1968), 8–11; H.B. Fant, "The Labor Policy of the Trustees for Establishing the Colony of Georgia in America," *Georgia Historical Quarterly* 16 (Mar. 1932): 1–16. Fant presents by far the best single account of the labor program in Georgia between 1735 and 1750. During these years while slavery was prohibited. the Trustees reserved the right to sell or dispose of any Negro slave apprehended in the colony.

4. Peter H. Wood, *Black Majority: Negroes in Colonial South Carolina from 1670 through the Stono Rebellion* (New York: Knopf, 1974), 308–325. The Stono Rebellion of 1739 caused much apprehension among Georgians; this apprehension is expressed in the *Colonial Records;* William B. Stevens, *A History of Georgia* . . . ., 2 vols. (New York: E.O. Jenkins, 1847; rpt. Beehive Press, 1972), 1:288–89. Spanish emissaries along the borders made a regular practice of encouraging slaves to escape from South Carolina into Florida. The promise of freedom and protection for all runaway slaves by the Spanish governor at St. Augustine seemed to offer an opportunity to escape bondage, and many did stage successful escapes. A Spanish regiment composed of Negro runaways, fully equipped and armed as Spanish troops under command of Negro officers, served and fought with Spain's army in Florida. Had slaves been allowed in Georgia, the very existence of the new colony would have been in peril, for they could have been encouraged to stage insurrections, to murder whites, and to run away.

5. *Colonial Records*, 4:283–84, 5:153–58, 164, 21:161–62; Stevens, *History of*

In defiance of the Negro Act of 1735, freeholders along the Savannah River brought slaves into Georgia from South Carolina under pretense that they were hired laborers. The cost of the hire was based on the value of the slave. It would have been difficult for colonial officials at Savannah to enforce the prohibition against slavery even had they cared to do so. With the exception of the Scots at Darien and the Salzburgers at Ebenezer, the residents of Georgia desired slavery. As early as 1735 a petition signed by seventeen freeholders stating the necessity for slave labor was presented to the Trustees. Again in 1738 a petition signed by 117 freeholders was presented, citing the two reasons for the distressing condition of the colony: the land tenure system and the restriction against slave labor.[6]

There is no doubt about the benevolent intentions and reforming zeal of Oglethorpe, though he himself owned slaves and a plantation in South Carolina. He also was deputy governor for the Royal African Company that king, parliament, and merchants supported; the African slave trade was considered "the great pillar and support of the British plantation trade in America." George Whitefield, the distinguished evangelist who founded Bethesda Orphanage near Savannah, and James Habersham, a colonial official within the governing body of President William Stephens, both strongly supported the movement to make slavery legal in Georgia. Whitefield launched Bethesda with monies received from his investments in land and slaves in South Carolina.[7]

Georgia, 1:283, 293, 295; Flanders, *Plantation Slavery in Georgia*, 10; Gray, *History of Agriculture*, 1:97–98.

6. Fant, "Labor Policy of the Trustees," 6–15; Hugh M'Call, *The History of Georgia, Containing Brief Sketches of the Most Remarkable Events up to the Present Day*, 2 vols. (Savannah, 1811–16), 1:48–67; Bonner, *History of Georgia Agriculture*, 5–8. See Betty C. Wood, "Thomas Stephens and the Introduction of Black Slavery in Georgia," *Georgia Historical Quarterly* 58 (Spring 1974): 24–40. Wood contends that Thomas Stephens, the son of William, must be credited with responsibility for the introduction of slavery in Georgia. Thomas acted as spokesman for the Georgia malcontents and presented their proslavery arguments to the House of Commons in 1742 and 1743.

7. *Colonial Records*, 3:281; Stevens, *History of Georgia*, 1:286–88, 308–310. See James R. Hertzler, "Slavery in the Yearly Sermons (1731–1750) Before the Georgia Trustees," *Georgia Historical Quarterly* 59 (Supplement 1975): 118–26; Phinizy Spalding, "Some Sermons Before the Trustees of Colonial Georgia," *Georgia Historical Quarterly* 57 (Fall 1973): 332–46. Hertzler and Spalding contend that the yearly sermons did not reinforce the Trustees' stand but instead implied that slavery, tempered with Christianity, could be beneficial to master and slave.

The arguments of Whitefield, Habersham, and others prompted a large number of residents to present to the Trustees, again in 1749, a petition requesting that slavery be permitted in the colony, to which William Stephens now affixed the official colonial seal. The petition was read before the Trustees, who reacted favorably in resolving to repeal, in 1750, the act that prohibited Negro slavery. At the same time the Trustees removed the restrictions that prohibited a fee simple title to the land and the amount of acreage that a freeholder might obtain. The period of the trusteeship also came to a close, and Georgia became a royal province in 1752.[8]

And so, despite the desires of Oglethorpe and his associates to create a society of yeomen farmers in Georgia, the suitability of the land for producing staple commodities such as rice and indigo prompted her more aggressive entrepreneurs to demand that a liberal land policy and slavery be introduced in order to create a "free enterprise" system. The program of the Trustees, though idealistic, was impracticable, and only when it was supplanted by a colonial system that offered opportunity for the merchant and planter capitalist did Georgia's economy begin to grow and to compare favorably, on a smaller scale, with the economies of the plantation provinces to the north.

Abandoning the restraints upon land and slaves brought to an end the artificial equality under which the colonists had lived, and also the hopes of the Trustees to create an agrarian peasant society based upon the concepts of eighteenth-century liberal thought. Men of means and influence now commenced to acquire large tracts of land while the role of the yeoman was eclipsed. This class could afford no slaves and was gradually pushed to the interior to develop small farms, while the nabobs in Savannah and the surrounding area petitioned for royal grants to lands suitable for cultivation. These Georgia aristocrats—Sir James Wright, royal governor; John Graham, lieutenant governor; James Habersham, John Morel, Francis Harris, and others—had viewed with some envy their enterprising Carolina neighbors who were making fortunes producing rice and indigo with the use of slave labor. Carolina growers also eyed the Georgia lowlands with the view in mind to expand their investments along the Georgia coast. Thus, a frontier movement developed, as swamp lands were cleared and

8. Enoch M. Banks, *The Economics of Land Tenure in Georgia* (New York: Columbia Univ. Press, 1905), 12–13; Bonner, *History of Georgia Agriculture*, 5–8.

prepared for cultivation of rice, and other lands for indigo and subsistence crops.[9]

This development of the tidewater frontier largely extended the Carolina rice belt, with striking creation of an extensive plantation system based upon capitalistic enterprise similar to the great plantation-slave units of South Carolina and the West Indies. By 1765 flourishing rice plantations were operating along the Savannah and Ogeechee rivers, as well as in the region of the great Altamaha Delta and further southward along the Satilla River. John Bartram commented upon these plantations during his travels in coastal Georgia and was impressed with the suitability of the country for such an enterprise. He described the highlands as being interspersed "with bay and cypress swamps very proper for rice." His son, William Bartram, traveled the same route several years later and observed numerous rice plantations north of the Altamaha River and its tributaries. The swamp lands in proximity of these waterways were filled with slaves who were "daily clearing and improving them into large fruitful plantations."[10]

In South Carolina in the 1750s the introduction of the tidal flow method revolutionized rice culture. This innovation is attributed to McKewn Johnstone, who perfected the system in the Winyah Bay region of Georgetown County. Prior to this time rice and indigo were produced on more inland fields in moderate amounts. These were the staple crops, though they had nothing in common except their need for a temperate climate. The inadequate water supply often resulted in poor rice yields. The tidal flow method marked a turning point in the economic history of South Carolina and, at the same time, marked the beginning of the history of rice culture in Georgia.[11]

9. Heath, *Constructive Liberalism*, 50–51; Alexander Hewatt, *An Historical Account of the Rise and progress of the Colonies of South Carolina and Georgia*, 2 vols. (London: Alexander Donaldson, 1769), 2:266.

10. *Diary of a Journey Through the Carolinas, Georgia, and Florida, 1765–66* (rpt. Philadelphia: American Philosophical Society, 1942), 30–31; *Travels in Georgia and Florida, 1773–74* (rpt. Philadelphia: American Philosophical Society, 1942), 36; Deed Records, Book DD, p. 175, Book X, 2:759–60, Chatham County; Savannah *Georgia Gazette*, July 5, 1764, Apr. 19, 1769, Mar. 22, 1775; *Collections of the Georgia Historical Society*, 6 vols. (Savannah, 1870–80), 3:232, 376–78 (hereafter cited as *Collections*). Alexander Wright, the son of Gov. Wright, and Lt. Gov. John Graham acquired extensive tracts of land suitable for rice culture along the Satilla River. See Richard B. Sheridan, *Sugar and Slavery: An Economic History of the British West Indies, 1623–1775* (Baltimore: Johns Hopkins Univ. Press, 1973), for an account of large-scale agro-industrial enterprises, plantation organization, and the slave labor system.

11. Doar, *Rice and Rice Planting*, 7–12; Gray, *History of Agriculture*, 1:279–80;

The era of the royal governors (1752 to 1776) witnessed a spectacular growth in population and economic prosperity. In 1750, 4,200 whites and 1,000 Negro slaves were in Georgia; in 1760, 6,000 whites and 3,578 Negro slaves; in 1770, 12,750 whites and 10,625 Negro slaves;[12] by 1776, 17,000 whites and 16,000 Negro slaves.[13] The great majority of the white population was composed of small farmers and their families, who had pushed into Georgia from the Piedmont region of the Carolinas and Virginia by crossing the Savannah River near Augusta to claim the western lands opened for settlement under the governorship of James Wright. The black population was concentrated along the coast, where the creation of rice plantations had transformed the area into a tidewater society inhabited by a preponderance of Negro slaves and a small elite planter class composed of crown officials, their associates, and migrants from South Carolina and abroad.[14]

Commercial records reflect Georgia's agricultural growth during the two decades prior to the American Revolution. Exports from Savannah in 1755 included 2,299 barrels of rice, 4,508 pounds of indigo, timber, staves, shingles, and deerskins. From

---

Heyward, *Seed From Madagascar*, 11–12; Dennis T. Lawson, *No Heir to Take Its Place: The Story of Rice Planting in Georgetown County, South Carolina* (Georgetown: Rice Museum, 1972), 5; Wood, *Black Majority*, 119–23. Wood presents evidence to show that blacks brought the knowledge of rice planting and other agricultural crops with them from Africa. Carman, *American Husbandry*, 283; Douglas C. Wilms, "The Development of Rice Culture in 18th Century Georgia," *Southeastern Geographer* 12 (May 1972): 49; *Georgia Gazette*, Nov. 24, 1797. The first rice produced in Georgia was on inland swamp lands where water from springs or streams was stored in reservoirs to be used for irrigation. Because of the uncertainty of sufficient water in dry seasons and the devastating effect of floods resulting from excessive rains, inland rice fields gradually gave way to the more effective and productive tidal flow system. However, as late as 1797 in Liberty County, a 900-acre inland rice plantation was advertised for sale by the owner. On this estate there were three large reservoirs connected by a canal to the 100 acres of swamp lands planted in rice. These fields annually produced 8–10 barrels of rice per hand.

12. *Historical Statistics of the United States: Colonial Times to 1857* (Washington, D.C.: Bureau of the Census, 1860), 756. Colonial records refer to several hundred slaves in 1750; the U.S. Census refers to 1,000.

13. *A Century of Population Growth from the First Census of the United States to the Twelfth, 1790–1910* (Washington, D.C.: Bureau of the Census, 1909); J.D.B. DeBow, *Industrial Resources of the Southern and Western States*, 3 vols. (New Orleans, 1852), 3:130. The total slave population in the North American colonies in 1776 numbered 502,132. DeBow's *Industrial Resources* shows the slave population in each province at that time: Conn., 6,000; Del., 9,000; Ga., 16,000; Md., 80,000; Mass., 3,500; N.J., 7,600; N.H., 629; N.Y., 15,000; N.C., 75,000; Pa., 10,000; R.I., 4,373; S.C., 110,000; Va., 165,000.

14. Gray, *History of Agriculture*, 2:1025; Bonner, *History of Georgia Agriculture*, 8–9. Under the governorship of James Wright, four land cessions were

this meager beginning, exports for the year 1763 increased to 7,500 barrels of rice, 9,633 pounds of indigo, 1,250 bushels of corn, plus deer and beaver skins, naval stores, and timber. These staple commodities were valued at £27,021. Ten years later, export of these commodities increased to reach a value of £121,677. The British occupation of East Florida in 1763 at the end of the Seven Years' War secured the Georgia coast and encouraged a great expansion in the rice industry. By the close of the colonial era annual rice exports from Georgia averaged 25,000 barrels. This figure does not account for rice produced along the Savannah River and marketed at Charleston, South Carolina. Rice exported annually from that colony on the eve of the Revolution approximated 165,000 barrels; a portion was produced in Georgia.[15] (See Appendix A, Table A-2, for barrels of rice exported from Charleston and Savannah from 1755 to 1773.)

During these years of economic prosperity in colonial Georgia, Savannah and Sunbury were the only ports of entry. A lively commercial trade developed at these two centers, as seafaring vessels docked at their wharfs to unload rum and sugar from the West Indies and rum, flour, biscuits, and other provisions from the northern colonies. These ships were then loaded with the commodities produced locally and returned to the destinations from which they came. The number of vessels entering Savannah for trade increased from 41 in 1760 to 171 in 1766; the number entering Sunbury is not known, though Governor Wright reported on the condition of the province in 1772 and stated that Sunbury was a close rival of Savannah in commercial importance, evidenced by the variety and frequency of ships entering and clearing her port annually, loaded with rice, indigo, lumber, shingles,

---

negotiated with the Indians that considerably increased lands available for whites in Georgia. In 1763 the area between Savannah and Augusta was relinquished by the Creek Indians after whites had settled on their lands as squatters. In 1765 the area located between the Altamaha and St. Marys rivers, and already claimed by the English, was formally granted by the Indians. The largest land cession was made in 1773 when two tracts were acquired. One, the area above Augusta known as "New Purchase," contained 1.5 million acres, and the other was land lying west of the original cession made to Oglethorpe, between the Ogeechee and Altamaha rivers. The "New Purchase" tract was ceded by treaty with the Creeks and Cherokees to satisfy a debt of £40,000 that the Indians owed to British traders. "New Purchase" was organized as Wilkes County in 1777.

15. Gray, *History of Agriculture*, 1:289–90, 2:1021–22; Hewatt, *An Historical Account*, 267; "Letters of James Habersham, 1756–1775," in *Collections*, 6:132, 142, 190, 213, 216; Carman, *American Husbandry*, 278–79. Rice was shipped in barrels of 230 lbs. at an average price of 60 shillings per hundredweight or 3 cents per lb. After 1800 rice was also shipped in tierces of 710 lbs., and in casks of 624 lbs.

corn, peas, livestock, barreled beef and pork, all of which were produced in lower Georgia. The bulk of the slave population in coastal Georgia was supplied at Charleston, though occasionally a slave ship arrived at Sunbury. At Savannah, these "slavers" entered the harbor more frequently to supply the increasing demand for labor as the plantation frontier pushed southward.[16]

Crown policy encouraged unlimited land grants and contributed to the rapid growth of rice plantations and slavery in coastal Georgia. Under the family right system, each head of a family was entitled to 100 acres as a headright grant as well as 50 acres for each member of a family, including slaves, up to a total of 1,000 acres. Additional land was easily obtained when the grantee increased his ownership in slaves and demonstrated ability to place more lands under cultivation. This liberal land program stimulated the growth of a slaveholding aristocracy composed of merchants, landlords, and royal officials, who constituted a very small percentage of the white population. The accumulation of extensive holdings in the hands of these few, who became as feudal lords, was entirely in keeping with imperial aims, designed to encourage a plantation economy geared to produce staple commodities for export and to discourage the production of finished goods that might compete with those of British manufacturers.[17]

By 1773 sixty persons in Georgia owned 2,500 acres or more of land, for an aggregate of about 350,000 acres. These sixty persons constituted less than 5 percent of the total landholders and had acquired about 20 percent of all lands granted by the government.

16. Stevens, *History of Georgia*, 1:311, 2:53; Charles C. Jones, Jr., *The Dead Towns of Georgia*, in *Collections* 4 (1878): 157–58, 171. *Georgia Gazette*, Oct. 25, 1764, Feb. 14, 1765, Apr. 8, 1767, Mar. 21, May 23, 1770; Phinizy Spalding, "Colonial Period," in Kenneth Coleman, ed., *A History of Georgia* (Athens: Univ. of Georgia Press, 1977), 51–53. Ebenezer, the German Salzburger settlement located about 25 miles northwest of Savannah, as well as Augusta, 125 miles northwest, were inland communities on the Savannah River. Augusta, at the fall line of the river, was of some commercial importance and served as a thriving frontier center for trade with the Indians. Couriers entered the back country from Augusta to exchange goods in return for furs, mostly deerskins. These furs were then transported along the river to Savannah where they were exported. See Chapter 6 for arrivals of slave ships at Savannah and Sunbury.

17. W.W. Abbott, *The Royal Governors of Georgia, 1754–1775* (Chapel Hill: Univ. of North Carolina Press, 1959), 17; Lee Ann Caldwell Swann, "Landgrants to Georgia Women, 1755–1775," *Georgia Historical Quarterly* 61 (Spring 1977): 23–33. In royal Georgia, 164 women received a total of 67,000 acres in individual grants. Though the majority of these grantees operated small farms, 16 of them accumulated tracts of 1,000 or more acres.

Since 2,500 acres represented a headright of forty-nine family members, most of whom were Negro slaves, the average number of slaves owned by an individual with this amount of land was from forty to forty-five. Of the sixty landlords, there were twenty who owned 5,000 acres or more, and a few owned from 15,000 to 27,000; such large holdings were representative of multiple units under operation.[18]

The royal governors exercised authority over all land grants. James Wright and his friends acquired large tracts during his governorship from 1760 to 1771 and again from 1773 to 1776. By 1771 Wright owned eleven plantations, an aggregate of 24,578 acres, and 523 slaves. His plantations were located along the Canoochee, Ogeechee, and Savannah rivers. The average size of a plantation was forty-seven slaves; slightly more than half were field hands. A force of thirty laborers under direction of a slave driver was utilized as a balanced ratio to cultivate rice fields ranging in size from 150 to 200 acres.[19] Wright's son, Alexander Wright, owned two plantations and an appropriate number of slaves to labor on these units.[20]

John Graham, lieutenant governor, the largest single landowner in colonial Georgia, emigrated from Scotland in 1753 and opened a factorage house at Savannah. He was appointed a member of the Royal Council by Governor Wright in 1764. During the years that followed he acquired, by grant and purchase, various tracts of land ranging in size from 300 to 2,000 acres and eventually owned a total of 26,578. He also owned 277 slaves. Located on the Savannah River were Monteith, Mulberry Grove, and New Settlement Plantations. In lower Georgia near the Altamaha Riv-

18. Heath, *Constructive Liberalism*, 63–64.

19. Flanders, *Plantation Slavery in Georgia*, 43; Gray, *History of Agriculture*, 2:730–31. The average annual output of work for a full hand in cultivating rice and subsistance crops was from five to six acres, though Gray states that seven acres per hand might be realized when mules and plows were used by laborers to prepare the land for planting. See David LeRoy Coon, "The Development of Market Agriculture in South Carolina, 1670–1785" (Ph.D. diss., Univ. of Illinois, 1972), 179–80, for a description of rice planting on inland swamps. Coon states that Gov. Glen of South Carolina recommended thirty slaves per overseer as a proper ratio; each slave was expected to cultivate three acres of rice in addition to food crops and caring for livestock.

20. Conveyance Book X, 2:759–60, Deed Records, Chatham County; *Colonial Records*, 9:696; *Georgia Gazette*, Apr. 19, 1769. Alexander Wright married Elizabeth Izard of South Carolina in 1769. She was the daughter of a wealthy planter and, no doubt, brought to her husband in marriage a handsome dowry.

er, Graham owned 1,500 acres; on St. Simons Island, 500; and along the Satilla River, 1,000.[21]

James Habersham, Georgia's leading colonial merchant and acting governor from 1771 to 1773, serves to illustrate again the manner in which wealth and social standing were attained by those individuals who were among, or associated with, the governing staff of royal officials. Habersham owned Silk Hope Plantation on the Little Ogeechee River. This unit comprised 15,000 acres of land, contained 200 slaves, and was managed as two separate units. Acreage improved in rice fields is not known but an aggregate yield of 700 barrels of rice was produced annually on these units in the 1770s, reflecting a gross annual return of some £1,250. Habersham's factorage business in partnership with Francis Harris provided another source of profit. He marketed the rice crops produced on the plantations of his friends and charged the usual commission for this service.[22]

Such notable South Carolinians as Jonathan Bryan and Miles Brewton migrated to Georgia during these years to engage in rice planting. Bryan arrived in 1752 and over a period of five years accumulated, by grant and purchase, 1,400 acres along the Savannah River, where he established Walnut Hill Plantation. In 1765 Bryan sold a portion (500 acres) of Walnut Hill to Brewton for £1,400 and moved with his family to Brampton Plantation on the Savannah River west of the city. The acreage that Brewton purchased consisted of rice fields already improved, a residence, houses for Negroes, and other outbuildings. Brewton acquired additional land to expand his planting interests and eventually owned 2,500 acres.[23]

21. Conveyance Book DD, 175, Deed Records, Chatham County; *Collections*, 3:232, 376–78; *Georgia Gazette*, July 5, 1764, Mar. 22, 1775; *Royal Georgia Gazette*, Feb. 1, 1781. John Graham was given the hollow title of lieutenant governor by the British crown when he was forced to flee with his family from Georgia in 1776. See *Collections*, 377.

22. "The Letters of Hon. James Habersham, 1756–1775," *Collections*, 6:75–76, 219; Record of Land Grants, *Colonial Records*, vols. 6–11; *Columbian Museum and Savannah Advertiser*, Mar. 26, 1810.

23. *Register of Colonial Grants*, Book A, p. 78, Department of Archives and History, Atlanta; *Colonial Records*, 7:154–55, 334; Conveyance Book C, 2:807–808, 840–41, Chatham County; *Revolutionary Records of the State of Georgia*, 1:229; George M. White, *Statistics of the State of Georgia* (Savannah, 1849), 125; *Georgia Gazette*, July 27, 1768; J.H. Redding, *Life and Times of Jonathan Bryan, 1708–1788* (Waycross, Ga., 1901), 33. Bryan was a prominent figure in the local community and a member of the King's Council. He chose, however, to identify with the Patriots during the American Revolution, was imprisoned for a time by the British, and then was released. He and Brewton owned considerable property

John G.W. DeBraham spent several years in Georgia as surveyor-general for the British government. After observing a number of rice plantations in operation he estimated the total cost of undertaking such an investment to be £2,476. This estimate was made on land already cleared, drained, and dyked. Itemized expenses included the purchase of forty working hands at a cost of £1,800; 200 acres of land, £100; incidentals such as slaves' clothing, oxen, horses, plantation tools, medicine, doctor's fees and provisions, £206; timber and boards to build a barn and pounding machine, £22; overseer's wage, £50; loss of Negroes due to death, £100.[24]

DeBraham also estimated the return on capital invested. He expected forty working hands to cultivate 130 acres planted in rice and 70 acres in provision crops, and his expected rice harvest to yield 350 barrels, or an annual income on investment of £28. In time, as expended capital decreased, income on investment would increase to £29. DeBraham's estimated figures on yields appear to be correct, as 2½ to 3 barrels of rice per acre or 8 to 10 barrels per hand were considered average. The price of rice varied with its quality and fluctuated with changing demand and supply in the market; the average price from 1719 to 1773 was 2.1 cents per pound; from 1789 to 1860, 3.3 cents per pound. On the assumption of available annual prices for the period between the Revolution and the Civil War, prices were above average in 1795 at 5.9 cents as a result of increased demand for grain caused by the war in Europe. From 1802 to 1807 prices rose above average to 4.5 cents but fell to 3.3 from 1808 to 1812. The War of 1812 increased the demand for foodstuffs, and so the price rose and remained above average at 4.3 cents until 1819. From 1820 to 1836 prices were below average at 2.9 cents, reflecting a greater production of rice. The period of low prices continued until 1845; the high prices of 1845 averaging 3.5 cents were due to the failure of grain crops in 1844. Except for the year 1858 when the average price

---

in South Carolina before coming to Georgia. Brewton and his family were drowned at sea while on a voyage from Charleston to Philadelphia, where Brewton was going to represent South Carolina in the Second Continental Congress. Philip M. Hamer, George C. Rogers, Jr., David R. Chestnutt, Peggy J. Clark, eds., *The Papers of Henry Laurens*, 3 vols. (Columbia: Univ. of South Carolina Press, 1976), 3:404–405, 433–54. In 1763 Henry Laurens of South Carolina petitioned for and was granted 3,000 acres of land on the south bank of the Altamaha River near Broughton Island. Laurens transported slaves to the area and developed a thriving rice plantation, though he directed the operation of this unit as an absentee owner.

24. *History of the Province of Georgia, With Map of Original Survey* (Wormsloe edition, 1849).

dropped to 2.9 cents, 1852 to 1861 was a period of better prices, averaging 3.5. (See Appendix A, Table A-3, for annual average prices from 1719 to 1860.[25])

The indigo industry in Georgia made little progress during the last twenty years of the colonial era. Reasons for the lack of a noticeable increase in production prior to the American Revolution are not clear, though the growth and profitability of the rice industry must have been a contributing factor in its decline. In South Carolina indigo production increased from 590,728 pounds in 1772 to 747,219 in 1775, whereas in Georgia production decreased from 19,900 pounds to 11,882. Indigo was cheaper to produce than rice because capital investment was comparatively low, but the quality of indigo produced in Georgia and Carolina was inferior to that of indigo produced in East Florida and the French West Indies. French indigo sold for 8 to 10 shillings per pound, but indigo manufactured in Carolina and Georgia sold for 2 shillings. The American Revolution brought to an end the British demand for and bounty on indigo.[26]

The tidewater experiment in rice planting and the liberal land policy evinced during the twenty-four years of royal government created a society of exclusive slaveholding planters in coastal Georgia, not unlike the society along the coast of South Carolina. These Georgia aristocrats, representing a small minority of the white population, attained wealth in land and slaves because of the benefits accruing to them from imperial policy. As a result their conservative ideals were nurtured to such an extent that, with few exceptions, this first generation of Georgians identified with the British ruling class and remained loyal subjects of the crown at the time of the American Revolution. Governor Wright's treaties with the Indians had opened vast lands in the interior and gave the small farmer, as he pushed westward, opportunity to

25. Gray, *History of Agriculture*, 1:289–90, 2:275–76. Inventories and appraisals of estates contain annual accountings with factors and merchants listing rice shipped and prices received from Charleston and Savannah in the nineteenth century. These accountings are among court records within the six counties involved in this study: Chatham, Bryan, Liberty, McIntosh, Glynn, and Camden; Carman, *American Husbandry*, 278–79.

26. DeBraham, *History of the Province of Georgia*, 51; Gray, *History of Agriculture*, 1:290–95, 2:1024. A description of the planting and manufacturing of indigo is contained in the following references: General John Floyd, "On the Cultivation and Preparation of Indigo," *Southern Agriculturist* 2 (Mar. 1829): 105–107, 154–62; Phillips, *American Negro Slavery*, 91–93; Elise Pinckney, ed., *The Letterbook of Eliza Lucas Pinckney, 1739–1762* (Chapel Hill: Univ. of North Carolina Press, 1972), xvii–xix.

obtain acreage; thus, he was less aware of the social injustice caused by the accumulation of, in the hands of a few, the most desirable lands along the coast.

Leadership in the movement for independence came primarily from the second generation of Georgians, the sons of Tory fathers—planters and merchants. Noble Wimberly Jones, the son of a wealthy planter and crown official, was the first of these young "democrats" to express vocal opposition. Joseph Clay, Samuel Elbert, John and Joseph Habersham (the sons of James Habersham), and Andrew McLean and Edward Telfair were among the younger generation of merchants who became revolutionary leaders.[27] During the Revolutionary War the great rice plantations of both Loyalists and Americans fell into disrepair and their slaves escaped, approximately 7,000 fleeing to the British lines, where they were granted freedom.[28] Others fled into the back country to find refuge with the Creek Indians and into Florida with the Seminoles. After the war, the rice coast was slowly rehabilitated and the plantations of this area once again became thriving units.[29]

27. Deed Records, Book W, p. 421, Book 2G, p. 280, Book D, p. 409, Chatham County; *Records of the Commons House of Assembly, 1770–1773*, in *Colonial Records*.

28. For the most complete coverage of the American Revolution, see Kenneth Coleman, *The American Revolution in Georgia, 1763–1789* (Athens: Univ. of Georgia Press, 1958); Benjamin Quarles, *The Negro in the American Revolution* (Chapel Hill: Univ. of North Carolina Press, 1961), p. 163; Allen P. Tankersley, "Midway District: A Study of Puritanism in Colonial Georgia," *Georgia Historical Quarterly* 32 (Mar. 1948): 149–57.

29. Gary M. Walton and James F. Shepherd, *The Economic Rise of Early America* (New York: Cambridge Univ. Press, 1979), 192, 198–200. Rice recovered less rapidly than did most other crops. Walton and Shepherd stress the adverse effects of the American Revolution on the national maritime trade and the overall American economy. The war interrupted the growing specialization in production, an expanding agricultural productivity, and the beginnings of urbanization. However, by the early 1790s trade and exports were increasing, and New York and the New England states (except New Hampshire) had recovered from trade disruptions; the southern states were slower to recover. Two events in 1793 stimulated the American economy: the Napoleonic Wars broke out and Eli Whitney invented the cotton gin. These events offered possibilities for industrial development and encouraged an unprecedented economic growth.

CHAPTER TWO

Expansion of Slavery and Profitability of Tidewater Plantations in the Nineteenth Century

During the American Revolution those Loyalists in Georgia who chose to identify with the British were declared guilty of treason, and their properties were subject to escheat under the Confiscation Acts of 1778 and 1780. A board of commissioners directed the distribution and resale of their estates. Approximately 200,000 acres, much of which constituted choice rice fields, were claimed by the new state government. In the distribution of this property several Revolutionary War heroes were favored with gifts of large plantations, two of whom were Nathanael Greene and Anthony Wayne.[1]

Greene was the recipient of the confiscated property of John Graham. This valuable 2,171-acre tract on the Savannah River, called Mulberry Grove, was presented to Greene in 1785. The plantation was described as having 500 acres of rice fields "under good dams and well drained," and 200 acres of highland suitable for cotton and provision crops. Improvements on the plantation included a rice mill, barns, overseer's house, a handsome residence, slave quarters, gardens, fruit orchards, and a variety of

1. Robert Watkins and George Watkins, eds., *Digest of the Laws of the State of Georgia* (Philadelphia, 1800), 209, 211; *Colonial Records*, vols. 1–3; Samuel G. McLendon, *History of the Public Domain in Georgia* (Atlanta, 1924), 178–82; Bonner, *History of Georgia Agriculture*, 32–40; Heath, *Constructive Liberalism*, 70. Among the Loyalists who lost their estates were James Wright, John Graham, Josiah Tattnall, James Hume, John Mullryne, Alexander Wylly, William McGillivray, George Kincaid, Joseph Farley, and Basil Cowper. Headrights and bounty grants exceeding 3 million acres in Georgia were conveyed to veterans of the

shrubs. Greene was in the process of restoring the plantation to make of it a productive unit when he died suddenly in 1786, leaving the estate heavily indebted. His widow had to sell Mulberry Grove in 1800 for $15,000 to satisfy Greene's creditors. This plantation later became one of the most productive rice units in Chatham County after it changed hands several times.[2]

Anthony Wayne received, in 1786, Richmond and Kew plantations, the confiscated property of James Wright. This estate contained 1,300 acres, of which 275 were rice lands valued at £13 per acre. The financial story of Anthony Wayne, in successfully directing the management of his plantation, ends much like that of Nathanael Greene. Wayne's creditors, the firm of James and Edward Penman of Charleston, foreclosed on Richmond and Kew to satisfy an indebtedness of £5,000 due them. William Bulloch, the next owner of Richmond and Kew, maintained the plantation as a productive enterprise for thirty-five years. A severe economic depression immediately followed the American Revolution. The financial reverses of Greene and Wayne may have been partially caused by this condition; nonetheless, overextension of credit with insufficient collateral contributed to their losses.[3]

Other patriots of the Revolutionary War had conveyed to them, or were given the opportunity to purchase at public auction, choice lands that had belonged to Loyalists; the grants and purchases launched their financial careers. Samuel Elbert, James Jackson, James Habersham, and John Morel were but a few who obtained desirable tracts in recognition of their contribution during the war. John Morel was presented with Tweedside Plantation, a 450-acre tract on the Savannah River. Morel's slaves reclaimed the rice fields on Tweedside and his planting interests brought profitable returns; he sold several hundred bushels of seed rice, carefully selected from his 1796 crop. The price of seed rice averaged from 15 to 20 cents per pound; rice shipped to market averaged 3 cents. Morel died in 1802, leaving a substantial estate to his heirs: three plantations, numerous slaves, and the harvested rice on Tweedside valued at $8,400.[4]

Revolutionary War. Less than one-third of the conveyances, however, went to Georgia veterans. Most of the land was granted to migrants from the Carolinas and Virginia, who poured into the interior of Georgia after the Revolution.

2. Deed Book U, p. 129, Deed Book W, pp. 279, 281, 283, Chatham County; *Columbian Museum and Savannah Advertiser*, Oct. 26, 1798, July 8, 1800.

3. Deed Book H, p. 562, T, p. 66, 2D, pp. 21, 494, 515, Chatham County.

4. Will of John Morel, box M, fol. 90, Probate Records, Chatham County;

Competent slaveholders like Morel restored and improved their properties in less than a decade after the war and were setting the pace for the progressive growth of rice culture that would continue to the period of the Civil War. When the first census was taken in 1790, the total population of Georgia was 82,548, classified under three districts. (See Appendix A, Table A-4, for the distribution of population within these districts.[5])

The heaviest black population was to be found within the Lower District in Chatham and Liberty counties, in which slaves outnumbered whites by nearly four to one. Early tax returns for these two counties are not available, but estate inventories indicate that individual ownership in slaves was large even at this early date. Glynn and Camden counties were sparsely settled; Bryan and McIntosh counties were not created until 1793 after the first census was taken. As the frontier advanced southward along the coast, these counties composing the rice belt became inhabited with large slave populations where desirable lands had been reclaimed and developed into productive plantations. The counties of the Upper District and Middle District were inhabited by many farmers whose ownership in land and slaves was small. The total number of families in 1790 throughout the state was 9,867 and only 25 percent were slaveowners; the majority owned fewer than twenty.[6]

The successful production of rice benefited from cheap labor, and Negro slaves furnished the only available supply. The slave population increased as the rice belt advanced. By 1820 slaves numbered 70 percent of the total population of 33,691 in Chatham, Bryan, Liberty, McIntosh, Glynn, and Camden counties; by 1850 they numbered 72 percent of the total of 52,530. An increase in the white population of Chatham County, partially the result of an increase in the merchant class located at Savannah,

---

Revolutionary Records, 1:426; *Collections*, 3:33, 38, 60; *Columbian Museum and Savannah Advertiser*, May 3, 1796, Mar. 21, 1797.

5. *United States Census Returns*, 1790 to 1860. Effingham County, within the Lower District, lies northwest of Chatham County along the Savannah River and was not a rice-producing area, being too far inland for its swamp lands to be sufficiently affected by the push of tides from the Atlantic Ocean.

6. Ruth Blair, ed., *Some Early Tax Digests* (Atlanta: Georgia Department of Archives and History, 1926), 29–30; *United States Census Returns*, 1790 to 1860; Harper, "Development of Agriculture in Lower Georgia from 1850 to 1880," 112–15. Harper's agricultural statistics for lower Georgia, taken from the 1860 census, show the slave population to be 54% in the coast strip and inhabitants per farm, 95. The rice coast continued, throughout the antebellum era, to have the most valuable farms and the most machinery, slaves, horses, and oxen per farm.

Figure 2. Percentage of Slaves to Total Population, 1860. (Drawing by Leonora Quarterman.)

caused the ratio of blacks to whites to drop by 1860 to slightly less than 70 percent of the total population of 58,250 within the six rice belt counties.[7] (See Appendix A, Table A-5, for population growth in the rice coast counties from 1800 to 1860, and Table A-6, for population growth of Georgia from 1800 to 1860.)

Rice production became large scale early in the nineteenth century. Native Georgians who had engaged in rice planting before the American Revolution expanded operations. Carolina planters, faced with declining profits due to rising costs and soil deterioration, expanded their interests in Georgia; their plantations often functioned as outpost organizations, managed by the sons and relatives of the rice kings of Charleston and Georgetown.[8] John Potter of Charleston invested in rice lands on the Georgia side of the Savannah River to launch the careers of his two sons. Potter purchased Colerain Plantation in 1817; his son, James, managed the plantation for several years, then was given title to the land and slaves. In 1832 the younger son, Thomas, was given Tweedside Plantation with its slaves. These two plantations were highly profitable; in 1845, on 500 acres planted on Tweedside, 30,000 bushels of rice were produced, representing a gross profit of $40,000; the yield from 550 acres on Colerain was slightly less.[9]

Stephen Elliott, Daniel Blake, and Arthur Heyward, sons of wealthy Carolinians, exemplify the movement into the Ogeechee River district, where extensive rice plantations were developed. Elliott purchased 500 acres in 1795 and later purchased land contiguous to this original tract, enlarging his ownership to include 1,100 acres known as Vallambrosa Plantation. In 1827 Elliott sold Vallambrosa to Daniel Blake of South Carolina. Blake and his family resided on Vallambrosa and in Savannah, dividing their time between the two places. By 1834 Blake had enlarged

7. *United States Census Returns*, 1790 to 1860.

8. House, *Planter Management*, 4.

9. Mary Granger, ed., *Savannah River Plantations*, Savannah Writers' Project (Savannah: Georgia Historical Society, 1947), 228–33. Other Carolinians who owned rice plantations along the Savannah River in Georgia were Louis Manigault and Jacob Read of Charleston. Manigault purchased Gowrie and East Hermitage in 1833; his son, Charles, managed these estates. Read began purchasing rice lands in 1783; by 1806 he owned 3,700 acres known as Drakies Plantation, and 208 Negro slaves. Read continued to live in Charleston, where he practiced law. At the time of his death in 1816, there were 265 slaves on Drakies; the crop of rough rice was valued at $24,500. William Wightman of Charleston was the next owner of Drakies; Wightman died in 1837 and John A. Fraser of Charleston purchased the plantation.

Vallambrosa to include 2,692 acres of land and an indeterminable number of Negro slaves, 183 of whom were included with the original purchase. Blake also owned three steam-powered rice mills in Savannah and the sloop *Othello*, which was used to transport rice from his plantation and his neighbor's to the mills. Daniel Blake died intestate in 1834 and his estate was divided between his two sons and two daughters. One daughter, Louisa, was married to Arthur Heyward of South Carolina. By 1840 Heyward and his wife had bought out the interests of the other beneficiaries in Vallambrosa on the Ogeechee River with its 314 slaves, in addition to the rice mills in Savannah.[10] One mill was described thus: "Upper Steam Rice Mill on the Savannah River, in Oglethorpe Ward, has three engines; two of forty horse power, and one of twenty horse power; number of buildings, seven; all of brick. Beats out 150 tierces of rice per day, or 16,000 tierces per year. Employs about the mill 48 persons, and four or six months in the year about 50 colored women in addition: consumes 1,600 cords of wood per annum."[11]

Among those Carolinians who settled along the Altamaha and Satilla rivers in lower Georgia were Duncan L. Clinch, William R. Gignilliat, Hugh Fraser Grant, Robert Hazelhurst, William H. Hazzard, and T. Pinckney Huger. Grant was the son of Dr. Robert Grant of South Carolina, who migrated to Glynn County after the American Revolution and secured title to land along the Altamaha River; by 1825 he owned 1,500 acres known as Elizafield Plantation. In 1833 Grant retired and divided his estate between two of his sons, Charles and Hugh Fraser.[12]

Duncan L. Clinch acquired choice land along the Satilla River in Camden County where he developed a rice plantation shortly after the War of 1812. Bishop Henry Benjamin Whipple visited Clinch in 1843 and described the plantation: "Gen'l Clinch has one of the largest rice plantations in this section of the country. He plants about 500 acres and has over one hundred field hands. The land is of the richest alluvial soil, and owing to the deposits made upon it by the influence of the tide, is inexhaustable." The rice

10. Mary Granger Collection (typewritten), box 3, Georgia Historical Society (hereafter cited as GHS), contains a description of Vallambrosa Plantation. Vallambrosa is spelled Vallambrosia on several old maps; Unpublished Census Returns, 1840, 1850; Deed Book, 2-S, fol. 198, Records of the Superior Court, Chatham County.

11. Granger Collection.

12. House, *Planter Management*, 7; Unpublished Census Returns, 1840, 1850.

yield in 1843 was about 25,000 bushels (1,150,000 pounds). Clinch's rice lands were of prime quality; according to Whipple, they were worth from $100 to $200 per acre.[13]

The prosperity evidenced in Georgia during the 1850s was the result of a great expansion in the rice industry and the cotton industry of middle and southwest Georgia. Much of the cotton was marketed by merchants at Savannah. Though the subject of short staple cotton is not within the realm of this study, the preponderance in production of short staple cotton in terms of wealth caused the state's center in total population and political influence to shift by 1830 to middle Georgia. Milledgeville, the state capital, located in the heart of the cotton belt, served as the center for a surrounding hinterland of some ninety miles, where two-thirds of the inhabitants of Georgia lived. By 1860 there were 462,198 slaves, 3,500 free blacks, and 591,588 whites living within the state, an aggregate population of 1,057,286. The population of the rice belt represented less than 6 percent of this total.[14]

Because of the unusual requirements necessary to develop tidal flow rice fields and the limitation of available land for such a purpose, not more than a total of 30,000 acres was planted in rice along the rivers of coastal Georgia when production of the staple reached its height in 1860. Rice fields varied in size from 200 to 600 acres. Louis Manigault listed twenty-one plantations and their acreage planted in rice in 1860 on the Georgia side of the Savannah River. The average size per unit was 425 acres, slightly less than the average size of 572 acres for those located along the Altamaha River.[15]

The unpublished census returns for 1850 list seventy-one persons in Georgia whose annual yields in rice ranged from 100,000 to 600,000 pounds; a few had yields of well over a million pounds. These individuals owned from 1,500 to 3,000 acres of land, about half of which was improved and only a portion planted in rice.

13. *Bishop Whipple's Southern Diary*," 1843–44, in Willie Lee Rose, ed., *Documentary History of Slavery in North America* (New York: Oxford Univ. Press, 1976), 506; Will of Duncan L. Clinch, Book C, 207–20, 1849, Probate Records, Camden County. Clinch was a descendant of Nathanial Heyward of South Carolina and grandfather of Duncan Clinch Heyward, author of *Seed From Madagascar*.

14. *United States Census Returns*, 1850, 1860. For the best single account of the rise of the upland cotton belt, see Bonner, *History of Georgia Agriculture*, 47–59.

15. Louis Manigault Plantation Records, 1855–76 (typewritten), GHS; Charles Spalding Wylly, *These Memories* (Brunswick, Ga.: Glover Brothers, n.d.), 40. Wylly was a grandson of Thomas Spalding, a prominent cotton planter of Sapelo Island, McIntosh County.

Rice was also grown on Sea Island cotton plantations along the coast in smaller quantities, but this study is primarily concerned with the planter who specialized in growing rice and whose production was of the dimensions cited above.[16]

Characteristic of the rice plantations in coastal Georgia that produced 100,000 pounds or more of rice annually was Wild Heron in the Ogeechee River District, owned by Francis Henry McLeod. Over the years this plantation and others like it were expanded with increased labor forces to attain for owners a "springtime" in production and prosperity by the mid-nineteenth century. Wild Heron's relic dikes and drainage canals of abandoned rice fields with their ditches, trenches, drains, and quarter-drains are still visible. From the outside bank that enclosed the fields can be seen the main canal that leads to the Ogeechee River and was used to irrigate McLeod's fields. To the east of Wild Heron's abandoned fields are the low country marshes that extend toward the Atlantic Ocean. This setting illustrates the engineering skill of owner and slaves in controlling fresh water tides with an intricate system of trunks and locks that were used to flood and drain fields at intervals while rice was being cultivated. The ruins of the brick rice mill, originally three stories high, are located on high land near the canal. The milled rice was shipped from this point on flatboats to the Ogeechee River, then along this river and to the Savannah River by another canal. At Savannah the rice was deposited at a factorage house to be marketed for the planter.[17]

The acreage that composed Wild Heron was originally land granted in 1747 and 1748 by the Trustees to four settlers who came to Georgia. Several years later, Francis Harris, speaker of the House in the Colonial Assembly, was granted land in the area. In time, Harris purchased his neighbor's tracts and eventually owned 3,400 acres. Harris had two children by his marriage to Mary

16. Unpublished Census Returns, 1850, 1860. Earlier returns were also reviewed but are not as satisfactory, as property values and crop production are not classified separately. The *United States Census Returns* gives the following breakdown by counties for rice (in number of pounds) and Sea Island cotton (in 400-lb. bales, ginned) produced in coastal Georgia in 1860: Bryan, 1,609,676 and 402; Camden, 10,330,068 and 630; Chatham, 25,934,160 and 933; Glynn, 4,842,755 and 688; Liberty, 2,548,382 and 2,405; McIntosh, 6,421,100 and 752.

17. Observations made by the writer during a field trip to Wild Heron Plantation. Judge Shelby Myrick, Jr., owner of Wild Heron, was most helpful in pointing out the remains of the rice fields and their irrigation canals, locks, and trunks that were used to control the tidal flow of water. Myrick stated that Gen. William Tecumseh Sherman stood on the outside bank of the rice fields in Dec. 1864 to direct the bombardment of Fort McAllister, not far from the plantation.

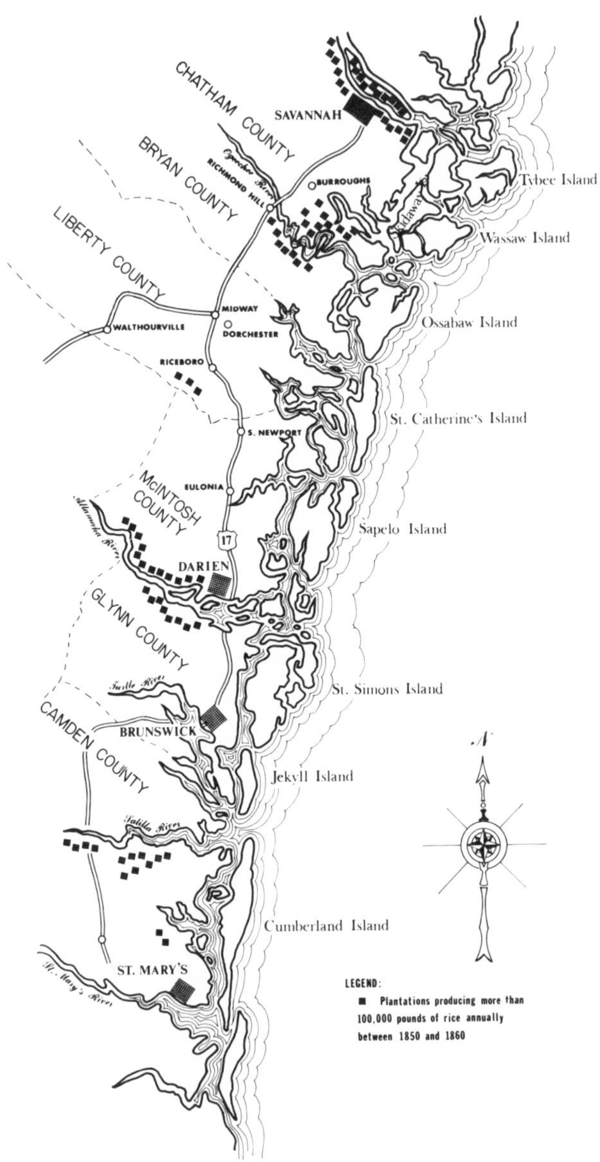

Figure 3. Plantations Producing More than 100,000 Pounds of Rice Annually, 1850–1860. (Drawing by Leonora Quarterman.)

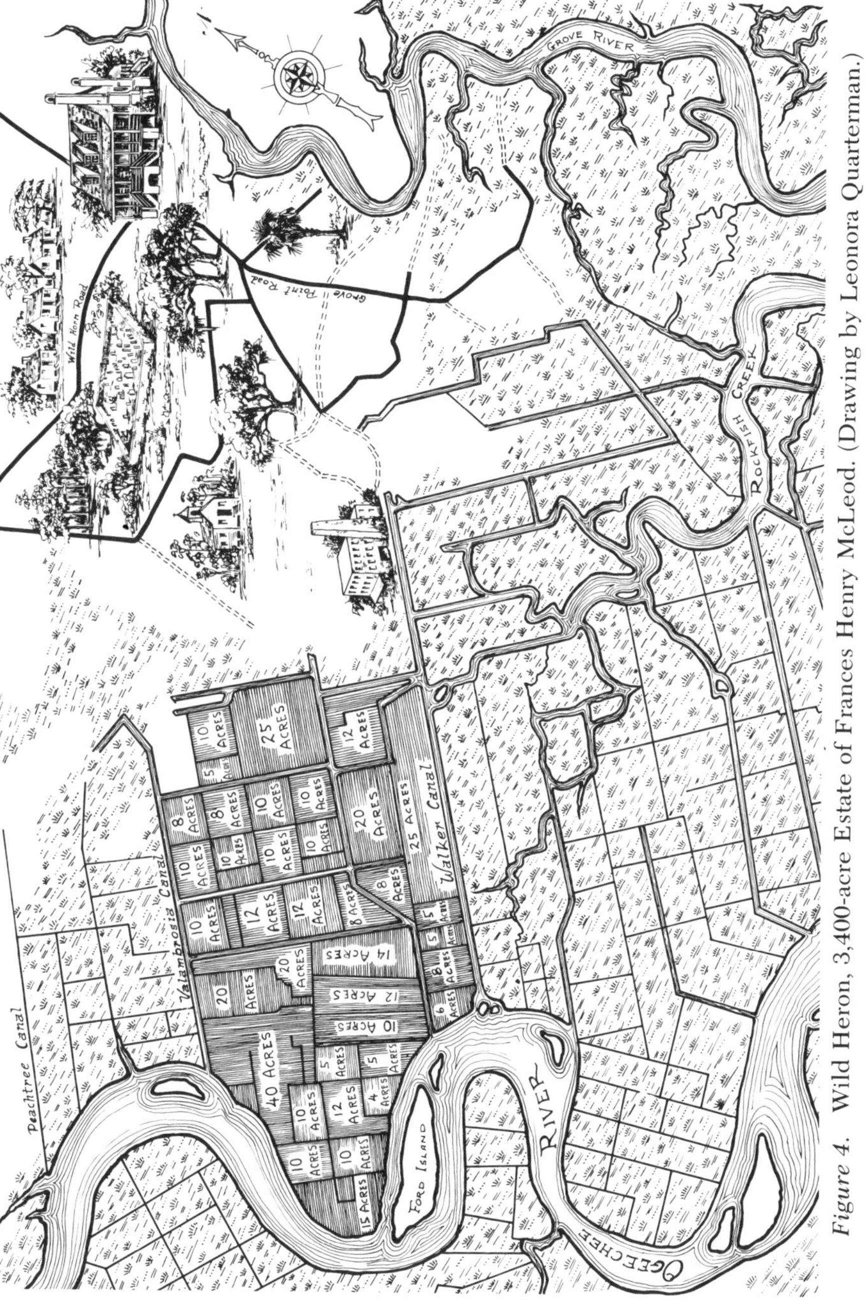

Figure 4. Wild Heron, 3,400-acre Estate of Frances Henry McLeod. (Drawing by Leonora Quarterman.)

Goodall, an English heiress. The son, Francis Henry Harris, was killed during the Revolutionary War. The daughter, Elizabeth, married Dr. Donald McLeod. One of the children of this union was Francis Henry McLeod, who inherited Wild Heron and managed the plantation successfully for over sixty years. On 450 acres planted in rice in 1859, the yield was 1,144,000 pounds, representing a gross return of $34,320.[18]

McLeod died in 1865 leaving an estate valued at $263,905. His land was appraised as follows: 450 acres planted in rice, $45,000; 310 acres of rice fields unplanted, $15,500; 2,000 acres of highlands, $30,000; 1,000 acres of swamp land, $10,000; 100 acres of pine land in Bryan County, $1,000. Also included in the appraisal of McLeod's estate were animals and farm equipment valued at $1,956; $4,000 in gold; $91,095 in Confederate bonds and treasury notes; $76,354 in 129 slaves. His Confederate money and slaves were considered to be of no value at the time of his death but were included in the accounting of his estate.[19]

Inventories and appraisals of estates help to complete a picture of plantation life, for they list specifically the articles that were necessary equipment for operating the plantation. The inventory of Ralph E. Elliott's estate, dated 1854, contains a long list of such items as machinery, ox wagons, flatboats, spades, plows, harrows, blacksmith tools, chains, hoes of many kinds, rice hooks, and various sorts of harness and gear. Elliott's livestock included nine mules, two horses, seventeen oxen, eighty sheep, and eleven cows. The 135 slaves on this plantation, Beech Tree, were valued at $62,158. Among them were skilled laborers worth $1,000 each, and field hands ranging in value from $400 to $900, plus others who were aged or infirm and had no value. The harvested rice on Elliott's plantation was valued at $11,336, and provision crops such as corn, peas, and oats, at $905. Elliott also owned a townhouse and twelve house servants in the city of Savannah. The total value of his estate was $91,785.[20] (See Appendix B, for brief

18. Will of Francis Henry McLeod, Chatham County; MSS in possession of Judge Shelby Myrick, Jr.; Unpublished Census Returns, 1850, 1860.

19. Inventories and Appraisements. Book M, N, 1860–1868, Chatham County, 226–29. Estate appraisals often list ownership in pine lands in the back country away from the plantation, sometimes located in an adjoining county. Pine lands were considered healthy as a place for retreat from the low country. During cholera epidemics slave children were sent to the pine lands, and planter families often retreated there in summer when they had no recourse to a beach area like St. Simons Island in Glynn County or a residence in Savannah, Darien, or St. Marys.

20. Inventories and Appraisements, Book K, 82–86, Chatham County.

sketches of the financial careers of other noted rice planters.)

During the two decades prior to 1850, the typical rice plantation of coastal Georgia represented a capital investment of from $50,000 to $100,000. An average slave cost from $300 to $500, uncleared rice swamps about $40 an acre, and improved rice fields, $80. More often than not, the rice planter was a son, son-in-law, or relative of an established planter and was financed initially by this individual through a loan on long-term credit, by means of an outright gift, or as a beneficiary through inheritance. Hugh Fraser Grant of Glynn County exemplifies this process. Grant was a son of Dr. Robert Grant of South Carolina, who migrated to Glynn County after the American Revolution and began securing title, by grant and purchase, to swamp land on the south bank of the Altamaha River at a location about seven miles inland from its mouth. By 1825 he owned 1,500 acres known as Elizafield Plantation, a choice site composed of swamps suitable for rice culture, pine lands for living quarters for his family and slaves, and fertile highlands for the production of food crops.[21]

Grant retired in 1833, transferring title of Elizafield with 105 slaves to his son, Hugh Fraser Grant, for the sum of $12,500. Evelyn Plantation with 113 slaves and contiguous to Elizafield was transferred to another son, Charles, for a like sum. Charles, a poor manager, became financially insolvent and was forced to sell Evelyn. Neighboring planters, one after another, purchased Evelyn but failed to realize profitable returns, and the plantation continued to revert to the Grant estate. During the years that Evelyn was being passed back and forth between owners, this 345-acre tract became known as Grantly. Hugh Fraser Grant planted these lands during the 1850s and kept a record of their crops along with the Elizafield crops in his plantation journal.[22]

Grant's journal covers the years from 1834 to 1861 and contains a daily account of the work routine on the plantation: slave lists, accounts with factors, relatives and neighbors, overseer's salaries, crop summaries, and scattered tax returns. Grant's managerial expertise is shown in the annual increase of net income from the sale of crops as he placed additional rice fields under cultivation with a greater labor force. In 1845 the yield from 200 acres planted

21. House, ed., *Planter Management*, 6–10, 42. Inventories and appraisals of estates in county court records list values of land, slaves, machinery, and improvements on the plantation. These values approximate the estimates made by House.

22. Ibid.; Deed Book G, 353, Deed Book H, 231, Deed Book K, 346–49, Glynn County.

in rice was 10,168 bushels (45 pounds to the bushel) and net profit, after all marketing costs were deducted, was $10,993. Capital investment for this year is not shown, but operating expenses were $6,483. In 1856 the yield from 345 acres planted in rice on Elizafield and Grantly was 13,971 bushels and net profit was $15,244; operating expenses were $6,527. Interest earned on total capital investment of $99,600 was 8.7 percent. During this year, Grant's tax return was itemized as follows:

420 acres rice land	
800 acres pine land adjoining	$45,000
400 acres and improvements at summer place	1,500
126 Negroes at $400	50,400
All other property	2,700[23]

When calculating their annual net returns, planters seldom included capital gains that accrued from appreciation in improvements on land and from natural increase in Negro slaves through birth. Estate accounts of Georgia rice and Sea Island cotton plantations reveal an average of five births per year for every 100 of total slave population. Hugh Fraser Grant's journal lists twenty-eight births for a six-year period from 1838 to 1845; nine infants died. Some pages are missing from Grant's journal, and so the exact number of slaves owned during these years is not known; however, on the unpublished census returns for 1850 Grant is shown as owning 124 slaves. Louis Manigault's journal lists four births on Hermitage Plantation in 1858 and again in 1859, where there was a total of 46 slaves; no infants died. George Kollock, who grew Sea Island cotton in coastal Georgia, owned 54 slaves in 1849; there were four births during this year and one infant died. In 1861 Kollock owned 72 slaves; there were five births and two infants died.[24] Fertility rates contributed to long-term capital gains. For example, an infant born in 1843, whose value was measured by the pound, ten years later was valued at from $350 to $450.[25]

If unpublished and published census returns are reasonably

23. House, ed., *Planter Management*, 186–88, 221–23, 263; Unpublished Census Returns, 1860. On the census returns, Grant's real estate was valued at $50,000, and his personal property, most of which represented the value of slaves, at $73,000.

24. House, ed., *Planter Management*, 255; Manigault Plantation Records, 1855–76; Kollock Plantation Books, 1837–61; Unpublished Census Returns, 1850, 1860.

25. Gray, *History of Agriculture*, 2:664–66. Gray lists prices quoted in 1853 by a slave broker in Richmond, Va.

correct, and if inventories and appraisals of estates and plantation accountings reflect true values, estimated rates for returns on capital investment for rice planting in coastal Georgia can be placed at 8 percent; individual earnings often exceeded that level. The Manigault family plantation records of rice planting on the Savannah River show average annual return on capital invested to have been 12 percent from 1833 to 1839; the Hugh Fraser Grant records of rice planting on the Altamaha River show annual return to have been 8.7 percent in 1856; the James P. Screven records show annual return to have been 13 percent in 1859.[26] Estimated rates for return on cotton plantations, with the same allowance given, have been placed at 6 percent.

Rice plantations were larger, more specialized, better managed, required more capital investment, and tended to have higher rates of return than cotton and sugar plantations. The rice industry required various skilled occupations: carpenters to build and repair floodgates and trunks, coopers to make barrels, mechanics to operate rice mills, blacksmiths, boatbuilders, boatmen, brickmasons, bird watchers, drivers, overseers, and trunk minders. Though rice plantations were fewer than plantations producing other staples, there was a greater concentration of large units among them. They existed only along a narrow strip of the Atlantic coast and were unique among the plantation systems of the Old South and New World.

In this chapter and the foregoing one, the rice industry in Georgia has been traced from its early beginnings in 1750 when slavery was formally introduced to the period of 1860 when growth reached its peak. During the American Revolution thousands of slaves escaped and the rice plantations fell into disrepair. After the war cargoes of slaves were imported to improve the land, and the plantations were slowly rehabilitated. As economic recovery advanced in the nineteenth century, transplanted Carolinians and native Georgians set about to expand their planting interests and proceeded to claim remaining lands in lower Georgia suitable for rice culture. Thus, well before 1850 plantations were strung out all along the Georgia coast from the Savannah River to the Satilla, impregnating the landscape with rice fields.

26. Manigault Plantation Records: House, ed., *Planter Management*, 6–10, 42; Deed Records, Book 3A, 300, Chatham County; Inventories and Appraisements, Book L, 1858–61, pp. 96–104, Chatham County.

It was only natural that the Georgia coast should develop plantation characteristics similar to those of the Carolina coast. Low country Georgia, like South Carolina, lent itself to the creation of large plantations suitable for rice fields. The majority of the Georgia planters had their roots in low country Carolina; they were the sons and relatives of Carolinians and were familiar with the technical procedures involved in growing rice. They were financed by their forebears or relatives or received properties through inheritance to commence their planting interests. They also inherited their status as planter aristocracy and were the elite of slaveholding society. They were a cultured class and theirs was a world of gracious living, sustained by the labor of their bondsmen. They were patriarchs, concerned with the general welfare of their "people" and, though they were local absentees for part or all of the time, they visited their plantations at regular intervals to observe the conditions of their crops and their slaves. With few exceptions they were efficient managers, as is shown in the steady increase in rice production, slave population, and annual returns from their investments. Labor-management needs on their plantations and the way slaves contributed to the life and economy of low country Georgia are the subject of the next two chapters.

CHAPTER THREE

The Labor of Low Country Slaves

Beside the ungathered rice he lay,
  His sickle in his hand;
His breast was bare, his matted hair
  Was buried in the sand.
Again, in the mist and shadow of sleep,
  He saw his Native Land.

He did not feel the driver's whip.
  Nor the burning heat of day;
For death had illumined the Land of Sleep,
  And his lifeless body lay
A worn-out fetter, that the soul
  Had broken and thrown away![1]

It was customary along the rice coast to perform all work by tasks. In the extremely laborious field work required in growing rice, the task system offered a more realistic method for work assignments than the gang system; the task system was also adopted on Sea Island cotton plantations. Task assignments were designed to produce effective performance and served as a convenient measurement of labor requirements on various projects. The standard measurement (daily assignment) was one-quarter of an acre, a square 105 feet on a side. The equivalent of this measurement was expected whether the work was planting, cultivating, harvesting, or preparing rice for market. Variations in this standard occurred when more strenuous assignments were per-

1. Henry Wadsworth Longfellow, "The Slave's Dream," Langston Hughes and Arna Bontemps, eds., *The Poetry of the Negro, 1746–1970* (New York: Doubleday, 1970), 459–60.

formed, like clearing and preparing new land for cultivation, or when lighter tasks were given, which justified more extensive work. When rice was being planted, the task of a full hand was from one to two acres; when hoeing was being done, the task was a half-acre or less, depending upon the density of the soil and weeds. When rice was being harvested, the task was three-quarters of an acre; threshing with a flailing stick, 600 sheaves for the men and 500 for the women.[2]

Clearing swamp lands to create rice plantations was a tremendous undertaking, and gangs of slave laborers performed such work. The area to be developed was first measured off and then cleared of all growth like cyprus and gum trees, including a jungle-like maze of undergrowth. When the swamp was cleared, an outside bank, or levee, was constructed to surround the proposed rice fields completely. This bank was built of mud and dirt thrown up while digging an inside ditch about twenty feet from it. The ditch created was approximately five feet deep and wide; later, when the fields were flooded, this ditch served as a canal along which flatboats traveled during harvesting. The outside bank had to be higher than the highest tides to insure protection against both salt water flood tides from the ocean side and high tides or freshets from fresh water rivers. It took several years to rejuvenate fields after the soil had been inundated with salt water pushed over the outside bank by hurricane winds or exceptionally high flood tides.[3]

2. House, "Labor-Management Problems on Georgia Rice Plantations, 1840–1860," *Agricultural History* 28 (Oct. 1954): 151–52; "Rules on Rice Estate of P.C. Weston," *De Bow's Review* 22 (Jan. 1857): 40; Easterby, ed., *South Carolina Rice Plantation,* 31; Coon, "Development of Market Agriculture." See Ira Berlin, "Time, Space, and the Evolution of Afro-American Society in British Mainland North America," *American Historical Review* 8 (Feb. 1980): 44–78, and Philip D. Morgan, "Work and Culture: The Task System and the World of Lowcountry Blacks," *William and Mary Quarterly* 39 (Oct. 1982): 563–99, for reasons why the task system came to characterize plantation cultivation in the low country. Berlin contends that environmental conditions of low country slaves resembled those in West Africa and that their isolation from the Anglo-American world caused them to retain their African cultural heritage more completely than slaves in other areas of the southern United States. The practice of field-crop production and technology was one aspect of this heritage. Low country slaves were familiar with the system of tasking and set the course of their work to conform with the strict requirements of rice production. Morgan suggests that production techniques involved in cultivating rice provided convenient units for task assignments; unlike sugar production where strict regimentation necessitated gang labor, rice, like coffee and pimento grown in the British West Indies, was "grown by a slave labor force organized by tasks rather than into gangs."

3. Doar, *Rice and Rice Planting,* 8–9; Heyward, *Seed From Madgascar,* 12.

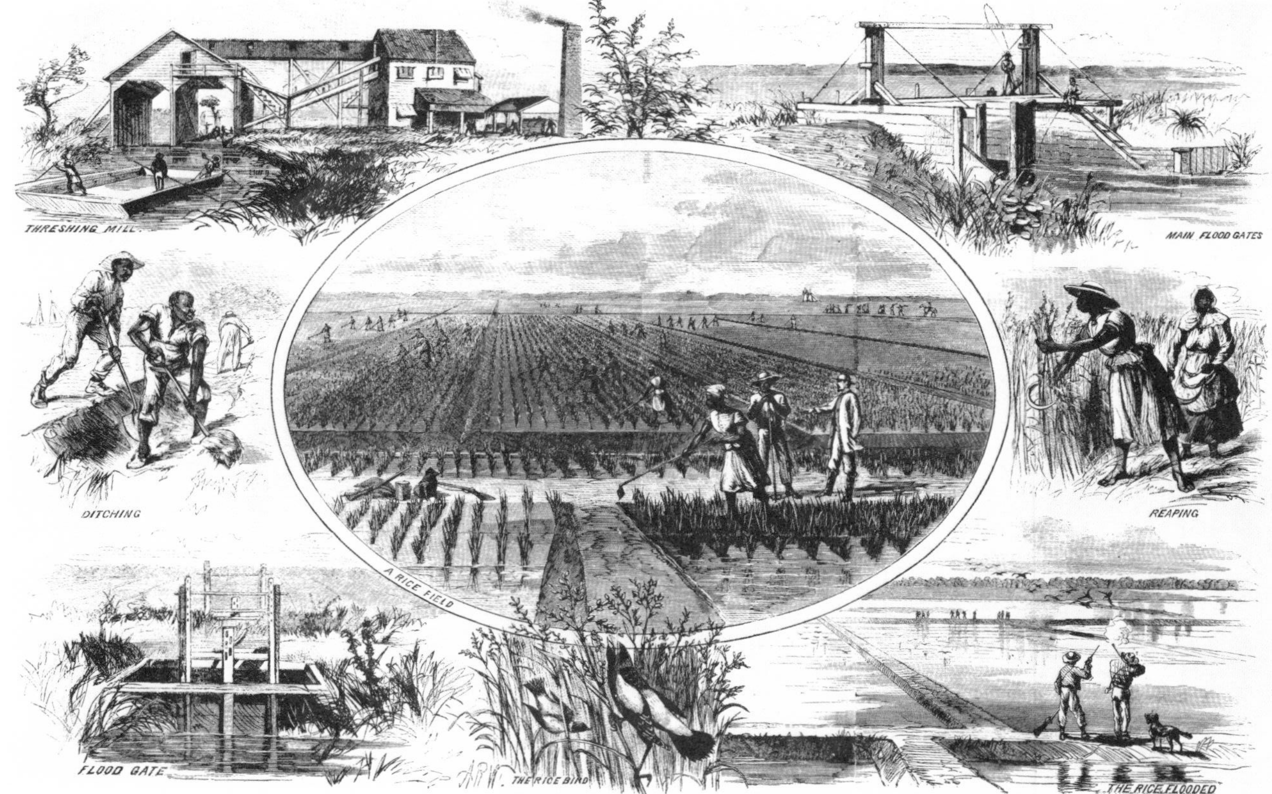

Figure 5. A Rice Plantation in Operation on the Ogeechee River near Savannah, Georgia. (From *Harper's Weekly*, January 5, 1867.)

The level of the land inside the outer bank had to be low enough to be flooded from fresh water rivers at high tide, yet high enough to drain properly at low tide. Before the enclosed area was ready for planting, floodgates were installed in the outside bank, all tree stumps removed, and the land drained and leveled off as evenly as possible. This area within the outside bank to be cultivated in rice was, on an average, from 200 to 500 acres. It was now divided into rice fields, the size of the fields varying from ten to twenty acres. Each field was subdivided into one-acre plots by drains called force ditches that were four feet wide and deep, sloping to two feet at the bottom. Each drain had shorter outlets called quarter-drains that ran through each acre. The quarter-drains were two feet wide, three fee deep, sloping to one foot at the bottom. This arrangement insured an adequate and consistent flow of water to and from each acre when fields were being flooded and drained. Trunks were installed in the larger inside banks (created by ditching) to control the flow to each field. The trunks provided individual irrigation at various stages of culture.[4]

The main floodgates, installed in the outside bank to connect with the river or a canal that led to the river, were constructed of heavy timbers strong enough to withstand the pressure of tidal flow. These gates were composed of two facing doors, fifteen to twenty feet apart, built on and bolted to a heavy wooden frame foundation. At high tide, if the fields were to be flooded, the outer door was raised by the trunk-minder, the slave responsible for that particular task, and the pressure of the water from the river or outside canal constructed to connect with it pushed the inside door open, filling the ditches and flowing into the rice fields. The water continued to flow until it reached the level of the river or canal. As the tide receded, the pressure of the water that flowed from the ditches forced the inside door to close and allowed the water to remain in the fields for the desired time.[5]

Rice fields were prepared for planting in March. Oxen and mules were used to plow and harrow the soft boggy soil. The mules were sometimes equipped with shoes or boots, placed on their hind hoofs to prevent bogging while they pulled the imple-

4. Lawson, *No Heir to Take Its Place*, 6. See Edmund Ruffin, *Agricultural Survey of South Carolina* (Columbia, S.C., 1843), and R.F.W. Allston, "Essay on Sea Coast Crops," *De Bow's Review* 16 (June 1851): 589–615, for descriptions of planting and processing rice for market.

5. Lawson, *No Heir to Take Its Place*, 6.

ments. These boots were made of leather, padded on the inside with straw, reinforced with soles of wood or iron, and tied to the animal's hoofs with leather thongs. Prior to planting, parallel trenches from twelve to fifteen inches apart were dug the total length of the field. Seed rice, which had been threshed by hand with a flailing stick, was used for planting—never mill rice, which might have been injured during the milling process. The rice was placed in the trenches and the water was let into the fields. This first flooding, the "sprout flow," remained from two to five days until the grain pipped. The fields were then drained and allowed to dry.[6]

When the seedling plants appeared, the fields were again flooded. During this second stage of irrigation, the "point" or "stretch" flow, the water again remained on the plants from two to five days; it was then drained off and the plants grew for about two weeks, during which time they were lightly hoed. The third irrigation, the "long" or "deep flow," occurred at mid-season and for several days completely submerged the rice. Dead weeds and other trash floated to the surface, to be raked off onto the banks. The water also killed any insects that may have infested the plants. It then was drained off gradually to a level of six inches and remained from two to three weeks before being drained completely from the fields. For several weeks the fields remained dry while the plants were given two vigorous hoeings. The rice plants were now ready for the fourth and last irrigation, the ' lay-by" or "harvest" flow. The fields were flooded and the water remained in the trenches from seven to eight weeks, supporting the rice plants as they grew and the heads of their stalks became heavy and ripened. The water was then drained off and the rice was ready to harvest, usually late in August and in September.[7]

Slaves worked barefooted in rice fields during summer temperatures ranging between 90 and 100 degrees, standing at times in water up to their knees while their driver stood on the bank with his whip, directing their work to keep them moving at a steady pace. While laboring in rice fields, the men rolled up their pants to keep them dry and the women pulled their skirts above their knees, using a cord around the waist or hips to hold up the slack.

6. "Directions for Planting Rice Given Overseer, 1842," MS, Arnold-Screven Papers, No. 3419, box 3, folder 39, Southern Historical Collection (hereafter cited as SHC). See also Doar, *Rice and Rice Planting*, 13–16; Lawson, *No Heir to Take Its Place*, 8–10.

7. "Directions for Planting Rice," Arnold-Screven Papers.

When harvesting rice, the female hands were described in one account as being more adept than the males: "Armed with the saw-edged, sickle-like 'rice hooks,' the cutters stretched across the squares, each seizing with her left hand as large a bundle of the heavy-headed stalks as she could conveniently grasp, which, with one stroke of her right arm, she quickly severed a few inches above the ground, laid the bundle on the stubble ready for those who tied into sheaves behind her, and, with a sweep of her left, gathered another handful."[8] Constant exposure to heat, humidity, dampness, insects, and poisonous reptiles made cultivating rice, without doubt, more objectionable and strenuous than cultivating dry culture crops and must account for the practice of tasking for work assignments.

Among the many hazards to the growing rice were the eating habits of ducks and birds. The yellow and black bobolinks, called rice birds, could strip a field of sprouted rice and destroy it completely as they headed north in May, or do the same in August and September as they returned to South America. Slaves classified as "bird-minders" used noisemakers such as clappers or muskets and built fires on the banks to protect the fields from these marauders. Alligators, rodents, and snakes were also destructive; sometimes they bored into the outside bank, loosening or undermining the earth that supported the floodgates and causing a break and damage to the fields from water flowing in.[9] Charles Manigault's overseer complained: "I have had two accidents at Gowrie lately. No. 14 trunk next to Mr. Taylor's went into the river at low water. I worked at it until Sunday before I put it together, and while I was at that, here went in about 50 feet of bank No. 12 next to Mr. Guerrard's."[10]

8. Ambrose E. Gonzales, *The Black Border: Gullah Stories of the Carolina Coast* (Columbia, S.C.: State Company, 1922), 135; Heyward, *Seed From Madagascar*, 180; Frederick Law Olmsted, *A Journey in the Seaboard Slave States*, in Mills Lane, ed., *The Rambler in Georgia* (Savannah: Beehive Press, 1973), 224. Heyward and Olmsted state that male and female hands wore cotton or woolen leggings or old rags wrapped around their legs and that sometimes the men wore shoes. Melville J. Herskovits, in *The Myth of the Negro Past* (New York: Harper, 1941), 160–61, writes, "the tradition of cooperation in the field of economic endeavor is outstanding in Negro cultures everywhere." This tradition, carried over into the New World, "found a congenial counterpart in the plantation system."

9. Heyward, *Seed From Madagascar*, 30–39. Rice birds and ducks were considered a delicacy when cooked and served on the planter's table.

10. Louis Manigault Papers, Duke Univ.

Figure 6. "Aunt Phebe," a Former Rice Plantation Slave in South Carolina. (From photograph in Essie Collins Matthews, *Aunt Phebe, Uncle Tom, and Others.*)

Figure 7. A Sheaf of Rice. (Drawing by Leonora Quarterman.)

Figure 8. An Outside Drainage Ditch Leading Away from Wild Heron's Rice Fields. (Drawing by Leonora Quarterman.)

James Potter's Argyle plantation journal serves as a record to show the work routine on rice plantations. Of the 118 slaves on Argyle in 1828, 66 were classified as field hands. These hands were divided into two forces, each under the direction of a slave driver responsible for overseeing their work. These laborers, like all others who worked under the task system, were classified as full hands or fractional hands according to their strength. Fractional hands were those males and females who for one reason or another were not able to do the work of a full hand. They might be adolescents going into the field for the first time, or men and women not strong enough or too old to be classified as full hands. But all fractional hands, whether classified as three-quarters, one-half, or one-quarter, were counted at their fractional equivalents when the number of full hands was totaled. For example, of the thirty-three slave hands on Argyle under direction of the driver, Tommy, thirty were classified as full hands and six as half-hands, of the thirty-three under the driver, Edmund, thirty were full hands, four were half-hands, one was three-quarters of a hand and one was one-quarter.[11]

The overseer's entries in the Argyle journal began in March, the month for planting rice. January and February were spent in preparing the fields: plowing, harrowing, breaking the soil with hoes, clearing off and burning old trash and stubble, cleaning ditches and drains, restoring banks, mending trunks and floodgates, and installing new ones where necessary. Rice was planted intermittently from the middle of March until early May. Those hands not planting rice were engaged in other field labor, and all slaves on the plantation, except children, the elderly, and those who were sick, had work assignments. On March 13, forty were engaged in planting rice, four in trenching, seven in raising banks, two in raking trash, two as watchman and gardener, two as cooks, one as trunkminder, two as drivers, two as nurses for the thirty-one children. On this day, seven slaves were sick, fifteen were working at Colerain, and three were superannuated. On May 22, sixty were hoeing rice while the watchman, gardener, trunkminder, cooks, nurses, and drivers were engaged in their usual tasks; five

11. Journal for Argyle Plantation, 1828–1831, James Potter Papers, GHS; Unpublished Census Returns, 1860. James Potter's holdings were vast. On the Savannah River, in addition to Argyle, he owned Colerain and Onslow, plus 440 slaves dispersed on these three units. The census taker made a notation on one sheet that the slaves listed belonging to Potter were "continued from another schedule, it being impossible for one to hold all of his Negroes."

slaves were sick, four were superannuated, two were minding "fowls and birds," and five were "differently employed."[12]

When the rice was harvested, all available hands were engaged in this important task. The stalks were cut with sickles (rice hooks) and were left on the bank for one or two days to dry. They were then tied together in sheaves and loaded onto flatboats and taken to the plantation yard to be stacked. Sheaves were stacked together on top of each other to a height of fifteen feet, tapering like a haystack so as to shed rain water. The outside measurement of the stacked sheaves was forty-five feet by twelve feet. Bundles of sheaves stacked in these measurements produced about a thousand bushels of rough rice when threshed. Stacking was done with great care; any wet sheaves were opened and dried before stacking to protect the stalks against moisture. The sheaves remained stacked for several weeks or longer while food crops were harvested.[13]

In November and December the rice was threshed, winnowed, and prepared for market. When rice was threshed by hand, slaves used flailing sticks (while the sheaves were still tied) to beat the grain from the stalks onto the clean hard ground, or a threshing floor especially designed for that purpose. After the seeds were threshed, they were taken to the winnowing house to be separated from the chaff (husks of the grain and grasses). The winnowing house was a room ten feet square, elevated from the ground about fifteen feet by supports, with an outside stairway leading up to the room. When the wind was sufficiently strong, the rice was thrown through a grating in the middle of the floor of the room to the surface below while the chaff was blown away. The rice was still in its outer shell and was called rough rice. Pounding or grinding was the next process used to separate the seed from the outer shell. Before pounding mills were perfected for this purpose, mortars made of hollowed out logs held the rice and a wooden pestle was used to pound it. Pounding produced the clean white rice and a residue known as rice flour.[14] Rice was shipped to market either as rough rice or white rice. Plantations like Gowrie and the Hermitage on the Savannah River, Wild Heron on the Ogeechee, and Hopeton on the Altamaha had mills where

12. Journal for Argyle, James Potter Papers.
13. House, ed., *Planter Management*, 51.
14. Doar, *Rice and Rice Planting*, 16–18; Lawson, *No Heir to Take Its Place*, 10, 12; House, ed., *Planter Management*, 60; inventories and appraisals of estates: Camden, Chatham, Glynn, Liberty, McIntosh counties.

Figure 9. The Winnowing House. (Drawing by Leonora Quarterman.)

machines threshed, winnowed, and pounded the rice to prepare it for market.[15] The entire process of growing, harvesting, and preparing rice for market was more intricate and demanding than the process involved in producing cotton, and capital investment in land, labor, and machinery was certainly greater.

Skilled slaves, those craftsmen whose special talents have not been recognized, made a distinct contribution to the total culture of coastal Georgia and the antebellum South. Thomas Spalding's skilled slaves built his mansion house on Sapelo Island, as well as his sugar mill, cotton gin, and other machinery, and supervised the operation of this equipment. The same was true on all plantations where machinery existed, and it did on larger plantations in the nineteenth century. James H. Couper, Thomas Butler King, Henry McAlpin, Francis H. McLeod, James Potter, and other planters whose outlays in equipment and machinery were extensive depended upon the talents of their skilled slaves and the labor of their other slaves for the fortunes they made from growing rice and Sea Island cotton, and for the luxurious style in which they lived.[16]

The skilled slave Sandy Maybank was Charles C. Jones's head carpenter and trusted foreman. Maybank directed the construction of Jones's rice mill and supervised all milling operations. During slack periods in the milling process Jones allowed Maybank to hire himself to neighboring plantations to do mill work. Jones's respect for and confidence in Maybank are shown in the following letter:

15. Estate Accounts, 1824–1829, Book C, 178, Probate Records, Chatham County. At this time Gowrie belonged to the estate of Nichol Turnbull. An entry on one accounting sheet reads: "139 rice tierces furnished for the Estate of Gowrie Mill and 138 bushels rice from the Estate pounded at said mill." The rice was then packed and transported to Savannah by boat to be marketed. Fanner baskets, made by slaves, were also used to winnow rice. These round flat baskets, two to three feet in diameter with small slanting rims, were attractive, sturdy, and utilitarian. Hucksters in coastal Georgia used them until fairly recently to carry and sell their produce, balancing the baskets on their heads as they walked along the streets crying their wares. This custom, like the art of basket weaving, was brought from Africa.

16. See E. Merton Coulter, *Thomas Spalding of Sapelo* (Baton Rouge: Louisiana State Univ. Press, 1940), for the work of Spalding's skilled slaves; also Coulter, ed., *Georgia's Disputed Ruins* (Chapel Hill: Univ. of North Carolina Press, 1937), which contains three essays, two of which relate to the tabby ruins of coastal Georgia; the third, written by Thomas Spalding, is a detailed account of the method used to cultivate sugar cane and to manufacture sugar. This essay is illustrated with sketches of Spalding's machinery. Estate accounts of planters verify the extent of their investments in machinery.

> As I wished to have some work done I thought it would be best to write you a letter that you could keep and so have it by you, that you might not forget anything. . . . You can attend to this work as soon as you can & Porter and William will assist you in it. Am glad to hear that you have been generally well all the season & hope you may continue so. . . . Tell Mary howdye for me—and your children. . . . Your mistress sends howdye for you and for Mary.[17]

Under the hiring system, there were opportunities for the slave to upgrade himself. The growing quasi-freedom of hired slaves was most pronounced in the two decades prior to the Civil War, when hired slaves in the cities and in industry had opportunity for greater mobility. They accumulated money from overtime work on Sundays or while "moonlighting" on another job; they might also receive an incentive wage to stimulate production or a cash bonus for extra labor performed beyond the work assigned. This upgrading of slave laborers into a "shadow-land of quasi-freedom was actually offset by the deteriorating status of the free negro," whose mobility, property rights, and job opportunities were curtailed during these years.[18]

Slave hiring had a significent bearing upon the economics of the labor system. Slaves were hired out to supply various demands: for income to support beneficiaries of deceased owners when there was a shortage of field labor, when skilled laborers were needed for a period of time, or when the owner was not using all of his labor forces for his own production. Advertisements were placed in the local newspapers by persons who wished to hire out their slaves and by those who wished to hire slaves for their own use. In 1788 John Peter Lange was short of labor and needed to hire "about 20 negro field slaves accustomed to rice planting, for whom good wages" would be paid; also "10 or 12 handy jobbing fellows, for assistance in laying the foundation of a rice mill." George Houston wanted to hire "ten or twelve good field hands"

17. As quoted in Starobin, *Industrial Slavery*, 106, 107. See Robert Manson Myers, ed., *The Children of Pride: A True Story of Georgia and the Civil War* (New Haven: Yale Univ. Press, 1972), 264, 305, 306, 307, 658, 659, 688, for references to Sandy Maybank. Maybank died Mar. 15, 1861, and Charles C. Jones referred to his death in a letter to his daughter, Mary S. Mallard: "Our old friend and faithful servant Sandy Maybank died at sunset last evening after a most rapid and desperate attack of pneumonia, which came suddenly upon him. . . . We feel his death, and will miss the cheeful and faithful man always. He has been with us twenty-seven years! Funeral here tomorrow."

18. Richard B. Morris, "The Measure of Bondage in the Slave States," *Mississippi Valley Historical Review* 41 (Sept. 1954): 230–40. See also John B. Boles, *Black Southerners, 1619–1869 (Lexington: Univ. Press of Kentucky, 1983), 116–24.*

to work on his plantation.[19] In 1819 "Six Prime Fellows and one Woman, all field hands, and the fellows axemen and otherwise handy on plantation work" were advertised to be hired out for one year. In another instance a construction firm advertised for "the services of 200 able-bodied negroes" for a period of five months; owners would be paid twelve dollars a month for each slave hired. Large gangs of slaves were needed for heavy construction work.[20]

The rate of hire depended upon the skill of the slave and the type of work to be done. Individuals, estates, or firms hiring slaves were responsible for furnishing them with adequate food, clothing, housing, and medical care; the agreement was made in a written contract. Slaves who belonged to the estate of Isaiah Davenport were hired by the month and year. The rates ranged from $4 to $7 per month.[21] Three slaves, Adam, Eve, and Prince, were hired for twelve months in 1825 by the estate of Nichol Turnbull for $150, and one slave, Amy, a quarter-hand, was hired for eight months in 1829 for $25. The four minor heirs of James Johnston, deceased, were supported and educated on the income from properties of the estate. In 1827 the income received by the children from slave hire was $6,676.[22]

Slaves and free white laborers were hired by the United States government for the construction of Fort Pulaski. Periodically, advertisements in the local newspaper announced that laborers were needed to work on the fort: "Wanted to hire by day, month, or year, ten black masons to work on fortifications at this place." At another time, "100 White or Black Laborers" were needed, as well as carpenters: "wanted to hire, four good steady ship carpenters—none but such need apply." The wage paid for each "prime slave" hired was $14 a month, "the owner to lose runaway time only and the Government to furnish physician and medicine. Any slave [could] be withdrawn from the work in one day's notice."[23]

Actually, few whites were recruited to work on Fort Pulaski because they refused to labor in the summer heat. It was an error to think that black laborers could withstand humid summer climate in the South and that white laborers could not. Blacks suf-

19. *Georgia Gazette*, Mar. 10, 1788, Mar. 1, 1789.
20. *Daily Georgian*, Jan. 18, 1819.
21. Inventories of Estates, Book B, 1819–24, p. 180, Probate Records, Chatham County.
22. Estate Accounts, Book C, 1825–29, pp. 178, 343–45, 457, Probate Records, Chatham County.
23. *Georgian*, Feb. 24, 1825, Dec. 13, 1831, Nov. 18, 1833, July 19, Aug. 4, Aug. 20, 1836.

fered and died from the depleting effects of humidity and disease caused by unsanitary conditions, while white laborers refused to work in such an environment. A cholera epidemic in 1834 among slaves who were on Cockspur Island working on Fort Pulaski caused many to die. Those remaining "were ordered home to their masters and the laboring force was seriously crippled."[24]

In 1837 and 1838 Irish immigrants were employed to work on the Brunswick and Altamaha Canal. Prior to their employment, slaves had been hired from local owners to dig the canal; the work was found to be too difficult for about 200 of the 500 slaves, who "were only accustomed to the light labors of the cotton field." The Irish workers soon fought among themselves, with those from Cork, Ireland, pitted against those from Kerry, and the local militia had to settle this fight. For several years, about 300 Irishmen and Negro slaves worked together digging the canal. The Panic of 1837 caused a shortage of money and credit facilities, and the canal was never completed.[25]

A trend toward replacement of Negro laborers with free white laborers occurred in certain occupations such as canal and railroad building, stevedoring, and textile manufacturing. Many companies, however, after experimenting with white labor, converted back to slave labor. Immigrants, with their Old World animosities, tended to be unruly and unreliable; quarrels sometimes erupted into brawls, and, on occasion, minor disputes erupted into riots that interrupted work and destroyed property. Free white labor proved to be more expensive and troublesome to the South than slave labor.[26] Free white labor did not replace Negro labor in Savannah. The Negro population in Savannah continued to increase, though the percentage to total population declined as a result of the greater-than-normal increase in immigrant population.

In 1859 the Savannah and Atlanta Railroad Company needed "thirty able-bodied men and women to work on repairs of the road." In 1862, 1,000 Negroes were needed "for important work in the neighborhood of Savannah." An appeal was made to the plant-

24. Rogers W. Young, "Major General Joseph King Fenno Mansfield" (typewritten), Fort Pulaski, 1935.

25. Edward M. Steel, Jr., "Flush Times in Brunswick, Georgia, in the 1830's," *Georgia Historical Quarterly* 39 (Sept. 1955): 231–38; Margaret Davis Cate, *Our Todays and Yesterdays: A Story of Brunswick and the Coastal Islands* (Brunswick, Ga.: Glover Brothers, 1930), 208–210. Thomas Butler King of Glynn County promoted the Brunswick and Altamaha Canal project.

26. Starobin, *Industrial Slavery*, 116–17.

ers of Georgia to furnish this force without delay. The value of each Negro would be appraised and if he "fell into the hands of the enemy" (Union troops), the owner would be reimbursed in the amount of the appraisal. Owners would receive $11 per month for each field hand, $13 for railroad hands, $15 for carpenters, $20 for drivers. Food, clothing, quarters, and medical expenses would be furnished.[27]

Generally the life of the hired slave was not easy, though hired slaves, like plantation slaves, expected, as reasonable, a certain level of production. Employers seldom abused the system, for bad treatment was economically counterproductive. Industrial slaves received money bonuses for extra work; this incentive prompted many to work overtime and was a decided advantage, for it allowed opportunity to express initiative and freedom of choice in deciding the amount of work to be performed above what was expected.[28]

Rice plantation slaves, like hired slaves, had an advantage over those who worked from sunup to sundown under the gang system and had little uncontrolled time to call their own. The gang system was a general practice on plantations throughout the South. The task system was a general practice only on rice and Sea Island cotton plantations in low country Carolina and Georgia. The task system served as a convenient measurement of labor requirements; the standard measurement or daily assignment was one-quarter of an acre or the equivalent thereof. When the task was completed, the slave had leisure time to engage in personal pursuits. Contemporary travelers commented upon the merits of the system: Basil Hall noted that slaves preferred the "method of tasking," and that "active hands" completed their work "generally by the middle of the day, others in two-thirds of the day." Charles Lyell noted: They "begin work at six o'clock in the morning, have an hour's rest at nine for breakfast, and many have finished their assigned task by two o'clock, all of them by three. . . ." Frederick Law Olmsted reported that task assignments were not unreasonable and that "the more industrious and active hands finished them often by two o'clock."[29]

The successful production of rice required precise workmanship throughout the various stages of cultivating, harvesting, and preparing the grain for market; the labor involved was more de-

27. *Daily Morning News*, Aug. 22, 1859, June 6, 1862.
28. Boles, *Black Southerners*, 123–24.
29. Lane, ed., *Rambler*, 66, 197, 225.

manding and objectionable than that required in the production of dry culture crops and was more suited to the performance of an individual worker rather than a gang of workers. The demands involved in producing rice were more effectively met when laborers were assigned individual tasks, which is why the task system was superior to the gang system for work assignments. The system encouraged initiative among slaves to complete the work within a reasonable length of time, the reward for which was free time.

Low country slaves used their free time to good advantage in a variety of ways: for leisure; to socialize; to make handcrafts, casting nets, and canoes; to hunt and fish; or to cultivate their garden plots; they also raised poultry. They sold their wares, boats, and produce for money, or exchanged them for tobacco and other choice items—in this way, they maintained a lifestyle somewhat different and perhaps less debilitating and demeaning emotionally than slaves in other plantation belts. Though they were more isolated and less acculturated than slaves in other areas, they could claim a modicum of self-esteem.

Whatever may have been the origins of tasking (scholars are not in full agreement), it was put to efficient and productive use as a labor system for slaves along the Carolina and Georgia coast. Many of the slaves transported to South Carolina and Georgia in the eighteenth century were from the Grain Coast of West Africa and had cultivated rice in their native land for home consumption and for market. (See Chapter 6 for slave importations into Carolina and Georgia.) They brought the knowledge of rice growing with them, along with their agricultural practices for determining work assignments. It is logical to presume that their familiarity with rice culture was utilized by owners and overseers in determining more effective and efficient methods for growing rice.

One need only travel along the mighty Altamaha River in Georgia, the Wacamaw in South Carolina, or others that were utilized to irrigate rice fields to be reminded of the special features that characterized rice plantations and the contributions of those slaves who kept them in operation. The shorelines of these rivers are indented with relic floodgates and canals that served to control the tidal flow of fresh water to and from fields. Beyond the shorelines are the deteriorated fields, overgrown with marsh grass, with the outline of their banks, drains, and quarterdrains barely visible. These remains serve as testimonials to the ingenuity of low country slaves who developed and worked these fields to produce the staple for a world market, and without whose labor such an industry could not have existed.

CHAPTER FOUR

Overseers and Drivers

White overseers as a class have been characterized as uneducated and uncouth, sometimes inhumane in their treatment of slaves. Undoubtedly many of them were, especially in the lower South where a large floating population of amateur overseers, inexperienced and incapable of managing large groups of slaves, moved from one plantation to another at the end of each year. It was this group that contemporary writers described when they traveled in the South and created a stereotyped image of the overseer.[1] Overseers were not always of this class. Some were the sons of planters who acted as managers of plantations for the valuable knowledge to be gained. Others were professional managers, experienced and responsible persons who directed the successful operation of plantations and management of slaves for the owner. This last group often accumulated acreage and slaves for themselves, and some even moved into the planter class.[2]

It has been suggested that the overseers employed on rice plantations were generally more competent and reliable than

1. William K. Scarborough, *The Overseer: Plantation Management in the Old South* (Baton Rouge: Louisiana State Univ. Press, 1966), 192–93. Scarborough reexamined the overseer and gave him a new image; not inevitably gross, the overseer was sometimes literate and articulate in expressing his views concerning agricultural reform.

2. Smith, *Slavery in Antebellum Florida,* 3, 53, 57–66, 102–103. Numerous essays are to be found in southern contemporary periodicals proclaiming the shortcomings of overseers and the rapid turnover in this occupation. The occupation was certainly not a prestigious one. The salaries were not commensurate with the duties and responsibilities demanded on the job, and, on the whole, it simply did not attract the South's more talented individuals. It was the exception when an employer retained an overseer for more than one or two years.

their counterparts in other plantation belts.[3] Perhaps some were, for the intricacies of rice planting demanded not only experience, knowledge, and the competent supervision of large numbers of slaves but also the overseeing of the condition and maintenance of rice fields and of such equipment and machinery as threshing and pounding mills. The overseers on R.Q. Mallard's rice plantation had to meet these requisites: "skill, experience, and ability to manage Negroes." They were usually married men with families; they received a salary and were allowed the use of a house, horses, servants, food, and firewood. Frequently they "saved enough to become in turn an owner of slaves and [a] plantation."[4]

In spite of Mallard's impression, overseers along the rice coast often failed to give full satisfaction to their employers, and their shortcomings are seen in the rapid turnover of their employment. Hugh Fraser Grant hired Thomas Skinner in January, 1842, and "discharged [him] on August 29 for Non attendance to Business," paying him $233 for eight months' wages.[5] Charles Manigault complained of the poor quality of his overseers and hired a new one each year until 1837. Between 1837 and 1865 the caliber of his overseers improved and their tenure was longer. The best of them was William Capers, who remained on the plantation from 1857 to 1865.[6]

The contract with the overseer enumerated the countless duties assigned to him and also expressed the attitude of the planter toward his slaves concerning care, health, and punishments. That the driver, not the overseer, carried out the punishments shows that the planter trusted his humanity and self-discipline more than that of the white man. Also, whipping more closely identified the driver with the whites, and it reinforced his power among the

3. Scarborough, *Overseer*, 56.

4. *Plantation Life Before Emancipation* (Richmond, Va.: Whittet and Shepperson, 1892), 56.

5. House, ed., *Planter Management*, 267–69.

6. Clifton, *Life and Labor on Argyle Island*, xxx. See also Manigault Plantation Journal, GHS, and Lewis Manigault Papers, Duke Univ., for references to Manigault's overseers, as well as the Kollock Plantation Books. Kollock changed overseers each year, though his was a cotton, not a rice, plantation. The qualities desired in an overseer were honesty, sobriety, and an understanding of the management of slaves. Typical advertisements in the *Georgia Gazette* and other contemporary newspapers referred to these qualities: "Wanted—An overseer for a Rice Plantation, no great distance from Savannah, a single man. Any person well recommended may meet with good encouragement, but none need apply unless he can produce a sufficient testimonial of his sobriety and capacity, etc. as an overseer."

slaves. The contract made between Richard J. Arnold and his overseer, John B. Gross, for the year 1844 reveals this fact. Gross was not allowed to whip the slaves. They were to be punished by the slaver drivers:

> The said Gross agrees to serve the said Arnold in the capacity of an overseer at his plantations in Bryan County, Georgia & to reside at Cherry Hill, & to manage his thrashing & pounding mill should he erect one.
>
> He is to devote his whole time & attention to the said Arnold's business . . . to attend to the sick at all times they may require & to do all in his power to keep the negroes from trading at the grog shops &, as far as in his power, to keep them at home & to do all in his power toward making good crops. He is not to chastise the negroes with severity or to use any other article than the lash in punishing them—& to do it through his drivers.[7]

P.C. Weston of South Carolina enumerated the qualities required of overseers for effectiveness in managing rice plantation slaves: "In nothing does a good manager so much excel a bad, as in being able to discern what a hand is capable of doing and in never attempting to make him do more." No slave should be given a task that could not be completed with "tolerable ease" or be punished for not finishing tasks, it being "contrary to justice to punish what cannot be done." A task on Weston's plantation was "as much work as the meanest field hand [could] do in nine hours working industriously." Before the slave left the field, the driver examined the completed task to approve of the work done.[8]

Drivers were foremen who directed the work of field laborers; they were also middlemen who represented management and were responsible for the successful production of crops. The mode of crop production along the rice coast and the prevailing task system of labor demanded that there be a supervisor to set work loads and to measure the performance of laborers through each successive stage of the growing process. Drivers possessed certain talents that qualified them for leadership and were

7. Arnold-Screven Papers, MSS, SHC. White Hall was Arnold's other plantation in Bryan County. Gross's contract was renewed for the next year, 1845, but with certain reservations concerned with crop production: "In the event of the Rice Crop at Cherry Hill falling short of eighteen thousand baskets, the cotton crop at both places falling short of thirty bags of clean cotton prepared for market, and the corn crop at both places falling short of three thousand bushels, the said Gross, in that event, is to receive as wages the sum that bears an equal porportion to the crop made, as eight hundred dollars bears to the crop stated above. . . ."

8. Rules on Rice Estate," 38–44. See James O. Breeden, ed., *Advice Among Masters: The Ideal in Slave Management in the Old South* (Westport, Conn., Greenwood, 1980), 69–70, for excerpted passages from Weston's essay.

selected from among the slave population upon that basis. They were usually tall, strong men, competent and reliable, able to display fair judgment in carrying out their duties. They helped get the slave gang out in the mornings, assigned tasks, set the work pace, and, at the end of the day's work, examined the quality of the work performed. Their authority was not limited to directing labor in the field. They were responsible for the general conduct of slaves. They had to keep order in the settlement and had authority to discipline slaves and punish them. They also helped issue rations and clothing and, on occasion, when the overseer and owner were absent from the plantation, they had sole responsibility for plantation operation.[9]

On cotton, rice, and sugar plantations where large numbers of slaves were worked, the overseer generally made use of several drivers. One was designated as the head driver and acted as a suboverseer, and the other drivers were responsible for the work of a smaller group of from thirty to forty field hands.[10] A study of the records of numerous rice plantations in Georgia confirms this ratio. For example, in 1834 the overseer of Hugh Fraser Grant's Elizafield Plantation in Glynn County worked thirty-seven prime hands under the direction and supervision of the driver, John.[11] In 1830 the overseer on James Potter's Argyle Plantation in Chatham County worked thirty-three hands under the driver Tommy, and another thirty-three under the driver Edmund. In 1839 Charles Manigault's overseer worked forty hands on Gowrie under the driver Edmund. In 1839 Charles Manigault's overseer worked forty hands on Gowrie under the driver Robert, and twenty-eight hands on East Hermitage under the driver Ishmael. These two plantations were on Argyle Island in the Savannah River and joined James Potter's rice fields.[12]

Recent studies on the role of slave drivers have shown them to be less brutish and inhumane than contemporary writers portrayed them: as a rule, they were not sadistic oppressors of their fellow bondsmen but, rather, were sympathetic with those under their charge as opposed to the interests of the white owner or

9. "Rules on Rice Estate," 38–44; Heyward, *Seed From Madagascar*, 157–58; Margaret Armstrong, *Fanny Kemble, A Passionate Victorian* (New York: Macmillan, 1938), 216–17; Olmsted, *Journey in Seaboard Slave States*, 222–23.

10. Kenneth M. Stampp, *The Peculiar Institution: Slavery in the Ante-Bellum South* (New York: Vintage, 1956), 40.

11. House, ed., *Planter Management*, 252–54.

12. Clifton, ed., *Life and Labor on Argyle Island*, 64–66. See also Louis Manigault Plantation Records, GHS.

overseer.[13] Notwithstanding such an interpretation, references to driver treatment of field laborers, culled from interviews with former slaves and other literature, express a wide range of attitudes and responses.[14] Apparently, some were brutal and relentless when directing the work of slaves and when punishing them, whereas others were fair and reasonable. The stereotype of the cruel driver was more valid during the eighteenth century when the coast still reflected the impact of Barbados and other West Indian Islands. The drivers there were apparently often cruel, although a disquieting number joined and helped lead slave revolts. The West Indian system was different, but it did shape the early coastal plantation system in this country.

An officer with the British forces that occupied Savannah in 1779 observed the condition of slaves who worked in rice fields on surrounding plantations and attributed much of what he saw to the "great cruelty" of the driver: "The Negro Women [were] two-thirds naked and very disgusting to the eye." The driver, with whip in hand, was directing their work.[15] George Lewis observed slaves who were working in a rice field along the Georgia coast in 1844. The barefoot women wore shifts and "dirty turbans on their heads." One young slave was wearing an iron collar with a bell attached that rang as he moved along. He was an habitual runaway, and floggings had failed as a form of punishment. Lewis was impressed with the slow movement of these laborers: "They moved their arms and hoes at the slowest, even when the black overseer [driver] was looking on and crying now and then, 'Mash the clods!' "[16]

As to driver cruelty, there were many incidents that justified the indictment so often made. On Charles Manigault's rice plantation in Chatham County the slave London committed suicide rather

13. William L. Van Deburg, *The Slave Drivers: Black Agricultural Labor Supervisors in the Antebellum South* (Westport, Conn., Greenwood, 1979), 5, 68–73; Leslie Howard Owens, *This Species of Property: Slave Life and Culture in the Old South* (New York: Oxford Univ. Press, 1976), 121–35.

14. Norman R. Yetman, ed., *Life Under the "Peculiar Institution": Selections From the Slave Narrative Collection* (New York: Holt, Rinehart and Winston, 1970), 12, 24, 35, 37, 55, 94, 96, 119, 142, 189, 192, 193, 196, 213, 224, 225, 271, 288, 294, 297, 312. See also Charles L. Perdue, Jr., Thomas E. Barden, Robert K. Phillips, eds., *Weevils in the Wheat: Interviews with Virginia Ex-Slaves* (Charlottesville: Univ. Press of Virginia, 1976), 26, 108, 110, 156, 266, 267, 274, 290, and MSS copies of the Slave Narratives, Library of Congress.

15. Catherine S. Crary, ed., *The Price of Loyalty: Tory Writings from the Revolutionary Era* (New York: McGraw-Hill, 1973), 273.

16. *Travels Through Lower Canada and the United States of America, Impressions of America*, in Lane, ed., *Rambler*, 181.

than be subjected to another whipping from the driver George. London's body was found floating in the Savannah River. The white overseer ordered that "no one touch the corpse; it will remain, if not taken off by the next tide, to let the negroes see when a negro takes his own life [he] will be treated in this manner." The overseer informed Manigault of this incident and advised him to sell George: "My advice to you about George is to ship him; he is of no use to you as a driver and is a bad negro, he would command a good price in Savannah where he can be sold in a quiet manner."[17] Roswell King, the overseer on Pierce Butler's plantation in Glynn County, was critical of the abuse practiced by the drivers on the slaves working in the rice fields; he commented:

> The grand point was to suppress the brutality and licentiousness practiced by the principal men . . . the drivers and tradesmen [skilled slaves]. More punishment is inflicted on every plantation by the men in power, from private pique, than from a neglect of duty. The owner or overseer knows, that with a given number of hands, such a portion of work is to be done. The driver, to screen favorites, or apply their time to his own purposes, imposes a heavy task on some. Should they murmur, an opportunity is taken months after, to punish those unfortunate fellows for not doing their own and others' tasks. Should they not come at the immediate offenders, it will descend on the nearest kindred. As an evidence of the various opportunities that a brutal driver has to gratify his revenge . . . let any planter go into his field, and in any negro's task, he can find apparently just grounds for punishment. To prevent this abuse, no driver in the field is allowed to inflict punishment until after a regular trial. . . . An order from a driver is to be implicitly obeyed as if it came from myself, nor do I counteract the execution (unless it is injurious) but direct his immediate attention to it. It would be endless for me to superintend the drivers and field hands too, and would of course make them useless. . . . It is a great point in having the principal drivers men that can support their dignity; a condescention to familiarity should be prohibited.[18]

The head driver on Pierce Butler's rice plantation was given full responsibility when the white overseer was away on one of Butler's other plantations. He assigned the tasks, pronounced punishments, gave permission for the men to leave the island, and performed many other duties in addition to giving out food allotments to the slaves. "Trustworthy, upright, intelligent, extremely well mannered, always clean and tidy in his person, with a cour-

17. Clifton, ed., *Life and Labor on Argyle Island,* 300–301. George was shipped from Savannah to Charleston, where he was sold to a slave trader.

18. "On the Management of the Butler Estate," *Southern Agriculturist* 1 (Sept. 1828): 523–29.

teousness of demeanor far removed from servility," he was admired and respected by the other slaves.[19]

A deterrent to driver cruelty was the threat and dishonor of being demoted, of being cast out of that favored circle of Negro aristocracy: drivers, carriage drivers, house servants, carpenters, and other skilled slaves. The driver's demotion "occurred frequently enough to exercise a wholesome restraint upon the strong passions of [that] Negro official." Though drivers carried whips to encourage a steady pace of work and to discourage shirking or careless habits while planting, cultivating, or harvesting, as a rule they refrained from using them in the field; whippings were reserved for a later time. The whip was carried more as a "symbol of authority than an instrument of service." On Charles C. Jones's plantation in Liberty County the whip was short "with a heavy handle and tapering thong, plaited in one piece." It was usually worn around the driver's shoulder and was known as a "cotton planter."[20]

There are many horror stories of driver brutality to be found in slave testimonials, though what sometimes appeared to be driver brutality or cruelty was not deeply internalized. References in slave narratives verify instances in which drivers sympathized with their fellow bondsmen; they played the role of punishing with great intensity when, in reality, the punishment was a mockery. Solomon Northup became a driver and learned to use the whip "with marvelous dexterity and precision, throwing the lash within a hair's breadth of the back, the ear, the nose, without, however, touching either of them." All the while, the slave "would squirm and screech as if in agony."[21]

An effective driver had to discipline and punish slaves when plantation routine was not followed; this did not mean that he was not respected by the other slaves. Attitudes of slaves toward the driver can be seen in the rhymes and songs they created to express their feelings.

> Dar is ole Uncle Billy, he's a might good Nigger
> He tote all de news to Mosser a little bigger

19. Frances Anne Kemble, *Journal of a Residence on a Georgia Plantation, 1838–1839* (New York: Harper, 1863), 44–45.

20. Mallard, *Plantation Life*, 40, 41, 46.

21. Solomon Northup, *Twelve Years a Slave*, ed. Sue Eakin, Joseph Logsdon (rpt. Baton Rouge: Louisiana State Univ. Press, 1972), 172.

> When you tell Uncle Billy you wants free er a fac'
> De nex' day de hide drap off'n yo' back.[22]

On James Hamilton Couper's plantation in Glynn County each gang worked under a driver who assigned their tasks and whose authority was limited to his gang. On this plantation, like many other large units, a head driver or foreman had authority over all the drivers. John D. Legare visited Couper's Hopeton Plantation in 1833 and gave the following report on the task system used there:

> Task work is resorted to . . . and working in gangs as is practiced in the West Indies and the upper country, is avoided. . . . The advantages are equalizing the work of each agreeably to strength, and the avoidance of watchful superintendance and incessant driving. As the negroes work in adjoining tasks, they are excited to exertion to a certain extent by emulation, and as the task of each is separate, imperfect work can readily be traced to the neglectful worker. By reference to the *Journal of Plantation Work*, it may be ascertained months after the execution of any work, by what driver's gang it was done, and through the driver, by what individual accountability is in this way readily established.[23]

On another rice plantation in coastal Georgia, the head driver was considered to be the de facto manager. He was a trusted foreman, was discreet in controlling the slaves under his charge, and, because of his long experience and knowledge of the techniques of growing rice, was given orders directly from the owner in the management of the plantation. The overseer was not consulted in the various stages of crop production or in governing the slaves, and he remained on the plantation only because the law required the presence of a white man wherever slaves were used.[24]

In recognition of their authority, the drivers on Duncan Clinch Heyward's rice plantation in South Carolina were provided houses "a little larger and somewhat better than the rest," at the end of each row street, facing the slave houses. Early in the morning the driver stood in his door and blew a horn to awaken the field hands on his row. After their breakfast they gathered together and walked to the rice field, the driver leading the way.

22. Thomas W. Talley, "Negro Folk Rhymes, Wise and Otherwise, with a Study," review by E.C.M., *Georgia Historical Quarterly* 6 (Mar. 1922): 86–89.
23. *Southern Agriculturist* 6 (Sept. 1833): 571–73, 576.
24. Olmsted, *Journey in Seaboard Slave States*, 226–27.

The field had been laid off in half-acre tasks. The slaves sat on the bank while waiting for their names to be called to be given their tasks: "Fall en yeh, Lizabet; you, Scipio, Tek dat tas' hed of Tom; Gal, ona fall en behine Isrul; chillun, ona tek de tas' longside ob yo ma, and mine, don't fool wid me today.' "[25] Orders similar to these were heard daily along the rice coast as drivers called out the assigned tasks for the field hands.

James H. Hammond of South Carolina believed the head driver to be the most important Negro on the plantation; he should not be required to work like other slaves. " 'He is to be treated with more respect than any other negro by both master and overseer. . . . He is to be required to maintain proper discipline at all times; to see that no negro idles or does bad work in the field, and to punish it with discretion on the spot. . . . He is a confidential servant, and may be a guard against any excesses or omissions of the overseer.' "[26] A good driver who performed according to Hammond's expectations kept the slaves working as steadily as possible, used the lash on those who were shiftless to maintain respect from those whose work was satisfactory, had a decent respect for unfeigned illness and individual weakness, and, at the same time, had the owner and overseer understand that work demands had to be reasonable.[27]

William Capers, the overseer on Gowrie Plantation, advised Charles Manigault to purchase the driver John, who was being sold from a South Carolina plantation, for "there [are] but few negroes more competent than he . . . John is about 45 years old, & if he is the man that I had as Driver at Mr. Pringle's, *buy him by all means*." Manigault purchased John, and Capers found him to be "as good a driver as when I left him on the Santee."[28]

Emily Burke was impressed by the quality of the driver while visiting a cotton plantation in Georgia. He was "an active, intelligent colored man, very gentlemanly in his deportment and much respected by the white people and beloved by the slaves." The

25. Heyward, *Seed From Madagascar*, 102, 157, 158, 179, 180.

26. Phillips, *American Negro Slavery*, 272; see also Phillips, *Plantation and Frontier Documents, 1649–1863*, 2 vols. (Cleveland: Clark, 1909), 2:32, 94. Hammond, at one time, was governor of South Carolina, and his cotton plantation was located on the Carolina side of the Savannah River about 16 miles below Augusta.

27. Genovese, *Roll, Jordan, Roll: The World the Slaves Made* (New York: Pantheon, 1974), 379.

28. Phillips, *Plantation and Frontier*, 1:337–38. See also Clifton, *Life and Labor on Argyle Island*, 304–305, for the same correspondence from Capers to Manigault.

owner preferred to have this slave acting as his overseer rather than a white man, and relied upon his advice and judgment in all matters concerning the plantation. According to Burke, the owner "had more peace and order upon his plantation and much more work done than when he employed white men for that purpose." The slaves received better treatment and "consequently were happier and more contented with their lot."[29]

Owners were adept at encouraging their slave drivers to remain loyal while directing the work of the plantation. They appealed to their religious sense of discipline and to their pride, flattered them and praised them for their services, expressed concern for their welfare, and stressed the fact the master and slaves benefited from an efficiently managed plantation.[30] Charles C. Jones's letters to his drivers manifest such motives. Jones was the owner of several plantations (rice and cotton) in Liberty County; he was also a Presbyterian minister and was absent from his plantations much of the time. To stay within the law, he employed two white overseers, Thomas J. Shepard and John S. Stevens, and through them maintained correspondence with his drivers: Cato, the driver at Montevideo; Andrew, the driver at Maybank, and Sandy Maybank, the head carpenter. The overseers read Jones's letters to these slave foremen and wrote back as they dictated. The intricacies of the relationship between owner and slave supervisors are revealed in the following correspondence.

> *Charles C. Jones to Cato, January 28, 1851.* I got Mr. Shepard's good letter this morning, in which he gives me a very particular account of all your work and business on the Plantation, and it pleases me well. . . . I hope God will be with you & give you good health again. You know our life and health are in His hands, and it is a great comfort to me to have a good hope that you love Him, and do put all your trust in our Lord and Savior Jesus Christ. . . . We have been together a long time, and I have always had a great attachment to you and confidence in you: and you have always been a good and faithful man to me. . . . Mr. Shepard will point out some one of the men who can take a look after things when you are not able to be as

29. *Pleasure and Pain: Reminiscences of Georgia in the 1840s*, introduction by Felicity Calhoun (rpt. Savannah: Behive Press, 1978), 88–89. Emily Burke came to Georgia in 1840 to teach at the Female Orphan Asylum in Savannah. She spent ten years in Georgia and, during much of this time, visited and taught on several plantations; she never identified the places where she worked.

30. Genovese, *Roll, Jordan, Roll*, 374–75. See also Genovese's whole section (365–88) on slave drivers and foremen for a detailed analysis of the functions of these "men between." See also Owens, *This Species of Property*, 121–35, and Van Deburg, *Slave Drivers*, 3–330, for similar accounts.

much about as you wish, and he can take directions from you and make his report to you.

Cato to C.C. Jones, September 3, 1852. Mr. Shepard brought me your letter last week, and I heard it read to me with great pleasure, and much obliged to you Master for your kind notice of me. I always feel satisfied that I have a good Shear of your Love and Confidence, but whenever I See you take the time & trouble, to write me your Servant a kind & I may say fatherly letter, it makes me feel more like crying with love and gratitude for So kind a master . . . and always feel it in my heart to say, I will try and be a better Servant than ever.

The letters contain lengthy discussions on the behavior and state of health of Jones's slaves, as well as detailed accounts of plantation work and crop production. These discussions indicate the extent of the driver's authority and reliability in directing plantation affairs: "Your people all seem to be doing very well. They attend praise & go to church regularly whenever there is preaching in reach. We have had a good deal of sickness among the children from worms, but no verry ill cases. . . . We have now all the women picking cotton & from appearance will have no more time to do anything else. . . ."

Jones and his drivers stressed religion as a means to control and discipline the slaves. Nonetheless, discipline was never complete among the slave population, as is revealed in Cato's correspondence concerning two recalcitrants, Phoebe and Cash.

Cato to C.C. Jones, March 3, 1851. As for Cash, I am afraid he has given up himself to the old boy, for Since his wife has been with him, he appears more petulent and has not only given up going to prayers, but I have several times heard him make use of bad words Whenever he was displeased, & have shamed and talked to him so often, that I have felt it my duty to report him to the church. . . . Phoebe and I get along So, So. She does her work very well, but there is a strong notion now and then to break out, but she knows well Enough how it will be if She does, and I am in hopes she will let her better judgement rule her passions.

Phoebe and Cash never did absorb the paternalistic ideals set forth in Jones's religious instructions, and their rebelliousness continued to harass Cato, who influenced Jones to dispose of them. In 1857 they and several of their children were shipped to Savannah, sold to a slave trader, then taken to New Orleans for resale. From New Orleans, Phoebe and Cash wrote the remaining members of their family in Liberty County, who were still owned by Jones.

Phoebe and Cash to Mr. Delions, March 17, 1857. Please tell my

> daughters Clairissa and Nancy a heap how a doo for me, Pheaby and Cash and Cashes son James. We left Savannah the first of Jany, we are now in New Orleans. Please tell them that their sister Jane died the first of Feby . . . we were sold for spite, I hope that it is for our own good. . . . Mr. Delions will please tell Cato that what [food] we have to trow away now it would be anough to furnish your Plantation for one season. Mr. Delions will please answer this letter for Clairissa and let me know all that has happened since I left. . . . Clairissa, your affectionate mother and Father sends a heap of Love to you and your Husband and my Grand Children, Give our love to Cashes Brother Porter and his wife Patience. Victoria gives her love to her Cousin Beck and Miley.
>
> I have no more to say until I get a home. I remain your affectionate Mother and Father.[31]

The futility in challenging the authority of the driver is well illustrated in the case of Phoebe and Cash, whose ultimate fate was determined by their refusal to respect the standards demanded by Cato. The close relationship and confidentiality between Jones and Cato is shown in their correspondence. Jones relied upon Cato's integrity in overseeing and reporting to him all matters concerning the plantation: crop production, the condition of the slaves, their performance in the field, and their general behavior.

The trusted driver had the confidence of the owner and acted as an informant to keep the owner abreast of all that went on within the plantation community. This was especially true on rice plantations, where the planter and his family seldom spent more than a part of each year on the plantation. Overseers came and left and seldom developed a close bond with the owner. Reliable and trusted drivers remained on the plantation for a lifetime and were of invaluable service to the owner.

31. The letters are located in the Charles Colcock Jones Papers, Special Collections Division, Tulane Univ. Library, New Orleans. For Jones's decision to sell Phoebe and Cash and certain members of their family, see his correspondence in Myers, ed., *Children of Pride*, 183–85.

CHAPTER FIVE

The Factorage System and Plantation Supply

The economy of the Old South was distinguished by the plantation system and was sustained by slave labor for use in the production of staple crops. The factorage system was the method used to market staple crops for the planter and, in return, to supply plantation needs. For example, whether cotton, rice, sugar, or tobacco was destined for domestic or foreign markets, it was handled first through the local factor or commission merchant, who forwarded the staple to factorage houses in New York where it was marketed.

The planter or local commission merchant received advances on or payment for the staple shipped, usually by means of sixty-day sterling bills or four-month New York drafts. Southern banks discounted these bills and drafts, and they were forwarded to New York to pay the debts of southern merchants and planters. Though needed services were provided, the system encouraged the excessive use of credit and made the South dependent upon the North for its banking and credit facilities. The entire operation of the plantation depended upon the factorage system, which constituted the main source of credit.[1] The system was based on the potential value of the unharvested crop. The bank, the factor, or the commission merchant gambled on the fickleness of crop futures. It was not unusual for the planter to go for months without cash, though he owned many acres, had enormous investments in slaves, and had valuable crops in the field. His factor or commis-

1. Robert R. Russel, *Economic Aspects of Southern Sectionalism, 1840–1861* (Urbana: Univ. of Illinois Press, 1924), 101. Factors often acted as commission merchants and vice versa.

sion merchant advanced cash payments to overseers, advanced him cash, paid debts due other persons, and performed many other services of this nature for the planter.[2]

The planter ordered the necessary supplies, which were debited against his account, and the annual interest or commission charged for such service was added to the total amount due. If the merchant was also a factor and handled the cotton, rice, or other staples, the commission charged for this service was also entered against the planter's account. If the planter dealt with a factor who was not his commission merchant, the merchant forwarded the bill to the factor for payment, charging a commission for this service.

The financial system enhanced northern business interests, though by no means did it deprive the planter of his profits. After service charges were deducted (interest rates at 5 percent) for the marketing of the crop and the supplying of the plantation, the planter was left with a substantial net return. The commission merchant always kept his ledger sheets itemized and up-to-date, indicating the standing of the planter at any given time. The method of paying an account with the merchant or factor was quite simple. When the planter's crop was sold, the merchant sent him a bill of sale indicating the number of pounds of cotton, rice, sugar, or tobacco involved in the transaction. Also included in the bill was an itemized list of charges made, which, when deducted, showed the net profit to the planter.[3]

During the early nineteenth century factorage houses in

2. Probate Records dated 1785–1860, Bryan, Camden, Chatham, Glynn, and Liberty counties. The records of McIntosh County were burned during the Civil War. Plantation accounts with merchants and factors found among estate inventories have proved to be the best sources for information on the factorage system.

3. Lewis E. Atherton, "The Problem of Credit Rating in the Ante-Bellum South," *Journal of Southern History* 12 (Nov., 1946): 534–56. Atherton studied records of a country storekeeper in the Old South and found that two-thirds to three-fourths of the goods were sold to the planter on credit. Just before the Civil War there was $131 million in credit extended to planters by factors. Philip S. Foner, *Business and Slavery: The New York Merchants and the Irrepressible Conflict* (Chapel Hill: Univ. of North Carolina Press, 1941), presents evidence to show that the South depended upon the North for credit. The New York business house would contact the local lawyer or storekeeper to check the rating of the planter before extending credit for merchandise from New York. The local lawyer acted as a collection agency for New York and charged a commission. It was necessary for the southerner to have a letter of recommendation from the lawyer to receive credit when shopping in New York. After the Panic of 1837 this informal system of credit changed and credit agencies were established in the South, though they were not totally effective until after the Civil War.

Charleston, South Carolina, marketed a large portion of the rice and cotton produced in coastal Georgia, while merchants in Savannah supplied plantation needs. After 1830 Savannah became a commercial center with its own factorage houses and banking facilities, and staple commodities were now marketed from this city. By 1850 these business houses had captured control of the rice market in coastal Georgia and were also marketing the rice produced on the Carolina side of the Savannah River.

Savannah also became an outlet for much of the short staple cotton produced in middle Georgia. The Savannah River became a bustling route along which barges, brigs, schooners, steamers, and other vessels traveled as far inland as Augusta to deposit orders made by merchants in that area for plantation supplies and to load cotton to be transported back to Savannah for deposit at factorage houses. From here, the cotton was shipped to New York. Savannah's harbor, with its high bluff overlooking the river, offered a natural setting for commercial growth. By 1860 business houses stretched all along this bluff, and walkways on the mall leading to these houses became known as Factor's Walk. Spacious warehouses were located under the business houses and opened below at the level of the Savannah River to receive cotton and rice. There, these staples were weighed and stored until ready for export.[4]

Of the numerous commercial houses in Savannah, the firm of Robert Habersham and Son was one of the oldest and most reputable. Some others were Benedix and Company, Caig and Company, Hunter, Pressman and Company, William Moore and Company, Padelford and Company, Poerier and Matthiesen, William H. Smith and Company, and W.M. Tunno; Tunno also had offices in Charleston. These firms offered a variety of wares and plantation equipment, designed to meet the needs in goods and services of a growing plantation society. Items such as cotton bagging, German Osnaburgs, glazed chimney tiles, window glass, Queen's ware in hogsheads, Madeira wine in half-pipes and quarter-casks,

4. *Directory for the City of Savannah*, 1859; C.H. Olmsted, "Savannah in the '40's," *Georgia Historical Quarterly* 1 (Sept. 1917): 243–53; the *Daily Georgian* for the year 1820 ran a continuous notice on the first column of the first page giving thirteen different shipping schedules: four ships went regularly to Liverpool, four to New York, one to Le Havre, one to Cowes (the Isle of Wight), one to Newport and New Bedford, Conn., one to Darien, Brunswick, St. Marys, and one to Mobile. The factorage warehouses have been remodeled into art galleries, boutiques, cafes, and museums, combining the old with the new to create a delightful atmosphere.

Figure 10. Mansion Designed by William Jay in 1818 for Richard Richardson, a wealthy factor and sometime president of the U.S. Bank. (Georgia Historical Society Collection.)

Figure 11. Side View and Balcony of the Richardson mansion. (Georgi Historical Society Collection.)

Havana cigars, wollens, linens, Manchester carpets, muslins, silks, stationery, gloves, hats, cutlery, guns, powder, shot, paints and oils, pickles, medicines, cord and twine, glassware, saddlery, shoes, perfumery, and spices were but a few of the various kinds of merchandise stocked by these houses.[5]

When the planter died and directed in his will that his estate be managed by an executor, this individual kept annual accountings of all transactions made for the estate. These accountings, along with those kept by merchants and factors, provide an accurate and meaningful source for determining the economic worth of plantations under the slave system; the ledger sheets show profit and loss for any given year. The estate accountings of Joseph Bryan for the years 1814 to 1827 serve to illustrate services performed by the merchant and/or factor and the executor for the estate, as well as commissions (or interest rates) charged by these agents in supplying goods, performing services, and for marketing the crop. The firms of Small and McNish and Robert Habersham and Son acted as merchants and factors for Bryan's estate, charging a commission of 2.5 percent on all transactions made to supply the plantation and to advance cash for support of three children; another 2.5 percent was charged for marketing the cotton. John Screven was appointed executor for this estate and charged 5 percent for handling the account; thus, a cost of 10 percent was debited against the estate for all transactions involved.[6]

For example, between July 1826 and April 1827 Haoersham's firm supplied Bryan's plantation with spades, corn, cloth for Negro clothing, and advanced cash for Bryan's children, who were in school at the North; discounted a note due the State Bank of Georgia; paid wages to an overseer; and performed other such services. Habersham added his 2.5 percent commission, and the total cost came to $6,263, which was debited to the account. Habersham credited to the account $4,653 from the net sale of 86 bales of Sea Island cotton after deducting charges for weighing and storing ($27) and his commission at 2.5 percent ($120) for selling the cotton. He discounted the executor's note of $1,500 due the estate and credited $1,484 to the account, along with $126

5. *Georgia Gazette*, Nov. 10, 24, Dec. 8, 1797; House, ed., *Planter Management*, 304–311.

6. Box B, fol. 106, Probate Records, Chatham County. Joseph Bryan's plantation on Whitmarsh Island produced no rice, only Sea Island cotton. Bryan was a grandson of the Revolutionary War patriot Jonathan Bryan, who fought in the war, was imprisoned by the British, then released. He died in 1788 at the age of eighty. See Redding, *Life and Times of Jonathan Bryan.*

Figure 12. The Firm of Robert Habersham and Company on Factor's Walk. (Georgia Historical Society Collection.)

Figure 13. A Rear View of the Old Factorage and Commerce Houses, Savannah, River Street. (Georgia Historical Society Collection.)

from the sale of 6 bales of cotton. Thus, $6,263 was credited to the estate at the end of a ten-month period.[7]

For the year 1816 George Herb, the executor of the estate of Robert S. Gibson, received a total income of $12,876 for the estate from several sources. His commission for receiving this income at 2.5 percent was $322, which he deducted from the income received. During the year Herb advanced cash for various needs of the estate, for which he charged another 2.5 percent. He paid the overseer's salary, made regular cash payments to Mrs. Gibson until her death, to the minister who performed her funeral ceremony, for the cost of catching a runaway slave, and for feeding the horses from the plantation when they were driven to town hauling produce. For this last service, Herb charged 37½ cents per meal per horse.[8]

Herb also paid the firm of Robert Habersham a total of $7,266 at different times during the year for supplies for Gibson's plantation; the cotton crop from the plantation was not marketed by Habersham but by Peter Guerard. The yield for the year 1816 brought a net income of $6, 507 after Guerard deducted 2.5 percent for marketing charges. Other sources of income for the Gibson estate during the year came from rental property in Savannah and from produce sold from the plantation such as butter, cabbages, grapes, hides, hogs, oranges, and poultry. As in the case of the Bryan estate, the total cost, or interest rate charged, for handling the Gibson estate was 10 percent. For local planters, factorage and mercantile charges continued to be 2.5 percent throughout the antebellum era, though marketing costs increased considerably over the years.[9]

Rice was shipped to market in barrels that held 200 pounds or more, in casks that held 600 pounds, or in tierces that held 700. The best quality of rice sold for an average of 3 cents a pound, though the price fluctuated at fractional amounts above and below this level; second quality rice and small rice averaged less than 3 cents. Rice flour, priced by the bushel at from 10 to 15 cents per bushel, was hardly worth marketing unless sold in bulk along with

7. Box B, fol. 106, Probate Records, Chatham County.

8. Box G, fol. 64, ibid.

9. Ibid.; Alfred H. Conrad and John R. Meyer, "The Economics of Slavery in the Ante-Bellum South," *Journal of Political Economy* 56 (Apr. 1958): 95–122, rpt. Harold D. Woodman, ed., *Slavery and the Southern Economy* (New York: Harcourt, Brace, 1966). See Woodman, p. 77, table 7, for factors' commission ranging from 2 to 2.5 percent in 1840.

rice and cotton. Accounts with factorage houses, however, show that rice flour was shipped. Barrels, casks, and tierces were often manufactured on the plantation, and the polished rice was sent to the local factor in these containers to be marketed; the best quality was sent in tierces. The owner was allowed 50 cents for each tierce deposited with the factor, and this allowance was credited to his account along with the proceeds from the sale of his rice.[10]

Those planters who did not have machinery to prepare their rice for market sent it as rough rice (in the husk or shell) to a mill nearby where it was pounded or polished and packed as white rice in tierces for shipment. Rough rice was sometimes marketed with the local merchant, though it was not sold in the world market until it was polished. Preparing rice for market away from the plantation involved an additional cost, which, when added to other charges and commissions, decreased the net profit to the owner. Nonetheless, the planter who sent his rice to the mill to be processed did not have the financial burden of money invested in heavy equipment that, in the final analysis of net profit, had to be reconciled. A bushel of rough rice when pounded made a yield of 45 pounds of white rice; twenty-one bushels of rough rice made a yield of 700 pounds, or one tierce of prime quality clean white rice, 66 pounds of clean small rice, and 75 pounds of rice flour.[11]

Since the net return on rice and cotton was affected by accessibility and transportation facilities in the local market, it was a significant advantage for the planters of coastal Georgia that they were close to the commercial markets at Charleston or Savannah. Prompt and safe delivery of the crop to the merchant at the propitious time meant that he could sell at the prime price. A close relationship existed between the factor and the planter; they were often friends and cooperated in their desire to have the crop marketed at the best possible time, since both stood to gain from premium prices. The rice planter's access to water transportation was an advantage when forwarding his crop to market; he might send rice to Savannah in his own barge or vessel, or, like Francis Henry McLeod of Wild Heron Plantation, might forward it by flatboat along one of the canals connecting with the Ogeechee River, then along the Ogeechee River Canal connecting with the

10. A perusal of numerous factorage accounts shown in inventories and appraisals of estates found in court records for Camden, Chatham, Glynn, and Liberty counties makes known this fact.

11. James Hamilton Couper, "Notes on Agricultural and Rural Economy," MSS, SHC.

Savannah River, to be deposited at Savannah. If not, the factor dispatched a freight vessel to the planter's dock or wharf where the rice was loaded and transported to the factorage house to be marketed. Sea Island cotton was bagged on the plantation and sent to the local merchant by wagon, or by boat if produced on the Sea Islands. Rice, like cotton, was marketed during the winter months between November and April.

Raymond Demere's account with the firm of Joseph Habersham may be used to illustrate marketing costs for the earlier part of the nineteenth century and to compare those rates with rising marketing costs of the 1840s and 1850s. A bill of sale for 182 tierces of rice that were marketed between November 1812 and March 1813 through six different factors shows that the rice was sold for $5,088; marketing costs (including commissions at 2.5 percent) were $354, leaving a net of $4,734, which was credited to Demere's account.[12]

James Hamilton Couper, as executor for the estate of James Hamilton, made annual accountings for the years 1829 to 1854 of all transactions involving Hopeton and Hamilton plantations. He charged 2.5 percent for paying out all debts accrued during the year and another 2.5 percent for all cash received from the sale of staples. He also drew a salary of $8,566 as manager for the two plantations and charged this amount as a debit against the estate. For the year 1833 the accounting kept by Couper shows a total credit to the estate of $22,016, representing cash received from the sale of cotton, molasses, rice, sugar, and syrup. These staples were marketed through R. Carnochan and R.M. King at The Thickets and at Darien in McIntosh County. An entry in Couper's inventory in 1833 shows that twenty-eight bags of cotton were sold at $1,734; marketing costs were $79, leaving a net of $1,655, which was credited to his account. Another entry shows that 135 tierces of rice were sold for $5,023; marketing costs were $429, leaving a net of $4,594, which was credited. And thirty hogsheads of sugar were sold for $2,033; marketing costs were $281, leaving a net of $1,752, which was credited.[13]

After 1840 several firms in Charleston, South Carolina, marketed Couper's rice and cotton: Gourdin Matthiessen and Com-

12. Box D, fol. I, Probate Records, Chatham County.

13. Wills and Appraisements, Book D, 299–305, Glynn County. R.R. Youngblood marketed rice from Hopeton for this year, and Hawes and Mitchell marketed molasses.

pany, James Chapman and Company, Bancroft, Goodwin, and Dawson, and Robert Mure and Company. Net proceeds from rice and cotton in 1851 (molasses and rice flour were incidental), after all costs for marketing were deducted, totaled $22,620. The rice crop was sold for $16,687 and the Sea Island cotton, for $6,258. Couper was now forwarding the staples to Charleston from Hopeton and Hamilton plantations in his own schooner, the *Hopeton*. After the staples were deposited with the factor, the boat was loaded with plantation supplies and returned to Glynn County.[14]

Though the commission to the factor for handling staples continued to be 2.5 percent, by the 1850s marketing costs had increased; added to cooperage, weighing, and storage was the cost of marine insurance. The market price for best quality rice had risen slightly, fluctuating at a fractional level above 3 cents a pound. The best quality of Sea Island cotton was selling for about 30 cents a pound, and the price continued to rise during the 1850s, to reach a spectacular high of $1.00 per pound at the beginning of the Civil War. A bill of sale for rice and another for cotton made by Robert Mure and Company at Charleston for James Hamilton Couper in 1851 reflects rising marketing costs: 316 tierces of rice were sold for $5,961 and marketing costs were $608; seventy-four bags of cotton were sold for $6,752, and marketing costs were $314.[15]

Prices that could cover the cost of marketing rice and Sea Island cotton from coastal Georgia varied slightly by locality, depending on the distance to market and methods used to move the staples. Total costs for handling and shipping rice appear to have ranged from $2 to $3 a tierce between 1810 and 1860. For example, in 1813 total charges for shipping and selling 182 tierces of rice from Raymond Demere's plantation through Savannah were $354. Total charges in 1833 for shipping and selling 135 tierces from James Hamilton Couper's plantation through Darien were $429; total charges in 1851 for 316 tierces from Couper's plantation were $608. Charges for marketing twenty-eight bags of Sea Island cot-

14. Record of Wills, Appraisements, Book E, 222–40, Probate Records, Glynn County. Net proceeds from cotton and rice produced on Hamilton and Hopeton plantations in 1850 and sold in the fall of that year and the spring of 1851 did not exceed net proceeds for the year 1833. The Panic of 1837 and the depression that followed and continued until the mid-1840s depressed the prices of staples. The southern economy recovered in the late 1840s, and the 1850s witnessed a great era of prosperity.

15. Ibid., 226.

ton for Couper in 1833 were $79; for marketing seventy-four bags in 1851, $314.[16]

In the 1820s total costs for handling and shipping short staple cotton from a plantation in middle Georgia averaged $6 a bale. Improved conditions in handling and shipping reduced costs slightly during the next decade and the average appears to have been nearer $4. Charges for marketing increased after 1840, averaging $5 per bale. For example, in 1844 total charges for shipping and selling forty-eight bales of cotton from William Bellamy's plantation in Jefferson County, Florida, through St. Marks to New York, were $242. Marketing costs increased during the 1850s; total charges for shipping and selling seventy-five bales of cotton from John Whitehead's plantation in Leon County, Florida, were $584; for thirty-eight bales from Isaac Bunting's plantation in Madison County, Florida, total charges from St. Marks to New York in 1859 were $287.[17]

The increased prosperity of the planter class in Georgia during the 1850s was reflected in the commercial growth of Savannah. By 1860 this city was a thriving business center, with ten local banks that had branches in middle Georgia to extend credit to the cotton planters of that area. Steamboats plying the Atlantic coastal trade arrived regularly to dispose of merchandise and passengers and to load cotton and rice. Most of the rice exported from Savannah was deposited in domestic ports: New York received 25 percent; Boston and Charleston, 10 percent; Baltimore, New Orleans, and Philadelphia, from 5 to 10 percent. A direct trade with foreign ports existed between Bordeaux, Hamburg, LeHavre, Marseilles, St. Petersburg, and Trieste; nonetheless, three-fourths of the rice exported from Savannah was sent to domestic ports.[18]

The planter paid for the services of his merchant and factor. The cost was not unrealistic at 5 percent for credit extension on plantation supplies and the service for marketing the crop. When the estate was managed by an executor for the beneficiaries of the deceased planter, an additional cost of 5 percent was charged for

16. Box D, fol. I, Probate Records, Chatham County; Wills and Appraisements, Book D, 299–305, Glynn County.

17. Gray, *History of Agriculture*, 2:716; an account of sales for cotton found among the papers in William Bellamy's estate file, dated July 16, 1844, File 33–43, Probate Records, Jefferson County; Book of Sales of Personal Estates, 1846–1860, p. 265, Leon County; an account of sales for cotton sold for the estate of Isaac Bunting, dated Jan. 22, 1859, MS in possession of Carlton Smith, Madison, Fl.

18. *Directory for the City of Savannah*, GHS; House, ed., *Planter Management*, 74–82.

this service.[19] Supplying the planter and marketing his crop was a profitable enterprise; that the system enriched the local factor and merchant is evidenced by the various charges made for handling the crop, financing the planter, and supplying his needs. The system by no means deprived the planter of his share of the profits from staples produced, though a contrary conclusion was often made by contemporary travelers and later by historians in the twentieth century. Nonetheless, the system was detrimental to the total southern economy because the New York merchants and factors, those middlemen who received and marketed the staples, were outsiders, and every dollar sent to them transferred not only that amount but the multiplier effect out of the South.

19. Inventories and appraisals of estates, also estate accounts, kept by executors, merchants, and factors, and recorded in county court records present evidence for these facts. House in *Planter Management* uses a rate of 2%, which he states was charged by the merchant and/or factor to market the crop. His contention is incorrect.

PART TWO

The Slaves

CHAPTER SIX

The Slave Trade International and Domestic

The sale began—young girls were there.
Defenseless in their wretchedness,
Whose stifled sobs of deep despair
Revealed their anguish and distress.

And mothers stood with streaming eyes,
And saw their dearest children sold;
Unheeded rose their bitter cries,
While tyrants bartered them for gold.[1]

From the colonial era onward, unrestricted ownership of land and slaves stimulated the growth of Georgia's plantation economy. The successful production of rice required a comparatively large force of laborers, and Negro slaves furnished the only available supply. As Georgia's economy took on new dimensions between 1750 and 1765, the demand for slaves increased accordingly. Prior to 1766 they were supplied mostly from South Carolina, though some were imported from Antigua, Barbados, Guadaloupe, Jamaica, Saint Croix, Saint Kitts, and Saint Martin in the West Indies.[2] See Table 1 for importations from America and the West Indies during these years. These slaves were carried to Georgia on merchant ships engaged in general trade, and their average arrival per ship was twelve. British West Indian and North American shippers specialized not in the slave trade but in a general

1. Frances E.W. Harper, "The Slave Auction," in Langston Hughes and Arna Bontemps, eds., *Poetry of the Negro, 1746–1970* (New York: Doubleday, 1970), 14.
2. Elizabeth Donnan, ed., *Documents Illustrative of the History of the Slave Trade to America*, 4 vols. (Washington, D.C.: Carnegie Institution of Washington, 1930–35), 4:612–19.

Table 1. Slave Importation into Georgia from America and the West Indies, 1755–1765
(number of ships in parenthesis)

Year	*America**	*West Indies*	*Total*
1755	43 (6)	8 (1)	51 (7)
1756		67 (4)	67 (4)
1757		8 (2)	8 (2)
1761**		69 (6)	69 (6)
1762		31 (3)	31 (3)
1763	20 (4)	115 (6)	135 (10)
1764	54 (5)	201 (16)	255 (21)
1765	113 (7)	291 (22)	404 (29)
Totals	230 (20)	790 (60)	1,020 (82)

SOURCE: Elizabeth Donnan, ed. *Documents Illustrative of the History of the Slave Trade to America,* 4 vols. (Washington, D.C.: Carnegie Institution of Washington, 1930–35), 2:612–19.

*Slave importations into Georgia from America between 1755 and 1765 originated mainly in South Carolina, Curacoa, and Granada. One ship arrived from Rhode Island and one from New York in 1755. The figures in the table do not represent the total influx of slaves into Georgia during these years. Georgians purchased slaves in Charleston to expand their planting interests and Carolinians migrated with their slaves to Georgia to develop new lands. Sunbury, below Savannah on the Georgia coast, imported 20 slaves in two shipments in 1764 and 7 in two shipments in 1765. All other importations were at Savannah.

**No importations are shown for 1758–60.

import trade that involved "a whole range of goods, including people."[3] There were no direct importations from Africa to Georgia until 1766.

Between 1766 and 1772, with the exception of six months in 1770 during which Georgia adopted the terms of the nonimportation agreement and did not import Negro slaves after July 1, large numbers were carried directly to Georgia from Gambia, Senegal, and Sierra Leone in West Africa. At the same time merchant ships carrying general cargo in the north Atlantic trade continued to supply Georgia with slaves on a smaller scale. In direct importations from Africa, slave arrivals averaged 146 per ship during this six-year period, as opposed to an average of 16 per general mer-

3. Herbert S. Klein, *The Middle Passage: Comparative Study in the Atlantic Slave Trade* (Princeton: Princeton Univ. Press, 1978), 125. See also 121–40 for Great Britain's trade with the West Indies and for the smaller trade in bringing slaves to North America from the West Indies and directly from Africa. The North American zones were largely Virginia, South Carolina, and Georgia, with South Carolina receiving the greatest numbers in the eighteenth century.

Table 2. Slave Importation into Georgia from America, the West Indies, and Africa, 1766–1771
(number of ships in parenthesis)

Year	*America*	*West Indies*	*Africa*	*Total*
1766	73 (7)	384 (27)	515 (5)	972 (39)
1767	63 (4)	199 (10)	205 (2)	467 (16)
1768		90 (1)	420 (2)	510 (3)
1769		20 (2)	517 (4)	537 (6)
1770			710 (3)	710 (3)
1771*			120 (1)	120 (1)

SOURCE: Elizabeth Donnan, ed., *Documents Illustrative of the History of the Slave Trade in America*, 4 vols. (Washington, D.C.: Carnegie Institution of Washington, 1930–35), 2:612–25.
*No importations are shown for 1772–73.

chant ship.[4] See Table 2 for importations from America, the West Indies, and Africa.

The figures from these two tables, giving a combined total of 4,326 slaves imported into Georgia from abroad between 1755 and 1771, by no means represent total slave population by 1772; population figures for this year are not known, nor are numbers of slaves imported between 1758 and 1760 and between 1772 and 1773. However, by 1773 the slave population in Georgia was 16,000, slightly less than half the total population of 33,000. Overland migrations from South Carolina, directed by owners, probably account for more than half the increase to 16,000 by 1773 from about 1,000 in 1755. In 1750, when slavery was introduced, there were already several hundred Negroes in Georgia, and by 1751 there were 420.[5]

The principal port of entry for slave ships in Georgia was Savannah, where Africans were landed, sold, and circulated throughout the plantation belt. Negro traders, whose factorage houses lined the business district along River Street, upon receiving news of

4. Donnan, *Documents*, 2:612–25.

5. *A Century of Population Growth*, 7:132; DeBow, *Industrial Resources*, 3:130; Stevens, *History of Georgia*, 2:53. Stevens, writing in the early nineteenth century, placed the total population in 1766, "nothwithstanding the ravages of the small pox two years before," at 18,000 (10,000 whites and 8,000 blacks). See Donnan, *Documents*, 2:569, for reference to the Seven Years' War that disrupted Britain's foreign slave trade to some degree between 1758 and 1760; not as many slave ships reached the African coast during these years. *Historical Statistics* shows a slave population of 1,000 in 1750.

the arrival of a slave ship, circulated broadsides and advertised the time and place of the forthcoming sale in the *Georgia Gazette*. George Baillie and Company advertised the sale of "a parcel of prime grain coast slaves, just imported from the West Indies"; barreled pork or rice were acceptable as payment. Johnson and Wylly had on hand to be sold "ten likely Gold Coast new negroes consisting of eight stout men and two women," also from the West Indies. Another auction involved a cargo from Gambia of "about 170 young and healthy new negroes, chiefly men, all of whom [had] had the smallpox." Ingliss and Hall advertised the arrival and sale of 340 "healthy new negroes, chiefly men, from the rice coast of Africa." An auction announced by Ewen and Bolton, "Vendue Masters," involved only two slaves, "a handsome young Indian princess, also a country born Negro boy."[6]

In the late eighteenth century British parliamentary acts regulated conditions on slave ships to reduce mortality rates during the voyage from Africa to America. The average number of slaves was now limited to conform to slaves per ton ratio of ships; inoculation and limited health standards were introduced; and to lessen time, hunger, and epidemics during the voyage, ships were reinforced with copper sheathing to increase their speed. Nonetheless, the loss in human life and the suffering was of great magnitude, especially during the Middle Passage from Africa to the West Indies.[7] In 1755, of the 390 slaves carried on the *Emperor*, only 270 survived to be delivered in Jamaica, many of whom were seriously ill. The mortality rate on the *Pearl*, which delivered a shipment at Charleston, was considerable. Of the seventy-one slaves on the *Concord*, only forty-nine survived the voyage to Antigua, and they were boys and girls, some too ill "for hopes of their recovery." The remaining Negroes sold from another shipment at Charleston consisted chiefly of adolescents who were not "accustom'd to destroy themselves like those who [were] older."[8]

Slave prices fluctuated, depending upon the market value of

6. *Georgia Gazette*, Oct. 25, 1764; Feb. 14, 1765; Apr. 8, 1767; Mar. 21, May 23, 1770.

7. Klein, *Middle Passage*, 174, 236–39. Klein attributes high mortality to disease and epidemics and compares eighteenth-century slave mortality with mortality of other seaborne immigrants to conclude that "they all experienced approximately the same rates of mortality." But by the nineteenth century, mortality rates of nonslave immigrants declined faster than they did among slave immigrants.

8. Hamer, et al., eds. *Papers of Henry Laurens*, 1:204, 267–69, 353. See Donnan, *Documents*, 2: 555, for a reference to the slave ship, *Zong*, where, in 1783, 60 of the

staple crops. Other conditions also affected the price in less degree: droughts that damaged food crops essential for maintaining slaves, wars and threats of wars, increases in duty regulations, moods and needs of individual planters, and the native or country origin of African immigrants. Buyer preferences were shown for western Grain Coast slaves who had cultivated rice in Africa, were familiar with the industry, and brought this talent with them; they were considered better workers than Africans from Angola, Calabar, or the interior.[9] There are no early references (before 1759) to slave values among Georgia records, though the correspondence of Henry Laurens, slave broker of South Carolina, contains many. These may be used to arrive at some idea of price ranges in the Georgia market prior to 1763.[10] In 1755 Laurens sold a group of slaves consisting of men, women, boys, and girls for an average of £29 sterling. At another time he sold "250 Angola Slaves" for an average of £33.17; of this group, prime men brought £40. Individual prices were determined by age, sex, strength, and physical condition. Generally, women sold from £3 to £6 less than men, and boys between ages thirteen and fifteen, from £4 to £6 less.[11]

During the summer of 1756, amidst the Seven Years' War, slave prices dropped sharply and, to make matters worse, a severe drought in South Carolina damaged crops, causing food shortages that created a special hardship for the slave population. Henry Laurens lamented the fact that "War struck our planters all of a heap and to this is now added such a drought that Our Indigo and Negro provisions is *[sic]* almost totally demolished, which happens at a time when the place is quite Clog'd with Slaves. . . . The planters won't offer half the price given a month ago." By 1757 the market had rallied and even slaves from Calabar, thought to be inferior as laborers, were bringing good prices, selling at £40 sterling.[12] In 1759 a Savannah correspondent reported that Negro

440 slaves were thrown overboard alive because of an epidemic. See also Daniel C. Littlefield, *Rice and Slaves: Ethnicity and the Slave Trade in Colonial South Carolina* (Baton Rouge: Louisiana State Univ. Press, 1981).

9. Donnan, "The Slave Trade into South Carolina before the Revolution," *American Historical Review*, 33 (Oct.–July 1927–28): 820–21. See also Wood, *Black Majority*, 62, for buyer preferences.

10. Hamer, et al., eds., *Papers of Henry Laurens*, 1:262–353. There is a 1739 reference in William Stephens's *Journal* to the price of a Negro slave who was taken to Georgia illegally and "sold back to Carolina for £23.5s." This reference is found in Stevens, *History of Georgia*, 1:299.

11. Hamer, et al., eds., *Papers of Henry Laurens*, 1: 265, 268–69, 353.

12. Ibid., 269; Donnan, "The Slave Trade," 821.

values in Georgia for "likely young slaves" were ranging from £37 to £40. By the 1760s John G.W. DeBraham estimated the cost of prime field hands in Georgia at £45. By now, average prices had risen from £35 to £40 in response to the growing demand resulting from the expanding plantation economies of Georgia and South Carolina.[13]

The treaty that ended the war between England and France in 1763 gave Florida to the British and extended the southern boundary of Georgia to the St. Marys River. The extended boundary opened for development desirable swamp lands for growing rice south of the Altamaha River and along the Satilla River in lower Georgia. Rice planters from the older tidewater regions of Georgia and South Carolina were quick to take advantage of the opportunity to claim these new lands and to transport gangs of slave laborers to the area to improve the swamps for cultivation. As a result, the ten-year period between 1763 and 1773 witnessed a great expansion in the rice industry along the Georgia coast, while the slave trade grew more intense until 1774, when nonimportation resolves brought an end to this highly profitable enterprise until after the American Revolution.[14]

Although the growth of the slave population in Georgia had been rather rapid, increasing from several hundred in 1750 to 16,000 in 1773, slightly less than half the total population of 33,000, the size of the slave population was small when compared with slave populations in Virginia (165,000), South Carolina (110,000), and Maryland (80,000). These older provinces to the north had maturing plantation economies even while Georgia was being settled.[15] During the Revolution slave populations in all of the colonies (now states) were depleted when thousands of Negroes seeking freedom with the British escaped to their lines.

Those merchants and factors who had engaged in the profitable business of buying and selling Africans looked forward with enthusiasm to the reopening of the slave trade in 1783. Joseph Clay displayed such enthusiasm: "Trade will expand here beyond conception; Negroes will be in great demand and will bring high prices. . . . Dry goods will answer very well [but] Negroes from

13. Donnan, *Documents*, 2:613; DeBraham, *History of the Province of Georgia*, 174.

14. See Hewatt, *An Historical Account*, 267. Hewatt, reporting on the economic progress in Georgia between 1763 and 1773, stated that "many settlements were made by Carolinians about Sunbury, and upon the great river, Altamaha."

15. *Historical Statistics; A Century of Population Growth*, 7:132; DeBow, *Industrial Resources*, 3:130.

Africa will do far better." Clay expounded upon the absolute necessity of the "Negro business" for the general prosperity of Georgia: "It is to the Trade of this Country, as the Soul to the Body." Clay, like James Habersham and John Graham, was a prominent Savannah resident, planter, and merchant. Graham, lieutenant governor and Loyalist, had fled during the Revolution and his property was confiscated, but Clay and Habersham identified with the Revolutionary cause and reestablished their firms at the end of the war. Unlike the later brokers and traders of Negroes in the nineteenth century, who were considered common and ill-bred, Clay and Habersham were, as Henry Laurens was in South Carolina, among the elite of Georgia's society.[16]

The foreign slave trade to North America continued to be a prime source for labor supply on Georgia plantations until 1799, when importation was disallowed by the Georgia state constitution. The disallowance was made because of expressed fears among the white population concerning the Haitian revolution and the threat that insurrectionary doctrine might be transported by Negro slaves from the West Indies. The prohibition was not strictly enforced, however, as is indicated by the steady increase in the slave population in Georgia after 1800. The act of the Georgia legislature, which prohibited importation from the West Indies, also prohibited importation from South Carolina unless the owner accompanied his slaves to Georgia for the expressed intention of using them as laborers; they were not to be sold or traded in Georgia.[17]

Prior to the 1799 disallowance of foreign importation, as provided in the Georgia constitution, slaves were carried to Georgia more frequently and in greater numbers from Africa and the West Indies than they had been before the Revolution. A sampling of advertisements placed in the *Georgia Gazette* between 1784 and 1799 referring to ship arrivals reflects the rate of increase: A shipment of 200 from the Isle of Delos in Africa was to be sold for "rice, tobacco, cotton, Indigo, or cash." At another time 360 "prime slaves" were to be sold for cash by Jeremiah Condy.

16. "Letters of Joseph Clay, Merchant of Savannah, 1776–1798," *Collections*, 8:187, 191, 194–95.

17. See DeCaradeuc Papers, 1751–1909, MSS, GHS, in which one seven-page item refers to the revolution in Santo Domingo. See also A.S. Clayton, *Compilation of the Laws of Georgia Enacted Between 1800 and 1810* (Augusta, 1813), 27; Helen Catterall, ed., *Judicial Cases Concerning American Negro Slavery and the Negro*, 5 vols. (Washington, D.C., 1926–37), 3:12. See Slave Owner Affidavits, 1818–47, Camden County, MSS, Department of Archives and History, Atlanta.

Kennedy and Parker announced the arrival and sale of "102 New Negroes, imported from the windward coast of Africa." Alexander Watt received 300 "Prime Young Negroes" from Angola, to be sold for cash, Sea Island cotton, or tobacco. Johnston and Robertson announced the sale of "Ninety-six choice and healthy New Negroes, consisting of men, women, boys and girls" from Bance Island, Africa.[18]

Notices of slave arrivals refer to African familiarity with rice growing. Many of the slave immigrants who arrived in Georgia and South Carolina during these years came from the west coast of Africa, where rice had long been a staple commodity and where natives had planted, cultivated, harvested, and processed rice for their own use and for market. Georgia rice planters may have preferred slaves from the "Grain Coast, the Rice Coast," or the "Windward Coast" where the peculiarities involved in growing rice were well known. As has been suggested in a recent study of Afro-Americans in colonial South Carolina, rice coast slaves most likely brought their special talents with them. In so doing, they made a distinct contribution to the total tidewater culture, which hitherto has not been recognized by historians.[19]

The methods used by Africans to cultivate rice—the methods of harvesting, threshing, winnowing, and pounding with mortar and pestle to produce the clean white rice—were much the same as methods used in Georgia and Carolina before threshing and pounding machines came into general use in the nineteenth century.[20] Francis Moor, a nineteenth-century traveler, observed planting customs and techniques on the west coast of Africa: the men cultivated corn, leaving the cultivation of rice entirely to the women and children. Moor also observed that rice was plentiful along the Congo River and in Angola.[21] There is no way to determine the percentage of Afro-Americans laboring on rice plantations in Carolina and Georgia who had backgrounds rooted in the

18. *Georgia Gazette*, Jan. 29, 1784, Aug. 18, 1785, Apr. 12, 1787, Aug. 16, 1792, June 21, Aug. 10, Sept. 3, Oct. 25, 1798; *Columbian Museum and Savannah Advertiser*, May 24, 1796. Between 1796 and 1801 the United States emerged as a major receiver of Jamaican reexported slaves, accounting for 23% of the total. Seasonal patterns of arrivals were determined by local weather, sailing conditions, and the American harvesting periods. See Klein, *Middle Passage*, 155–56.

19. Wood, *Black Majority*, 61–62; *Georgia Gazette*, Jan. 29, 1784, Aug. 18, 1785, Apr. 12, 1787, Aug. 16, 1792, June 21, Aug. 10, Sept. 3, Oct. 25, 1798. See also Littlefield, *Rice and Slaves*.

20. Lydia Parrish, *Slave Songs of the Georgia Sea Islands* (New York: Creative Age Press, 1942), 227.

21. See Donnan, *Documents*, 2:569, for a reference to rice growing in Africa in a

rice belts of their native land; references do offer credence for reasonable assumption that many were transplanted to an environment similar to the one they had left.

The federal constitution prohibited the foreign slave trade after 1807. There is no way to estimate the extent of illegal importations into Georgia after that date, nor their statistical significance for the economy. Even if only a small part of the total slave population, the incoming Africans provided a steady link between the slave quarters and West African culture. Locations along the Georgia coast that served as receiving centers for slave smuggling were Harris Neck, Darien, Cumberland Island, St. Marys, and Fernandina, across the St. Marys River in Florida.[22] Zephaniah Kingsley, slave trader of Florida, also supplied Georgia and Carolina planters, who were "always desirous of filling their quarters with Kingsley's niggers." Kingsley engaged in the "Triangular Trade" system from his base on Fort George Island near Jacksonville, sailing with his Sea Island cotton to Liverpool, England, then to the African coast where he purchased Negroes and carried them to Florida on his return trip. These Africans were trained or "seasoned" on Kingsley's plantation to become field hands and skilled laborers, then were sold in the domestic market.[23]

References to the illegal slave trade along the Georgia coast are to be found in testimonials made in the 1930s by former rice plantation slaves. Rosanna Williams remembered her father and grandfather who were tricked ("fool away wid a red hankuhchuh") by a trader in Africa and were carried to Glynn County, where they were purchased by Charles Grant. Patience Spauld-

---

contemporary account of the internal slave trade where black merchants purchased prisoners of war, then marketed their chattel on the west coast of Africa. These slaves were never procured until after the rice season. This was the custom of the rice country where there were many small independent states and frequent tribal wars. Prisoners of war were seldom disposed of until the "rice was in the ground or until it was cut."

22. MSS, in possession of Bessie Lewis, Pine Harbor, McIntosh County; Isaac F. Arnow, "History of St. Marys and Camden County, Georgia," *Camden County Tribune*, 1950–53. Descendents of slaves continued to live at Harris Neck (McIntosh County) until 1942, when the federal government claimed the 2,687-acre tract, which was land given to their forebears in 1865 by the Freedmen's Bureau. The residents were evicted in 1942 and the government later created the Harris Neck Wildlife Refuge. Today, about forty black descendants of the original residents are protesting and demanding that the land be "reclaimed with compensation" for their parents and grandparents.

23. Philip S. May, "Zephaniah Kingsley, Non-Conformist, 1765–1843," *Florida Historical Quarterly* 23 (Oct. 1945): 145–50. Kingsley was the son of Zephaniah Kingsley, a Loyalist who was forced to flee from Charleston, S.C., during the

ing, the grandmother of Ed Thorpe of Harris Neck, McIntosh County, was carried on a slave ship directly from Africa after having been kidnapped by traders who enticed her by displaying a piece of red cloth from their boat. Thorpe's grandmother explained that "all duh people in Africa loves red. Das how dey ketch um. I mean duh folks wut bring um yuh as slabes. Dey put up a red clawt weah dey would see it. Wen dey git close tuh duh boat, dey grab um an bring um yuh." A few elderly Negroes living on St. Catherines Island in the 1930s remembered their forebears who were brought from Africa on slave ships.[24]

Paul Singleton, a former slave of McIntosh County, recalled a slave ship's being pursued by a naval patrol off the Georgia coast; the fifty slaves on this ship were thrown overboard to get rid of evidence of the clandestine nature of the voyage. Robert Pinckney, who was taken by his new owner in the late 1850s from Clinch County to Wilmington Island, Chatham County, remembered that "deah was still some folks" on the island "what hab come from Africa," also that "duh las gang wuz brung attuh I git uah and dey come ovuh from Africa." Jim Myers of Camden County described the slave prison near Woodbine where Negroes, recently arrived from Africa, were chained to iron rings fastened in the floor and kept there until they were manageable: "They chained them wile [wild] Africans theah till they wuz tame. They'd take em out one by one and they'd give em a stick an put em in the fiel with people wut knowd how tuh wuk and that way they lun how too. They sket to give em a hoe. It's shshp [sharp] and they might frail roun with it."[25]

American Revolution. See Edwin L. Williams, Jr., "Negro Slavery in Florida," *Florida Historical Quarterly* 27 (Oct. 1949): 93–110, and 28 (Jan. 1950): 180–204. Kingsley also bred slaves for market. Gray, *History of Agriculture*, 2: 648–49. Gray gives a figure of 270,000 slaves that were brought into the United States illegally. See *Floridian and Journal*, Aug. 6, 1859, Nov. 10, 1860, for estimates that 250,000 slaves were imported illegally between 1808 and 1860.

24. *Drums and Shadows: Survival Studies Among the Georgia Coastal Negroes*, Georgia Writers' Project (Athens: Univ. of Georgia Press, 1940), 17, 70, 74, 105, 121. See Donnan, *Documents*, 2:568, 572, 573, for several practices used by traders to procure slaves: by burning and raiding villages, by trading legitimately with the overlord of a tribe in exchange for his prisoners, and by kidnapping Africans who unknowingly were attracted or enticed by a display of brightly colored goods or merchandise. See Klein, *Middle Passage*, 240–44, for a discussion of sex delineation when raiding villages for slaves as the reason for the failure of women to appear in the slave market as frequently as men. The widespread practice of using women exclusively for agricultural labor in West Africa was the basic cause, but strong emphasis upon matrilineal kinship also contributed to this phenomenon.

25. *Drums and Shadows*, 116, 187, 191–92. Reinforcing these testimonies as

The domestic slave trade was greatly stimulated when foreign importation ceased. The demand for labor in the newer plantation belts of the lower South caused a spectacular shift in slave populations from the border states to those more frontier areas. The states of the upper South became selling states, and Virginia ranked first among them. Between 1830 and 1860 Virginia exported approximately 300,000 Negro slaves. Virginia planters had so impoverished their soil they no longer received profitable returns from their tobacco (except their best, the "Virginia leaf"), and many now came to depend upon the sale of their " 'surplus negroes' " to " 'maintain a semblance of their former hospitality.' "[26]

Records of the Virginia legislature for the years 1831 and 1832 refer to "surplus Negroes" as a profitable enterprise for the state. Thomas R. Dew, president of William and Mary College, called Virginia "a negro raising state" and declared that she produced "enough for her own supply and six thousand for sale" annually to other states.[27] Antislavery writers frequently commented upon the system of rearing slaves for market as a source of income in Virginia and other border states of the South. The narratives of former slaves collected by the Works Progress Administration (later, the Work Projects Administration) in the 1930s reveal the significance of fertility rates. Procreation was rewarded and infertility punished. Annie Neely of Liberty County, Georgia, whose mother was a slave, stated that the "big husky-male slaves were encouraged to have children by female slaves," and that these females received fringe benefits for breeding. They were given better food and did not have to work so hard. Effie Wilson Winn of Liberty County recalled that her forebears were owned by John P. Stevens and that Stevens had favorite female slaves called breeders who were exempt from field work. Jim Cook of McIntosh County stated that owners encouraged healthy males to breed with females. George Noble Jones of Chatham County boasted that his force of 120 Negroes increased itself more than 10 percent in 1854. In 1860 Jones sold a group of laborers on another plantation since these slaves "had displayed no increase for some time."[28]

---

evidence of slave smuggling on the Georgia coast are Records of the Federal District Court, Savannah, on deposit at the Microfilm Records Center, East Point, Ga.

26. As quoted in Frederick Bancroft, *Slave Trading in the Old South* (New York: Frederick Unger, 1931), 69; Gray, *History of Agriculture*, 2:651, 661–63.

27. Bancroft, *Slave Trading in the Old South.* See Richard Sutch, "The Breeding of Slaves for Sale and the Westward Expansion of Slavery, 1850–1860," Engerman and Genovese, eds., *Race and Slavery*, 173–210.

28. Interview with Annie Neeley, Feb. 5, 1975, Richmond Hill, Liberty Coun-

Owners considered slave increase of prime importance and did not hesitate to boast of what they considered an annual growth in their estates accuring from their infant slave populations. Their slaves were encouraged to propagate since natural increase meant additional wealth. "Breeding slaves," "child-bearing women," "breeding period," and "too old to breed" are familiar terms in contemporary writings of the Old South.[29]

Georgia's total slave population in 1850 was 381,682, and in 1860, 462,236, an actual increase of 80,554. Of this increase, it is estimated that 8,000 were slaves imported from the Carolinas, Maryland, and Virginia to supply Georgia planters who preferred to purchase slaves outside the state where they were cheaper than those in Georgia. This inflow is not comparable to the outflow, estimated at 15,000 from 1850 to 1860. The outflow went to markets in Memphis, Natchez, and New Orleans to supply planters in the newer plantation belts of Alabama, Arkansas, Florida, Louisiana, Mississippi, and Texas, where opportunities to use slaves profitably on cheaper fertile land were greater than in Georgia.[30]

---

ty. Dorchester Academy in Liberty County was founded during Reconstruction by Neeley's father and several other Negroes, as was the Congregational Church at Dorchester. Neeley calls mulattoes "ishies" and says there were many such offspring in South Carolina who lived in the house with the owner as trained servants. Neeley's great-grandchildren look white; interview with Effie Wilson Winn, Jan. 21, 1975, Sunbury; interview with Jim Cook, Apr. 9, 1975, Darien, McIntosh county; Smith, *Slavery in Antebellum Florida*, 31. Jones directed the operation of his two Florida plantations as an absentee owner.

29. Bancroft, *Slave Trading*, 68; Olmsted, *Journey in Seaboard Slave States*, 57; Charles S. Sydnor, *Slavery in Mississippi* (New York: Appleton, 1933), 136–37; Coulter, *Thomas Spalding of Sapelo*, 39. See Sutch, "Breeding of Slaves for Sale," Engerman and Genovese, eds., *Race and Slavery*, 173–210. The techniques employed by Sutch to examine the extent and nature of slave breeding are based on data contained in the federal Census returns for 1850 and 1860. Sutch examined fertility rates in the buying and selling states to conclude that the selling states had a higher fertility ratio. He states that "The evidence on slave migration is ample to conclude that a substantial interstate trade in human beings took place and that eastern and border state planters sold slaves to this trade."

30. *United States Census Returns*, 1850, 1860; Bancroft, *Slave Trading*, 383, 384, 394, 399, 400. Georgia did not export many slaves prior to the Mexican War. To determine the approximate inflow of 8,000 slaves, Bancroft adds a natural increase of 23.4% to the slave population in 1850 and subtracts the same from the population in 1860; the difference indicates importation plus the natural increase. To determine the approximate outflow of 15,000 slaves, Bancroft adds to the 8,000 imported an 11.7% increase and divides the result by 1,117 to arrive at 15,875 exportations. Allowing for 875 emancipations and successful runaways, there remains 15,000. Bancroft's formula is as follows: 1850–60: 381, 682 × 1.234 − 462,198 + 8,936 (8,000 × 1.117) ÷ 1.117 − 875 = 15,000. See Bancroft, *Slave Trading*, 400 n. 32.

At the same time, the rice coast counties (Camden, Chatham, Bryan, Glynn, Liberty, McIntosh) experienced an inflow/outflow trade on a small scale. In 1850 the total slave population for these six counties was 35,278, and in 1860, 34,314, a decrease of 964. Though slave populations increased slightly in three of these counties, Chatham, Bryan, and Liberty, the decrease in Glynn County of 1,393, from 4,232 in 1850 to 2,839 in 1860, more than offset the increase. About one-third of Glynn's decrease was caused by the outflow of Pierce Butler's 436 slaves, who were taken to Chatham County for sale in 1859; the outflow from Camden (103) and McIntosh (566) counties was negligible.[31]

The large number of slaves in the labor market encouraged planters to buy and sell Negroes already in the area. Court records in coastal Georgia frequently relate transactions of this nature. In some instances the complete plantation was sold, including slaves, livestock, crops, farm equipment, buildings, and other property. Contemporary newspapers are filled with advertisements offering complete plantations for sale, such as this one:

> Executor's Sale, Plantation and Negroes. At the plantation of the late James Forrest, esq., about six miles from Savannah, on Friday, the 29th December, at 12 o'clock, will be sold at public sale, about 97 negroes, the property of the estate. These negroes have been brought up and lived long together, and have made on the place excellent cotton crops. A great proportion have been accustomed to go in the field, but few are old, and the rest prime healthy young people. There are among them several carpenters. At the same time will be sold the plantation called Oakland, about 550 acres of which is good planting land.[32]

When planters died insolvent, leaving their estates heavily indebted, their slaves and other personal property were sold at public auction to satisfy their creditors. The estate of Josiah Tattnall was insolvent at the time of his death in 1799. His widow was forced to sell a portion of the slaves on Bonaventure Plantation, as well as the cotton and rice crops; seven years later the remaining slaves who were mortgaged and other personal property on the plantation were sold: Lydy and Bines for $200; a mother and son, $705; a Negro man, John, $491; and Beck, who was "very old," $100.[33] The estate of George W. Allen was heavily indebted at the

31. *United States Census Returns*, 1850, 1860. See Appendix A, Table A-5, for population growth in the rice coast counties from 1800 to 1860.

32. *Daily Georgian*, Nov. 28, 1820; box F 64, fol. 64, Probate Records, Chatham County.

33. Box T, fol. 35, 42, Probate Records, Chatham County. The inventory of this

time of his death; all of the slaves and other personal property on his plantation, Beverly-Berwick, were sold to satisfy creditors.[34]

Since enslaved workers were regarded as property and served as collateral on mortgage loans, they were circulated in the market whenever foreclosures were made. The time and place of the auction was announced in advance: "Sheriff's Sale. On the first Tuesday of June next, will be sold at the Courthouse in the City of Savannah, between the hours of 10 and 4 o'clock, ten negroes, viz.: Cato, Hager, Lucy, Judy, May, Betty, Sophia, Ceasar, little Mary, Ned, levied on under a forclosure of a mortgage as the property of John W. Stirk, to satisfy the trustees of the White Bluff Congregation."[35]

At a sheriff's sale in St. Marys, two children were auctioned off to the highest bidder when Cook, Williford and Company levied upon the property of Francis Young to secure the debt he owed them. At another sale, a family of nine Negroes, Flora, Prissey, Luke, Roger, Lizzy, Jeney, Sarah, David, and Tom, were sold to the highest bidder to satisfy debt. A mulatto slave, Jane, and her child were sold the same day to satisfy a debt due John Haupt by Ashe Howe.[36]

Slaves were also advertised for sale with assurance that they were being sold for no reason other than personal circumstances of the owner. This meant they were desirable servants, there was no indebtedness accrued against them, and they might be purchased on credit instead of cash at the time of sale. A group of house servants in Savannah was advertised for sale with the understanding that they would not be removed from the city. These Negroes, a female slave who was a "good cook, washer and ironer," her two children, and two other servants were being sold "for no fault."[37]

The domestic slave market was representative of a large portion of the wealth in the South, and the demand for slaves continued to stimulate the economy so long as investments brought profitable

estate is quite interesting. The slaves were grouped and valued as families. The executor for the estate, Robert Mitchell, paid out $6 for "mourning gowns" worn by the two slaves, Nancy and Molly, at the funeral. He paid out $10 for the "carriage carrying the corpse," $60 to Farris for the coffin, $26.50 to Dixon for supplying the drapes for the coffin. Two Negro nurses, Betty and Hannah, were paid $31 for their services while nursing Tattnall before his death.

34. Box A, fol. 56, Probate Records, Chatham County.

35. *Daily Georgian*, May 2, 1823.

36. Ibid., Jan. 3, 8, 1823.

37. *Daily Morning News*, Sept. 5, 1859. Advertisements announcing private and public sales appear in this newspaper to the period of 1864.

returns. There were always those owners who, for one reason or another, desired to sell their Negroes and placed them in the market. As late as 1863, a sale of sixty Negroes was announced by H. Meinhard and Company in Savannah: "Just received a large lot of negroes, consisting of men, women, boys and girls, in families, and one fine house servant and carriage driver." The auctioneer and broker, E. Mendel, made known that his business house on Market Square had "accommodations for any number of Negroes at a moderate price for board" until they could be sold privately or at public auction. Another sale was announced by Clinkscales and Boozer:

> We have this day received a lot of negroes from the West, such as have generally given Georgians such undivided satisfaction. We have negroes of every class, men, boys, women, girls; also several families—cooks, washers, ironers, house servants, and a first-rate country blacksmith. We have lately rented the well known office and yard of Captain Joe Bryan, deceased. The ample and complete arrangements of this establishment for convenience and health are worthy of the attention of those who have negroes they want to sell.[38]

Captain Joe Bryan, referred to in this advertisement, was Joseph Bryan, the reliable and well-known Negro broker who directed the auction of Pierce Butler's slaves in 1859. This sale of Negroes by one owner was the largest to take place in coastal Georgia and perhaps in the South. Butler was forced to sell 436 Negroes to satisfy his creditors. His slaves were selected from two plantations in Glynn County and transported to Savannah in groups over a period of several days prior to the sale.[39]

Butler's slaves were classified and valued in family groups, though they were not always sold together. Field hands were sold separately at $1,200 each; a skilled carpenter, at $1,750; and one family, at $6,180. The total amount received from the sale of 426 Negroes (10 became ill and were not sold) was $303,850. The traders and planters who purchased these slaves were from Alabama, middle Georgia, and South Carolina. This sale occurred only a few years before blacks would be set free. Pierce Butler's daughter, Frances Butler Leigh, reported in 1866 that "nearly all who have lived through the terrible suffering of these past four

38. Ibid., Mar. 17, Apr. 9, Dec. 29, 1863.

39. *What Became of the Slaves on a Georgia Plantation? Great Auction Sale of Slaves, at Savannah, Georgia, March 2nd & 3rd, 1859. A Sequel to Mrs. Kemble's Journal* N.p.: American Anti-Slavery Scoeity, n.d.), 4, 12, 14, 19.

years have come back, as well as many of those who were sold seven years ago."[40] Most of Butler's slaves, unlike thousands of others who were sold separately and had to confront the deep and dreadful longing for a child, mother, brother, or sister and hope to overcome the shock of having been stripped of all family ties, were reunited with their families.

To insure the best possible price, a certain amount of grooming was done to prepare slaves for market. The men were given a fresh set of clothing to have them create a pleasing appearance, and the women were given bright, showy cotton prints or gaily figured bandannas. The men were often given a drink of gin or whiskey to make them seem spirited. Pierce Butler gave each of his slaves a new silver dollar before they were sold. Prospective buyers examined slaves carefully to make sure there were no physical defects or scars from whippings to indicate bad character. The value of the Negro was determined by his physical condition, his age, and his skill. Buyers were hesitant to purchase Negroes whose advanced age would prevent a profitable output of work. There were some exceptions when house servants or skilled laborers were being sold, though the average purchaser preferred young Negroes.[41]

Various classifications determined individual prices for slaves. For example, blacksmiths, carpenters, seamstresses, prime field hands, brick masons, and house servants were more valuable than other Negroes and brought higher prices. Sex, age, temperament, physical condition, skill, and experience were also determining

40. Ibid., 2, 7. Though his name was not mentioned, the sale of Pierce Butler's slaves was announced in the *Daily Morning News* well ahead of time, as well as in other newspapers throughout the South. Negro traders came from several slave states to attend the sale; Frances Butler Leigh, *Ten Years on a Georgia Plantation* (London: Bentley, 1883), 14, 22.

41. Buyers examined Negroes as they would animals, pulling open their mouths to see their teeth, feeling their limbs to know how muscular they were, and making them walk and bend to make sure they were not lame or arthritic. At private sales and at auction sales, examining rooms were used where Negroes were made to take off their clothing so that all of their body parts could be viewed with the purpose of making doubly sure they were strong and healthy. The Negro had to submit to these humiliations and show no emotion. *What Became of the Slaves on a Georgia Plantation?*, 8, 9; Sydnor, *Slavery in Mississippi* 134–40; Bancroft, *Slave Trading*, 113. For poignant descriptions of the Negro broker's display room, the courtyard, and surrounding barracks where the slaves were kept until time of sale and the standard procedure used to examine and classify them, see Nehemiah Adams, *South-Side View of Slavery; or Three Months at the South in 1854* (Boston, 1854), 64–81; William Chambers, *Things As They Are in America*, 141–50, and Frederika Bremer, *The Homes of the New World: Impressions of America*, both rpt. in Rose, ed., *Documentary History of Slavery*, 169–72.

factors. Negroes recently imported from Africa were considered less valuable than "country" Negroes from an older state like Virginia. Field hands between eighteen and thirty years of age brought more than older Negroes, and male hands brought more than female hands. Children were often priced according to height and weight, and infants were valued by the pound. Attractive females and skilled workers sometimes sold for triple the value, and in some instances, the buyer would pay more for a group of Negroes upon agreement that the old and infirm be excluded.[42]

At the time of Anna Matilda King's death in 1862, her 142 slaves ranged in value from $100 to $1,000. A few had no value. Alex, age thirty-three, and Delia, age twenty-three, were each appraised at $1,000; Frederick, age sixteen, at $700; Theresa, who was one year old, at $200; Edinborough, age twenty-seven, and Big Peter, age seventy-six, had no value.[43] In 1863 the 214 slaves belonging to James Potter on Tweedside Plantation, were valued at $115,250. On Colerain Plantation which Potter also owned, the 239 slaves were valued at $116,400. The slaves on these two plantations ranged in value from $1,500 to $50. Robert, age thirty-three, was appraised at $1,500; "Old Charlotte," age sixty, and "Old Minda, market woman," at $50 each; Nancy, age seventy-eight, had no value. Potter's total estate in real and personal property was valued at $380,825. His ownership in slaves represented more than 60 percent of this wealth. He also owned stock in various banks and railroads valued at $146,850.[44]

Owners often directed in their wills that their Negroes be sold. Priscilla Houstoun, after bequeathing favorite house servants to her children, requested that all of her other slaves be sold "at public outcry" within three months after her death.[45] Sarah Wright requested in her will that certain slaves be left to her four nieces. The slave Ishmael, his wife, Minty, and one of their sons, Adam, she gave to Margaret McQueen. The slave Diana, her three children, as well as June, his wife, Hagar, and their three children

42. Gray, *History of Agriculture*, 2:664–66. Gray lists prices quoted in 1853 by a slave broker in Richmond, Virginia: Best men (18–25), $1,200 to $1,300; Fair men (18–25), $950 to $1,050; Boys, five feet in height, $850 to $950; Boys, four feet, $375 to $400; Young Women, $800 to $1,000; Girls, five feet, $750 to $850; Girls, four feet, $350 to $450.

43. Record of Wills, Book G, 145–48, Probate Records, Glynn County.

44. Inventories and Appraisements, Book M. N. 1861–1868, 111–19, 134, 173, Chatham County.

45. Will Book B, 131–34, Probate Records, Chatham County.

she gave to Mary Ann Couper; another child of this slave family she gave to Eliza Mackay. The slaves Joe and Joseph, who were other sons of Ishmael and Minty, were bequeathed to Sarah Williamson. Wright directed that her attorney decide whether or not to sell her remaining slaves.[46] Sampson Neyle provided in his will that his executors have full power "to sell any unprofitable negro or negroes and replace them with others" so that his planting interests would continue to show profitable returns.[47]

William R. Waring requested that his plantation and slaves on Skidaway Island be sold after his death "at such time and in such manner" as his executors deemed expedient, "the proceeds of any such sale" to be reinvested by them and used as income for his children.[48] Thomas Spalding of Sapelo Island, who died heavily indebted in 1851, had requested that "the slaves continue to labor on Sapelo" and that the proceeds of his plantation be used to pay off his debts. There were 250 slaves involved in this estate, 15 of whom had no value because of their age or infirmity. While still in life, Spalding had given land and slaves to his six children and now at the age of seventy-eight the remainder of his property "yet incumbered with debt, a debt that has greatly imbittered my latter years" could not be distributed to his heirs. After signing his will, he added the following paragraph: "I am again unfortunate and must sell forty-nine Negroes and three old nurses in order to pay my debts to the State Bank. This will reduce one thousand dollars to five hundred dollars to my daughter Elizabeth to plainly educate her two oldest sons."[49]

Mitchell King, a wealthy slaveholder of Charleston, South Carolina, owned Retreat Plantation on Argyle Island in Chatham County, Georgia, in addition to properties in North Carolina. King was seventy-six years old and had eleven children when his will was made in 1856. He directed that at the time of his death his executors "sell and dispose of at public or private sale for cash or on credit, all or any part of" his slave property and the proceeds be reinvested for the benefit of his children. By 1862 King could

46. Will Book W, 114, Probate Records, Chatham County.

47. Box N, fol. 39, Probate Records, Chatham County.

48. Will Book H, 126, Probate Records, Chatham County.

49. Will Book, 49, Probate Records, McIntosh County. Thomas Spalding's will, dated 1848, along with the inventory of his estate, was destroyed during the Civil War when all of the probate records were burned. The recording of his will is a certified copy, made after the war. Spalding owed $10,000 to the State Bank of Georgia, $5,000 to his friend Mr. Molyneux, who was probably his factor, and $1,850 on a note that he guaranteed for his son, Charles.

predict the possibility of the loss of his great fortune in slave property. He added a codicil to his will:

> Many fearful changes have taken place in our beloved South, and in the condition and prospects of our families. My son Henry has laid down his life in defense of his Country, and I feel myself tottering on the verge of the grave. My financial arrangements are in sad disorder. My children will have a heavy task before them. My various small legacies given by my will to my Grand Children I hereby revoke and annul. God I trust will protect them. It is impossible to enter fully into the situation of my affairs or to form any estimate of my estate.[50]

The circumstances that prompted the sale of slaves were often beyond the control of the owner, and the harshness and callousness associated with slave sales did not always reflect the owner's attitude. In many instances, benevolent feelings were expressed by planters in their wills when providing, in the distribution of their slaves, that families not be separated when sold. To insure such direction, a redistribution of other personal property was sometimes provided to maintain a fair share among their heirs. Out of devotion and appreciation for faithful service, some left small legacies to favorite servants or stipulated that they be given to certain members of the owner's family to assure them a degree of protection as family servants.

It may be that rice plantation slaves benefited from the select type of owner who was born and bred in a traditional aristocratic slave society where benevolent and patriarchal attitudes had been nurtured over the years and were more pronounced than in the newer frontier plantation belts. Nonetheless, planter attitudes varied. Rice planters were sometimes callous and cared little for the destiny that might befall their slaves—incorrigible slaves were sold, and so were those who did not propagate.

When owners directed in their wills that their slaves be sold privately or publicly and that the proceeds be used for their beneficiaries, they admittedly cared little for the future condition of their slaves. On inventory sheets listing personal property of rice planters, slaves are frequently classified in family groups; the value of the family is given as well as the individual value of the slave. Such listings were necessary to execute promptly estate properties and were not expressly made to placate the owner's conscience by protecting the slave family. Family identifications

50. Will Book J, Chatham County, 15–29, Department of Archives and History, Atlanta.

on inventory sheets were not a guarantee against family separations through sales—husbands, wives, and children were often sold individually to different owners, never to see each other again.

Negro slaves were regarded as personal property, and there was no security against their sale and circulation in the market, which often resulted in the separation of families. Such conditions as the inevitable death of the owner and the division of his estate, over extension of credit with slaves mortgaged as collateral and the resulting foreclosure, or the consistent refusal by the slave to conform to the routine of work were contibuting factors in the sale of slaves. Slaves were victimized, dehumanized, and made to suffer irreparable emotional damage as a result of their being traded in the open market as chattel. The slave trade was one of the harshest aspects of slavery, and its impact upon the total condition and personality of those victimized under its system must not be minimized.

CHAPTER SEVEN

Care, Maintenance, and Health of Low Country Slaves

The quantity and quality of the slave's diet were affected by owner attitude, a knowledge of basic dietary needs, and the geographic location of the plantation. There were several major sources from which the slave received his food. The first and basic one was each slave's weekly allotment of corn and pork. Corn and pork were supplemented periodically with sweet potatoes, peas, turnips, fruits (in season), beef, mutton, salted fish, coffee, molasses, and, on rice plantations, rice and rice flour as a variation of cornmeal. Another source was the slaves' garden plots, located near their cabins. Here they grew green vegetables and kept chickens and hogs. A third source was the food they obtained by hunting and fishing; the availability of this last source depended upon the type of labor system in use on the plantation, upon owner latitude in allowing slaves to have guns for hunting wild animals and game, and upon the proximity of the plantation to rivers and streams.[1]

The weekly allowance of corn per slave was a peck of ground meal. There was no stinting on the recommended allowance of cornmeal, and some slaves had access to unlimited amounts. They preferred to grind their own corn; this was the custom along the Georgia coast, though not generally throughout the South, since some owners objected to the time consumed in the grinding process.[2] Georgia Bryan Conrad described the ancient method

1. Sam Bowers Hilliard, *Hog Meat and Hoecake: Food Supply in the Old South, 1840–1860* (Carbondale: Southern Illinois Univ. Press, 1972), 55–56.
2. For contemporary references to slave diet, see *De Bow's Review* 3 (1847):

used by slaves to grind their corn on her father's plantation on the Altamaha River: "Corn was ground in the Bibical handmill, 'two women grinding at a mill . . . .' Large stones, the upper one with a hole in it, were connected by a pole with the roof of the shed in which they stood. The women would take hold of this pole and turn the stone with a celerity and ease that was surprising." Conrad remembered the "whirring of the stones, the soft rustle of the meal as it fell into the basket placed to receive it, and the sound of the women's voices singing at the mill."[3] Edward J. Thomas remembered how the "young men and girls [slaves], on moonlight nights, would meet to grind their corn around the hand mills," and the plaintive songs they sang as they waited for their turn at the machine.[4]

Cornmeal, the core of the slave's diet, is a low quality protein, lacking three of the eight essential amino acids (methionine, lysine, and trytophan) contained in such high quality proteins as meat, fish, or fowl. Pork is also low in these same amino acids. Thus, the basic foods, corn and pork, were deficient in nutrients necessary to maintain health; food supplements helped to supply the nutrients necessary for a balanced diet. Such supplements were generally available to rice plantation slaves.[5] The frequent references in contemporary literature to the variety of food available for and consumed by rice plantation slaves suggest that their diet was high in carbohydrates, fats, and proteins, and was well balanced.[6]

419–20; 7 (1849): 380–83; 14 (1853): 177–78; 25 (1858): 224–27; *Southern Cultivator* 8 (1850):162–64. For general works that devote sections to slave diet, see Charles S. Davis, *The Cotton Kingdom in Alabama* (Montgomery, Ala.: Alabama State Department of Archives and History, 1939); Flanders, *Plantation Slavery in Georgia;* Phillips, *American Negro Slavery;* Todd L. Savitt, *Medicine and Slavery: The Diseases and Health Care of Blacks in Antebellum Virginia* (Chicago: Univ. of Illinois Press, 1978); James B. Sellers, *Slavery in Alabama* (University, Ala.: Univ. of Alabama Press, 1950); Sydnor, *Slavery in Mississippi;* Joe Gray Taylor, *Negro Slavery in Louisiana* (Baton Rouge: Louisiana Historical Association, 1963); Stampp, *Peculiar Institution.*

3. *Reminiscences of a Southern Woman* (rpt. Hampton, Va.: Hampton Institute Press, n.d.), 9.

4. *Memoirs of a Southerner, 1840–1923* (Savannah, 1923), 12; Margaret Davis Cate, *Early Days of Coastal Georgia* (New York: Gallery Press, 1955), 181. Opposite this page in Cates's book, Charles Alexander, a former slave, is shown holding an old round mill stone that was used by four generations of his family to grind corn into meal and grits.

5. Hilliard, *Hog Meat and Hoecake,* 62–66; Savitt, *Medicine and Slavery,* 91–92; Kenneth F. Kiple and Virginia Kiple, "Slave Child Mortality: Some Nutritional Answers to a Perennial Puzzle," *Journal of Social History* 10 (July 1977): 284–309.

6. *Autobiography of Joseph Le Conte,* ed. William D. Armes (New York: D. Ap-

The weekly allowance of pork per slave was from two to five pounds. Pork, with its fatty content, was considered more nutritionally valuable than beef or mutton as an energy-producing food, though large numbers of cattle were dispersed throughout the South and beef could have been utilized more consistently. On rice plantations beef was issued regularly to slaves as a variation from pork; two pounds of beef per slave were considered the equivalent in food value of one pound of pork. Nonetheless, pork was preferred and recommended; its "heat generating" qualities were thought to be healthful for blacks though harmful for whites. Thus, pork rations were increased during periods of especially heavy work loads in order to compensate for greater output of energy.[7]

Provision crops such as turnips (roots and tops), peas, and sweet potatoes were grown on the plantation and served as supplements to enrich the slave's diet. Turnips have a high iron and vitamin content and may have saved many a slave from having a serious deficiency disease. Peas are fairly high in proteins and contain some vitamins, and sweet potatoes are an excellent source for several nutrients and vitamins. Dried peas and sweet potatoes were easily preserved for extended periods of time, and so could be stored and given out intermittently during the year.[8]

The slave garden plot was a source of supply for green vegetables and was virtually universal in the plantation South. Contemporary travelers often referred to these patches when reporting on the slave system. John Lambert, traveling along the Savannah River in 1808, noticed "men, women, boys, and girls busily employed in hoeing and planting. Each had a separate piece of ground marked out for their day's work." When the task was finished, these slaves worked in their own gardens. They sold their surplus produce and some saved money "to purchase their freedom . . . generally equivalent to five or six hundred dollars."[9]

---

pleton, 1903), 27, 33; Conrad, *Reminiscences*, 7, 8; Coulter, *Thomas Spalding*, 85, 121; Charles Seton Henry Hardee, *Reminiscences and Recollections of Old Savannah* (Savannah, 1926), 11, 12; Thomas, *Memoirs of a Southerner*, 9–13; Charles Spalding Wylly, *The Seed That Was Sown in the Colony of Georgia: The Harvest and the Aftermath, 1740–1870* (New York: Neale, 1910), 50–51.

7. Hilliard, *Hog Meat and Hoecake*, 56.

8. Ibid., 65. J.D.B. De Bow, *Compendium of the Seventh Census* (Washington, D.C., 1854), lists Georgia as producing 6,986,428 bushels of sweet potatoes in 1850, the greatest amount for any of the states.

9. *Travels Through Lower Canada and the United States*, in Lane, ed., *Rambler*, 49.

It was to the owner's advantage to provide garden plots since they contributed materially to the slave's diet. The task system of labor used in growing rice allowed some free time, and the practice by owners along the rice coast of encouraging slaves to have gardens, and even to permit them to hunt and fish, contributed substantially to their diet.[10] The climate along the Georgia and Carolina coast permitted the growth of green vegetables such as cabbages, collards, and turnip greens throughout the year; these vegetables supplied the vitamins and iron necessary for physical well-being. By modern standards, the dietary intake of rice coast slaves was adequate.

Garden plots varied from one to two acres; half an acre per family was reported to be the size on one Georgia rice plantation.[11] Thomas Spalding's slaves, like others along the coast, in their spare time cultivated their garden plots, had chickens and hogs, hunted and fished, and sold their surplus produce.[12] Thomas Butler King's slaves sold their surplus produce to the King family. Produce was also purchased by this planter family from slaves who lived on plantations nearby. Accountings were kept of the transactions: "Quamina for 4½ bushels corn and eggs, $3.50; Sanders for 3 baskets, Fodder, 8 small chickens, $2.19; Hamilton's negro for fowls, $1.12; Amy for 5 ducks and 4 fowls, $2.75; Butler's negro, Jacob, for poultry, $10.50; Old Whiskey for 3 baskets, .56½; Hamilton's negro, 18 terrapins, .90."[13]

Foods not produced on the plantation were purchased from the merchant for slave consumption. Molasses (rich in calcium and iron), salt, sugar, salted fish, brandy, rum, tobacco, and corn were some of the items obtained regularly between 1791 and 1812 for the slaves on Raymond Demere's two plantations, Dublin and Cherry Hill in Chatham County.[14] Fortunately, estate account-

10. Gray, *History of Agriculture*, 1:564; Basil Hall, *Travels in North America in the Years 1827 and 1828*, 3 vols. (Philadelphia, 1829), 3:180; Sir Charles Lyell, *A Second Visit to the United States of America*, 2 vols. (New York, 1850), 1:327; Olmsted, *Journey in Seaboard Slave States*, 422, 682, 693.

11. Olmsted, *Journey in Seaboard Slave States*, 422.

12. Coulter, *Thomas Spalding*, 80–81, 85.

13. Thomas Butler King Papers, 1836–55, MSS, D, 1252, SHC. "Hamilton's negro" most likely refers to James Hamilton Couper's slave from Hamilton Plantation on St. Simons Island; "Butler's negro," to Pierce Butler's slave from Butler's Island. Both plantations were fairly close to the King plantation in Glynn County. The custom among blacks of having garden patches for growing green vegetables throughout the year survives today along the Georgia and Carolina coast.

14. Estate Account of Raymond Demere, 1791–1812, box D, fol. 1, Probate Records, Chatham County.

ings of rice planters are available among county court records. These contain listings of foods and other items obtained from the merchant to supply plantation slaves. James Hamilton Couper's annual accountings of all transactions involving Hopeton and Hamilton plantations in Glynn County serve as a meaningful source to evaluate the quality and variety of food consumed by his slaves. In 1833 purchases were made for "3,800 bushels corn, $2,978; 29 barrels prime pork, $185; 53 barrels no. 3 mackerel, $142; 2,710 lbs. Christmas beef, $95."[15]

The slave children on Couper's Hopeton Plantation were cared for and fed in a nursery, "remarkably neat and clean, well ventilated, and heated altogether by steam." At sunrise, the children (called the nursery gang) were taken by their mothers and nurses (unrated superannuated slaves) from the settlements to the nursery and delivered into the care of an elderly nurse who saw that they were washed and their hair combed. Their breakfast was served at eight o'clock and consisted of hominy and molasses; at two o'clock they were served a dinner of soup made of salt pork, Irish potatoes, okra, peas, or turnips. They were also given corn dumplings or sweet potatoes. The children were taken home at sunset.[16]

The 114 slave children on Pierce Butler's plantation received basically the same diet as the Couper children. The overseer, Roswell King, Jr., boasted that "it cost less than two cents each per week, in giving them a feed of okra soup with pork, or a little molasses or hominy, or small rice. The great advantage is, that there is not a dirt-eater [geophagy] among them." King associated dirt-eating with improper diet and referred to it as "an incurable propensity produced from a morbid state of the stomach."[17]

With regard to feeding the adult slaves on Butler's plantation, King wrote: They "have plenty of the best corn, well-ground, by water and animal power, with a portion of fish (No. 3 Mackerel),

15. Wills and Appraisements, Book D, 171–83, Glynn County.

16. *Southern Agriculturist* 6 (1833): 574.

17. Ibid. 1 (1828): 527. See Robert W. Twyman, "The Clay Eater: A New Look at an Old Southern Engima," *Journal of Southern History* 37 (Aug. 1971): 430–47. Twyman does not associate dirt-eating with hookworm disease nor iron deficiency. Evidence as to the cause may hinge upon tradition or habit that begins as an experiment, then becomes a craving. Dirt-eating is still practiced among thousands of southerners, black and white, and is identified in the dictionary as geophagy. See Savitt, *Medicine and Slavery*, 67, 68, where geophagy is referred to as being a "habit or custom, rather than a symptom of hookworm disease or dietary deficiency." According to Savitt, dirt or clay eaters "ingested millions of tiny roundworm eggs along with the clay," which infested them with intestinal worms.

Beef, Pork, and molasses, and when much exposed, a little Rum. To each gang there is a cook who carefully prepares two meals per day."[18] These basic foods were supplemented with peas and sweet potatoes, green vegetables from their garden patches, and poultry and hogs that they kept penned. They used their boats to catch fish, to cast for shrimp, and to gather oysters.[19]

Unlike the majority of plantation slaves who worked under the gang system from sunup to sundown and had little leisure time to hunt and fish, rice coast slaves had opportunity for such activity. Trusted slaves were allowed to have guns and many had boats, mostly canoes that they made from cypress trees. Owners encouraged the removal of cypress trees from swamp lands where new ground was to be cleared for planting. The woods, swamps, and salt water creeks were filled with fowl, deer, opossum, racoons, terrapins, alligators, crabs, fish, oysters, and shrimp. The low country terrain with its numerous creeks, streams, and rivers made canoes a practical mode for transportation from one plantation to another. Slave boat crews created their own rhythmical tunes as they rowed and sang.[20] Frederika Bremer noted that they sang "as they rowed their boats up the river on their return from the city, whither they had taken their small wares—eggs, fowls, and vegetables—for sale, as they do two or three times a week."[21]

With few exceptions, clothes for rice plantation slaves were made on the plantation by slave seamstresses. Materials used were rough durable osnaburgs, denims, kersey (a cotton and woolen weave), calicoes, twills, and plains. Red flannel was used to make garments for infants. Women and children wore osnaburg shifts, though the women's dress might consist, instead, of a blouse and skirt. The men wore pants and a jacket or shirt. The men on the Thomas Plantation in McIntosh County were given two suits of clothes a year, one of wool, the other cotton, two shirts, a pair of blankets, and a pair of heavy shoes. During the summer slaves went barefooted. Estate account records list regular purchases made for large amounts of cloth, blankets, and, less frequently, for shoes and hats. A blanket was generally given every other year. A few slaves were given socks but none were given

18. *Southern Agriculturist* 1 (Sept. 1828): 526.

19. Cate, *Early Days of Coastal Georgia*, 81, 175, 201.

20. Conrad, *Reminiscences*, 6, 7; Thomas, *Memoirs of a Southerner*, 11; *Autobiography of Joseph Le Conte*, 18; Coulter, *Thomas Spalding*, 190.

21. *Homes of the New World and Impressions of America*, trans. Mary Howitt. 2 vols. (New York: Harper, 1853), 1:305.

underwear, thought to be unnecessary garments. The men were given woolen hats for winter wear and straw hats for summer; the women wore bandannas.[22]

In 1804 the estate account of Raymond Demere contained annual listings of supplies purchased to maintain his slaves. The lists include such items as apple brandy, rum, hats, handerchiefs, as well as blankets and shoes in greater numbers, along with the usual amounts of corn, salt, molasses, tobacco, cloth, and accessories. No purchases were made for salted pork since there were hogs in sufficient numbers on Demere's two plantations; these animals were slaughtered, and the meat was cured and fed to the slaves as salt pork.[23]

James Hamilton Couper made annual accountings of all transactions involving Hopeton and Hamilton plantations in Glynn County. The accountings, like those of Raymond Demere's, serve as a meaningful source to evaluate treatment of slaves and costs for their care and maintenance. Hopeton, like Dublin and Cherry Hill, was not a self-sufficient unit in supplying basic foods or clothing for slaves. These necessities were purchased at intervals throughout the year. The inventory sheets list blankets, cloth, corn, mackerel, needles, pork, salt, shoes, soap, thread, and other items. Also listed are expenses for medical treatment, religious instruction, and the cost of reclaiming runaway slaves. Another entry worthy of mention reads, "cash paid negro woman for 36 weeks allowance—superannuated, $7.00."[24]

The slave houses of coastal Georgia were of substantial construction, good design, and were made of tabby, brick, clapboards, or batten boards place on wood; they were usually elevated from the ground. Tabby, a mixture of lime, crushed oysters shells, sand, and water, when dried, hardened like cement.[25] Numerous oyster

22. Conrad, *Reminiscences*, 7; Thomas, *Memoirs of a Southerner*, 9, 10; *Autobiography of Joseph LeConte*, 22. Leconte described the self-sufficiency of Woodmanston Plantation. All of the clothing, including shoes, were made on this plantation. The hides of slaughtered cattle were cured, and skilled slaves manufactured shoes from the leather.

23. Estate Account of Raymond Demere, 1791–1812, box D, fol. 1, Probate Records, Chatham County.

24. Wills and Appraisements, Book D, 171–83, Glynn County; Kollock Papers, 1799–1850, D 164, fol. 22, MS, Colonial Dames of America Collection, GHS; Kollock Plantation Books, MS, vol. 6, SHC. Kollock's overseer gave out shoes annually in December to all field hands; flannel shirts, knitted woolen stockings, and cotton socks were given intermittently.

25. Observations made by the writer. Tabby ruins remain today along the coast and on the islands as a reminder of the ingenuity and resourcefulness of the planter class and their slave laborers in making use of materials close at hand.

Figure 14. Charles Spalding's Tabby Slave Houses at the Thickets. (Drawing by Leonora Quarterman.)

beds on mud flats of creeks and rivers were accessible and the shells were a practical material for use in construction. Tabby was also used to build the owner's house, as were those of Poulain du Bignon, John Floyd, Thomas Spalding, Jacob Waldburg, and others. Slave houses made of logs, rather typical in other plantation belts, were not the style used along the Georgia coast, though Georgia Bryan Conrad recalled that the slave houses on her father's plantation were built of logs and "consisted of two rooms divided by a goodsized hall running straight through them. The rooms had large fire-places."[26]

The tabby ruins of four slave houses built by Charles Spalding's slaves still stand at a site called the Thickets, located on a rather high bluff near the Sapelo River a few miles north of Darien in McIntosh County. These houses were well built, attractive, unique in style, and are worthy of a description. They were double units (eight apartments), placed forty-two feet apart, and faced each other along the "quarter's street" that was forty-two feet wide; the structures were thirty-three feet in length along the street and fourteen in depth. Each apartment had a separate entrance with a hallway and small window at the far end, and two rooms with a small window in each. A brick chimney running up the center of the building provided a fireplace for each unit. The walls were eight inches thick, constructed of ten courses of tabby, ten inches to a course, making the building approximately nine feet high. The roofs were flat, made of tabby bricks laid on heavy timber supports and waterproofed with tar and sand. These houses were not elevated from the ground and their floors are thought to have been tabby, though this is not confirmed. In their day they were models of efficiency and good design and were in striking contrast to the more usual type of slave house made of wood, with a pitched roof and elevated from the ground.[27] Charles Spalding, the son of Thomas Spalding, is listed as owning forty-four slaves and eight slave houses in 1860; this ratio conforms with the average slave family that consisted of five persons per unit.[28]

26. Conrad, *Reminiscences*, 7.

27. Marmaduke H. Floyd, "Certain Tabby Ruins on the Georgia Coast," 1935, MS in possession of Picot de Beoufillet Floyd, Clearwater, Fl.; observations made by the writer while viewing the tabby ruins at the Thickets; Unpublished Census Returns, 1860.

28. Unpublished Census Returns, 1860. Thomas Spalding owned 252 slaves and 50 slave houses. It is possible that William Carnochan, a native of Jamaica, who owned and operated a sugar mill and rum distillery at the Thickets prior to his death in the 1830s, influenced the design of Charles Spalding's slave houses and

Robert Stafford's slave houses on Cumberland Island were constructed of English brick; they were slightly elevated from the ground and had steeply pitched roofs. These were single-family dwellings with one room and a loft above where children slept; like all slave houses, each contained a chimney with fireplace for cooking and heating. Several of Stafford's slave houses still stand, and the foundations and ruins of others are sufficiently apparent to reconstruct the plan of this slave community. The houses faced each other along a broad street on high ground overlooking the Cumberland River. North of the houses are the ruins of several larger brick structures, which may have served as a hospital, nursery, and overseer's house. Stafford owned 110 slaves and twenty-four slave houses in 1860.[29]

A fine example of brick quarters were the slave houses on Hermitage Plantation belonging to Henry McAlpin, rice planter and industrialist. These houses were one-family units, each with two rooms and separate kitchen with fireplace. A vegetable garden was located behind each unit, along with a chicken yard. These quarters were described in 1864 by a journalist with the Union army as it approached Savannah: " 'There are about 70 or 80 Negro houses, all built of brick and white-washed so they look very neat, and rows of live oaks between, making it the handsomest plantation . . . in Georgia. They keep about 400 hands at work burning brick and make a large fortune at it too.' " McAlpin's Hermitage Plantation was complete with a two-story brick slave hospital that provided separate wings for males and females, a substantial overseer's house, numerous brick outbuildings, and a handsome mansion, Regency in design.[30]

Destruction of the Hermitage was a great historical loss. The mansion, slave houses, and other outbuildings represented the

---

his father's mansion on Sapelo Island, for they were constructed in the style of houses in the English West Indies.

29. Unpublished Census Returns, 1860; observations made by the writer while visiting the site; interview with Mary Bullard of Cumberland Island. Bullard is a great-granddaughter of Thomas Carnegie, who owned a large portion of Cumberland Island in the early twentieth century. Descendents of Stafford's slaves lived on the island until fairly recently.

30. Granger, *Savannah River Plantations*, 438–40, 450; Unpublished Census Returns, 1850. McAlpin owned 200 slaves at the time of his death in 1851. As quoted in Medora Field Perkerson, *White Columns of Georgia* (New York: Rinehart, 1952), 101. Henry Ford purchased the Hermitage in 1935 and destroyed the slave houses, hospital, overseer's house, mansion, and all other buildings on the site. Two of the slave houses were dismantled and shipped to the Ford Museum at Dearborn, Mich. where they were reconstructed in their original design.

Figure 15. Slave Houses on Henry McAlpin's Hermitage Plantation. (Margaret Davis Cate Collection, Fort Frederica National Monument.)

Figure 16. Former Slaves Who Continued to Live on Hermitage Plantation After the Civil War. (From photograph in Essie Collins Matthews, *Aunt Phebe, Uncle Tom, and Others.*)

Figure 17. "Aunt Lucy," Oldest of Former Slaves at Hermitage Plantation. (From photograph in Essie Collins Matthews, *Aunt Phebe, Uncle Tom, and Others.)*

finest in architectural design and exemplified the efficiency of plantation operation as a self-sustaining unit with the use of slave labor. The mansion was one of the most beautiful antebellum houses in the South. Its architectural design expressed the talents of Henry McAlpin and his friend, William Jay, who designed a number of the more elegant town houses in Savannah.

The slave houses on Pierce Butler's plantation "were neat, and whitewashed, all floored with wood, each with an apartment called a hall, two sleeping-rooms, and a loft for the children." This description made by Frederick Law Olmsted twenty years later belies the one Frances Ann Kemble gave of housing conditions for her husband's slaves on Butler's Island. On another rice plantation described by Olmsted there were "thirty neatly whitewashed cottages with a broad avenue planted with Pride-of-China trees between them." These houses were wooden, framed with batten boards, and stood fifty feet apart. They had shingle roofs and brick chimneys. At the side of each house there was a vegetable garden and an enclosed pigsty. There was also a "sick-house" on this street in front of which Olmsted observed slaves wrapped in blankets, lounging in the sunshine on the steps and on the ground.[31]

On still another plantation slave houses were clapboard and of a slightly different style. They faced each other on two separate streets. A "well-house" was located on one street, and on the other, a "mill-house" where the slaves ground their corn.[32] A slave dwelling occupied by a house servant on Grove Point Plantation near the Ogeechee River is still standing. This one-room clapboard house is elevated from the ground, is of sound construction, has not been neglected, and so has not deteriorated, and tends to reinforce contemporary accounts that slave housing along the Georgia coast was adequate.[33] Georgia is not seen as above average when living conditions of slaves in other states are compared; however, research does indicate that rice and Sea Island cotton plantation slaves were provided better housing than slaves who lived on plantations of average size. The wealthy

31. *Journey in Seaboard Slave States*, 215. Whitewash was used on slave houses because of its lime content, which acted as a disinfectant. See Margaret Davis Cate Photograph Collection, RGI, ser. 2, p. 47, GHS, for a photograph of one of Pierce Butler's slave houses that was still standing on Butler's Island in 1925. The house was built of batten boards, stood well off the ground, had a steeply pitched roof, and was a double unit with a chimney running up through the center.

32. Olmsted, *Journey in Seaboard Slave States*, 215–16.

33. Observations made by the writer while visiting Grove Point Plantation.

Figure 18. Slave House Still Standing Near Owner's Residence on Grove Point Plantation. (Drawing by Leonora Quarterman.)

Figure 19. Interior of Slave House. (Drawing by Leonora Quarterman.)

Figure 20. Slave Houses made of Tabby on St. Catherines Island. (Drawing by Leonora Quarterman.)

planter of coastal Georgia provided elaborate dwellings more often than did the smaller slaveholders.

Generally, owners were concerned with the health of their slaves and provided them with medical care, though the quality of such care was poor by modern standards. Medical science was not advanced and the very primitive treatment (like bleeding and purging) used to cure the patient sometimes hastened death. The large numbers of Negro slaves concentrated on rice and cotton plantations along the Georgia coast and the frequency of their illnesses attracted prominent members of the medical profession. Many medical doctors came South, motivated by their interest in improving the science of medicine, and also in earning the lucrative fees paid by owners anxious to have the unusual diseases of their slave populations treated. Southern plantations, especially rice plantations, offered a fertile field for doctors to observe what were considered the "peculiar" illnesses of blacks.

Dr. Joshua E. White, a member of the Georgia Medical Society founded in 1804 at Savannah, was greatly concerned with improving the general health of slaves and observed while treating them that many of their ailments resulted from lack of proper clothing, poor housing conditions, and inadequate diet. He also noted that those who were recent arrivals from Africa were scantily clothed and could not acclimate to the cold winter months of the Georgia coast, nor could they withstand the humidity and constant exposure to dampness and water while working in rice fields during the summer. This environment made them susceptible to inflammatory disease.[34]

Basil Hall noted that slaves who worked in rice fields, standing ankle deep in mud "ditching, drawing, weeding, or turning over wet ground," were frequently affected by respiratory diseases and sometimes "sank rapidly under their hardships" when overworked.[35] Though contemporary travelers frequently commented upon the susceptibility of rice field slaves to pulmonary diseases caused by constant exposure to dampness from working in wet fields, mortality rates do not provide evidence for conclusions that slave deaths were greater in the rice belt than in other plantation belts throughout the South. Mortality schedules listing

34. Victor H. Bassett, "Plantation Medicine," *Journal of the Medical Association of Georgia* 20 (Mar. 1940): 115; Joseph I. Waring, "Colonial Medicine in Georgia and South Carolina," *Georgia Historical Quarterly* 59 (Supplement 1975): 141–59.

35. *Travels in North America*, 2:223.

Figure 21. Tabby Slave House on James Hamilton Couper's Hamilton Plantation. (Margaret Davis Cate Collection, Fort Frederica National Monument.)

slave deaths and causes for deaths indicate that slaves died from similar diseases regardless of their location, whether working on sugar plantations in Louisiana and Mississippi, rice plantations along the coast, or on cotton plantations in other areas of the South.[36]

Dr. Richard D. Arnold, who like Dr. Joshua E. White treated slaves on rice plantations, expressed the attitude that would gradually take hold and bring about improved health care and living conditions for slaves: "A planter loses so much capital by the death of everyone of his operatives, hence, to save his capital is to save his Negroes." Arnold, himself a slaveholder whose rice plantation was in Bryan County on the Ogeechee River, understood owner attitudes concerning the well-being of their slaves. As he explained, he deliberately chose coastal Georgia to practice his profession:

> It is amongst the slave population that I consider the greatest field to lie . . . . . The *interest* [investment], if [for] no other motive, causes the *Master* to obtain medical aid for his slave, & instead of looking to the laborer for his remuneration, the Physician looks to the *Employer*. This is the true reason why Physicians get into practice more readily at the South than at the North, and that *here* he stands some chance of making his bread while he has teeth to chew it.[37]

Dr. James Ewell of Savannah did much to encourage better health standards for slaves, publishing as early as 1807 *The Mariner's and Overseer's Medical Companion*. This book became a manual for owners and overseers to use, and by 1837 the seventh edition had been published. Ewell made numerous recommenda-

36. See Robert W. Fogel and Stanley L. Engerman, *Time on The Cross: The Economics of American Negro Slavery* (Boston: Little, Brown, 1974), fig. 36, p. 125, which compares the life expectancy of slaves in the United States in 1850 with that of white Americans. The life expectancy of slaves was 12% below the average of white Americans but was almost identical with the life expectancy in France and Holland and exceeded the life expectancy of urban industrial workers in the United States and Europe. See Joseph Bancroft, *Census of the City of Savannah. . . .* (Savannah, 1848), 54, where slave deaths were "but as 2 to 3 of whites" annually between 1810 and 1847. See also, Paul A. David, et al., *Reckoning With Slavery: A Critical Study in the Quantitative History of American Negro Slavery* (New York: Oxford Univ. Press, 1976), 130–31, 283–86, for slave mortality rates; in this study, Fogel's and Engerman's findings are refuted.

37. Richard H. Shryock, ed., *Letters of Richard D. Arnold, M.D. 1808–1876* (Durham: Duke Univ. Press, 1929), 13, 33. See Shryock, "Medical Practice in the Old South," *South Atlantic Quarterly* 29 (Apr. 1930): 160–78; Weymouth T., Jordan, "Plantation Medicine in the Old South," *Alabama Review* 3 (Apr. 1950): 83–107; Peter Wood, "People's Medicine in the Early South," *Southern Exposure* (Summer 1978): 50–53.

tions for the improvement of living conditions for Negroes, emphasizing the importance of cleanliness in slave quarters and the necessity for having an infirmary or hospital on the plantation, properly constructed with adequate ventilation, where slaves could be housed and nursed when ill and where pregnant mothers could deliver their offspring and both have proper care after delivery.[38] In 1832 the first public Negro hospital in America, the Georgia Infirmary, was completed at Savannah. Seriously ill Negroes were now taken to this hospital, where they received the best of care that the times warranted.[39]

Proper care and treatment of their slaves were emphasized by owners in their instructions to overseers. Overseers were permitted to treat minor ailments, but the physician had to be summoned when the slave's illness became serious. On larger plantations, like the rice and Sea Island cotton plantations of coastal Georgia where the slave community numbered from 70 to 300 or more, substantial hospitals were maintained where slaves who were ill could be cared for and where pregnant mothers could deliver their offspring. Medical care was administered by a physician whose services were retained by the owner. Health care for the slaves on James Hamilton Couper's plantation was described as follows:

> The sick present themselves every morning at the hospital, where they are examined and prescribed for. The hospital is an airy and warm building, 80 feet by 24, with four wards, an entry which answers as an examining room, a medicine closet, a kitchen, and a bathing room. One ward is for lying-in women, another for women, and two others for men. The whole is heated with steam, supplied by two small copper boilers, and this mode has been in use for 14 years. The accommodations for the sick are a cot for each person, with a straw mattress and pillar [*sic*], a pillar [*sic*] case, 2 blankets and a coverlid, with benches. The beds are refilled with clean straw once a month, and the cases and blankets at the same time washed. The wards are swept every day and washed out once a week, and the whole building whitewashed twice a year.[40]

The slave hospital on Retreat Plantation (owned by Thomas Butler King), St. Simons Island, was constructed of tabby and contained ten rooms. The rooms on the ground floor were used for

38. Bassett, "Plantation Medicine," 120.

39. Ibid., 116; Edith Duncan Johnston, *The Houstouns of Georgia* (Athens; Univ. of Georgia Press, 1950), 183. The Georgia Infirmary remained in use until 1974.

40. *Southern Agriculturist* 6 (June 1833): 573–75.

Figure 22. Liverpool Hazzard, Former Slave of Pierce Butler. (Margaret Davis Cate Collection, Fort Frederica National Monument.)

Figure 23. Ruins of the Slave Hospital on Thomas Butler King's Retreat Plantation, St. Simons Island. (Margaret Davis Cate Collection, Fort Frederica National Monument.)

the women, the second floor for the men, and the attic rooms were occupied by two slave nurses who lived in the hospital. The rooms had ample footage (twelve by fifteen feet), and each contained a fireplace and two windows. The stairway was located in a wide hall in the middle of the building. As was the custom, the hospital was located near the residence of the owner so that the condition of the slaves could be closely supervised by the mistress of the plantation, in this instance, Anna Matilda (Page) King. Mrs. King kept a record of the births, illnesses, and causes of deaths of the slaves. In 1856 twenty-eight children and two adults had measles. There were no deaths and five infants escaped this communicable disease.[41] (Infants have a natural immunity.) On Hermitage Plantation (owned by Henry McAlpin) in Chatham County, the slave hosital was constructed of Savannah "gray" bricks manufactured on the plantation; it was two stories high and had separate quarters for the men and the women. The hospital was located near the owner's house.[42]

The exceptionally high death rate among slave children in the United States is related to Negro adaptations in West Africa to geographic and environmental circumstances that were necessary for survival there. These adaptations altered the nutritional needs of Negroes and in their New World environment became a liability. One example is the sickle trait, a heritable hemoglobin characteristic that heightens resistance to malaria.[43] Dr. Richard D. Arnold of Savannah noted that blacks were less susceptible to malaria than whites and commented upon their immunity.

> I can, so far as an observation of twenty-four years in the malarial country goes, corroborate the fact of the less liability of the negro to all classes of our malarial fevers (by which I mean, Intermittent, Remittent, Congestive, etc.) But I cannot say that the negro is exempt entirely, for I have treated them for various forms of malar-

41. See Cate, *Early Days of Coastal Georgia*, 75, and 195 for a picture of and reference to "Old Sibby Kelly" who was a "granny woman" or midwife in Glynn County. See "Georgia's Baby Catchin Grannies," *Georgia Department of Archives and History Newsletter*, Aug. 1980, in which a brief sketch of Georgia's black midwives tells of Georgia's long-established custom of recognizing midwifery. For the role of the plantation mistress, see Catherine Clinton, *The Plantation Mistress: Woman's World in the Old South* (New York: Pantheon Books, 1982), and Anne Firor Scott, *The Southern Lady: From Pedestal to Politics, 1830–1930* (Chicago: Univ. of Chicago Press, 1970).

42. Granger, *Savannah River Plantations*, 440.

43. Kenneth and Virginia Kiple, "Slave Child Mortality," 285–86. See also Savitt, *Medicine and Slavery*, 27–34, 135–46, and Wood, *Black Majority*, 88, 89.

> ial fever. Still, even where they do have it, they have it in a very light form & I do not recollect ever to have lost a full-blooded African by a climate fever . . . . The negroes on the Rice plantations goes [*sic*] unscathed in an atmosphere which would bring certain death to an unacclimated white adult, unless he should use much precaution in fortifying himself against malaria, by avoiding early morning, evening, and night air.[44]

In a recent study on infant and child slave mortality rates, nutritional deficiencies and poor postnatal care were found to be primary causes for the exceptionally high mortality rates for slave infants and children as opposed to whites in the same age range. Diseases that most frequently caused death among slave infants and children were "convulsions," "lock jaw," "suffocation," "teething," "Tetanus," and "worms." Mortality rates among these slaves were four times greater than rates for whites in the same age range. Data were compiled from the Census returns for 1850 from the seven states of Virginia, North Carolina, South Carolina, Mississippi, Georgia, Alabama, and Louisiana, where 75 percent of the slaves resided. Slave infants and children accounted for 51 percent of all Negro deaths in 1850, whereas white infants and children accounted for 38 percent of all white deaths.[45]

Convulsions and teething were symptoms of a children's disease, which today is identified as tetany, not to be confused with tetanus. Tetany is caused by mineral deficiencies, or a lack of calcium, magnesium, and vitamin D in the body and is characterized by convulsions and muscle spasms. Tetanus (lockjaw), though imperfectly identified during slavery times, is an acute infectious disease caused by the specific toxin produced by the tetanus bacillus, which is introduced through a wound. Neonatal tetanus was a frequent cause of death among newborn slaves and

---

The trait when inherited from one parent is not detrimental but when inherited from both parents causes the offspring to suffer from sickle-cell anemia. Today, roughly one out of every 500 blacks has sickle-cell anemia. Another inherited nutritional liability for blacks in America is lactose intolerance caused by the absence of the lactose enzyme necessary to metabolize milk sugars for body consumption. Today, roughly 75% of the black population in the United States, as opposed to roughly 12% of the white, cannot tolerate lactose.

44. Shryock, ed., *Letters of Richard D. Arnold*, 66. See *Southern Agriculturist* 6 (Jan. 1846): 1, for recommendations on draining ditches in rice fields to prevent malaria. See also, Thomas Gamble, Jr., *History of the Municipal Government of Savannah* (Savannah, 1910), 141–46, for reference to the elimination of rice fields in the vicinity of Savannah as early as 1819 to discourage outbreaks of malaria.

45. Savitt, *Medicine and Slavery*, 135–46; Kenneth and Virginia Kiple, "Slave Child Mortality," 290.

occurred when sterile medical procedures were not practiced while handling the umbilical stump.[46]

"Smothering," "overlaying," or "suffocation" seemed to occur almost exclusively among newborn slaves. Until recently observers attributed infant death from suffocation to infanticide, claiming that mothers preferred to kill their infants rather than have them reared as slaves, or to neglect of slave mothers, who rolled over on their infants, cutting off their air supply. Recent medical evidence, however, identifies smothering (suffocation) as Sudden Infant Death Syndrome (SIDS) or "crib death." Today, "crib death" is the leading killer (10 to 30 percent) of black and white children between the ages of two weeks and eleven months.[47]

Hookworm disease was a malady that affected children and adults, though children most frequently were the victims. It was not identified during slavery times as being related to a serious malnutrition, though Dr. John Le Conte of Liberty County, while practicing medicine in Savannah, observed its effects, "dirt-eating," among Negro children and wrote a scholarly account of his observations.[48] Charles B. Jones of Liberty County sold his female slave Rose in 1845, declaring "her only disease is dirt-eating which is easily cured." Rose later died and the purchaser tried unsuccessfully to collect from Jones the amount paid for this slave, as well as the expenses of her illness and burial.[49]

Sporadic outbreaks of smallpox plagued city residents as well as plantation slaves. As early as 1764 inoculation was practiced, and after 1801 Jenner's vaccine was introduced by Dr. James Ewell for the protection of blacks and whites; in time, both received routine vaccinations with the serum. Separate infirmaries were used on plantations to isolate slaves while they were being treated for smallpox. In Savannah, sixteen cases of smallpox were reported in 1832; these stricken slaves were immediately sent to a temporary hospital seven miles from the city "to stop the progress of the disease"; all persons who had been exposed were vaccinated.[50]

46, Kenneth and Virginia Kiple, "Slave Child Morality," 291–93; Savitt, *Medicine and Slavery*, 120, 122.

47. Fogel and Engerman, *Time on the Cross*, 124–25; Kenneth and Virginia Kiple, "Slave Child Mortality," 294–96; Savitt, *Medicine and Slavery*, 122–28. See also, David, et al., eds., *Reckoning With Slavery*, 286–91.

48. Bassett, "Plantation Medicine," 117.

49. "Edmund Rogers vs. Charles Berrien Jones," Oct. 1846, MS, Superior Court Records, Liberty County.

50. "Minutes of the Board of Health, 1828–1832," MS, GHS.

Asiatic cholera was primarily a plantation disease that caused the death of many Negroes. Cholera was bred in unsanitary conditions and careless food habits among slaves. It was communicable and was often spread from one slave to another when Negroes secretly visited, without a pass, a wife or loved one on another plantation. A cholera epidemic in 1834 on plantations along the Savannah River resulted in a large death toll among slaves. In 1849 sixty slaves died of this dreaded disease on plantations near Savannah.[51]

Early in the nineteenth century medical care for slaves was provided under the contract system whereby the physician agreed to treat all slaves on the plantation throughout the year for a stipulated fee. Among the listings on Raymond Demere's account sheets for the year 1811 is an entry showing cash paid "Dr. Jenkins per agreement for year, $205."[52] An improvement over the contract system was the fee bill system, adopted in 1818 by the Georgia Medical Society. The fee bill system required an itemized statement of all visits made during the year for medical and surgical services to slaves, the nature of the illness, the medication given, and the amount charged. Under the new regulation physicians had to be qualified and licensed to practice.[53] Dr. P.M. Kollock, who cared for the slaves on William Mackay's plantation in 1838, charged $64 for twenty-two visits. He performed such services as extracting teeth for Christiana, Cuffee, Chloe, Isaac, and Sambo; the fee was $1 for each extraction. Foı "dressing Molly after dark," he charged $10, and for "amputating thumb for June and subsequent treatment," he charged $20.[54]

Dr. J.S. Sullivan in 1850 charged $346 for visiting and treating the slaves on Hopeton Plantation in Glynn County.[55] Dr. Lewis Turner, in the same year, charged $132 "by contract at one dollar per head" for medical services in treating the slaves on one of the

51. Kollock Papers, MSS, D 164, folder 22, GHS. In this same reference is recorded the deaths of five slave children from whooping cough (1848). Life in the slave community was a breeding ground for several year-round diseases that were contracted through respiratory secretions—whooping cough, measles, chicken pox, and mumps. These are usually identified as childhood diseases, though adults, when not immune, contracted them also. See Savitt, *Slavery and Medicine*, 55–56.

52. Estate Account of Raymond Demere, 1791–1812, box D, fol. 1, Probate Records, Chatham County.

53. Bassett, "Plantation Medicine," 114.

54. Mackey and Stiles Family Papers, 1741–1915, MS, ser. A, SHC.

55. Records of Wills, Appraisements, Book E, 228, Probate Records, Glynn County.

plantations belonging to the estate of William H. Mongin. On another plantation belonging to the Mongin estate the physician charged $371 for the first six months in 1851. A sampling of the treatment and charges are as follows: "Dressing Bob and applying leeches, $2.50; vaccinating two children from the island, $4.00; medicine for syphilis, Harry, $2.00; fitting truss for Jim, $1.00; visit 12 o'clock at night and dressing three wounds, Bob, $5.00."[56]

Generally, the plantation slaves in coastal Georgia were adequately fed, clothed, and housed, and received as good medical care as the times permitted. The familiar claim that nutritional deficiencies, poor housing facilities, unsanitary living conditions (though they existed and affected blacks and whites), and strenuous work assignments adversely affected the physical health of slaves cannot be substantiated for slaves in the low country, where the system was economically rational and efficient, and where the environment and an elitist type of owner had a positive effect upon the slave's way of life. Mortality was not abnormally high among adult slaves. An exception was the high mortality for slave infants and children as opposed to whites in the same age range—a phenomenon attributed to heritable nutritional liabilities, poor postnatal care, and "crib death," for which as yet there is no satisfactory explanation.

56. Estate Accounts, Book M, 151–53, Probate Records, Chatham County.

CHAPTER EIGHT

Marching to Zion: The Religion of Slaves in Coastal Georgia

The religious heritage of the Negro in coastal Georgia has an impressive past and dates from the middle of the eighteenth century when slavery was formally introduced. The English clerics Bartholomew Zouberbuhler and Joseph Ottolenghe were the first to Christianize Africans in Georgia and to transmit to them the religious beliefs and cultural ideals of Anglo-Americans. Zouberbuhler, a worthy successor of John Wesley and rector of Christ Episcopal Church in Savannah from 1745 to 1766, organized a church school for slave children and encouraged the regular attendance of adult slaves at his church services.[1]

In 1750 the Society for the Propagation of the Gospel and the Associates of Dr. Bray provided funds for the salary of Ottolenghe, who was sent from England to instruct the slaves in the tenets of the Church of England. At this time there were about four hundred Negro slaves in Georgia. Ottolenghe was assigned to teach the slaves to read and to understand the catechism, and to direct the silk filature in Savannah. Born in Italy of Jewish parentage, he had been trained in the culture and processing of silk. He then went to England, converted from Judaism to Christianity, and became a communicant in the Anglican Church.[2]

Ottolenghe faced serious difficulties in his new position in

1. *Society for the Propagation of the Gosepl,* 20 vols. (London: E. Owen, printer, 1744–63), Journal B, 19: 133; F. Bland Tucker, "Christ Church and the Negro, 1750–1860," MS in possession of Dr. Tucker, Rector Emeritus, Christ Episcopal Church; James B. Lawrence, "Religious Education of the Negro in the Colony of Georgia," *Georgia Historical Quarterly* 14 (Mar. 1930): 43–57.

2. Lawrence, "Religious Education of the Negro," 41–42. For general accounts of the religious education of blacks, see Carter G. Woodson, *The Education of the*

Georgia as schoolmaster, not the least of which were the "catechist uninspired" slaveholders who opposed his work in teaching slaves to read. These slaveholders thought the Negro to be "ten times worse when a Christian than in his state of paganism." Always the fear of knowledgeable slaves plagued slaveholders, who knew that Christian slaves often could read the Bible and were more prone to act upon insurrectionary thoughts than were the illiterate. Ottolenghe believed—and the great majority of slaveholders would later agree—that the slaveholder " 'would be a greater gainer if his servant should be converted to christianity,' " for in such a case, " 'he would have, instead of an immoral dishonest domestic, a faithful servant.' "A slave with this emotional ingredient was less likely to be dissatisfied with his condition in life.[3]

Ottolenghe's experience as schoolmaster was rewarding. He reported in 1753 that the slaves learned quickly, that several were reading "tolerably well," and that all had memorized the catechism. This was a distinct achievement, as Ottolenghe knew no African dialects and his students had to surmount a language barrier in a completely alien environment.[4] In 1759 Ottolenghe's work as schoolmaster and catechist to the Negroes ended, and he returned to England after having "discharged his duty with great care and diligence," according to the appraisal of Bartholomew Zouberbuhler.[5]

Zouberhbuhler's activities centered in Christ Church Parish, and his evangelical work among the slaves expressed his great interest in their welfare. He appointed itinerent catechists to travel in coastal Georgia and along the Savannah River to teach and instruct slaves on outlying plantations. Zouberbuhler died in 1766, leaving a rather large estate. He directed in his will that one of his plantations, Beth Abram, be held in trust and that the income from the plantation be used to employ a qualified person to teach the forty-three slaves thereon to read, and to hold regular church services for them. Zouberhbuhler's directions were fol-

---

Negro Prior to 1861 (Washington, D.C., 1919), and E. Franklin Frazier, *The Negro Church in America* (New York: Schocken, 1964).

3. As quoted in Tucker, "Christ Church and the Negro."

4. Lawrence, "Religious Education of the Negro," 44, 46, 48–49. Ottolenghe taught blacks and whites (indentured servants). His schoolhouse was a large room he constructed as an addition to his small frame house " 'for ye Instruction of ye Negroes, and such of ye White people who can neither read nor can give any Account of their Religion.' " As quoted in Lawrence.

5. Ibid.

lowed, and the work of his successor, Cornelius Winter, continued until the period of the American Revolution.[6]

Baptist missionaries were also active in Georgia in converting slaves to Christianity during the colonial era. The young slave George Liele, brought from Virginia by his owner Henry Sharpe, was converted and baptized in Burke County in 1774 by Matthew Moore, a Baptist minister. Liele was later ordained as a minister, and for his religious work among the slaves is acknowledged to be the first black Baptist missionary in Georgia. He had great oratorical skill and preached to slaves on the rice and indigo plantations along the Savannah River. He also preached on Sunday evenings in the white church in Burke County, where he was a member. He was manumitted by Sharpe, who was killed during the Revolutionary War. Sharpe's heirs had Liele jailed and tried to claim him as their property. He was befriended by a British officer who advised that he leave Georgia with the British evacuation in 1783. He did, though only after baptizing four slaves of Jonathan Bryan at Brampton Plantation. Liele went to Kingston, Jamaica, to found the first black Baptist church there.[7]

Andrew Bryan, one of the four slaves baptized by Liele and, like Liele, a gifted orator, began preaching at prayer meetings for slaves on plantations nearby and in Savannah. He was permitted to erect a wooden building in Yamacraw Village, a settlement on the west side of the city, on land belonging to a white man. The slaves whom Bryan converted had to have passes from the owner or overseer to leave the plantation to attend his church. When they did, they could be seen paddling along the Savannah River in their cypress canoes on Sunday mornings and evenings going to or having come from the church services. Baptisms were held on Sundays, four times throughout the year. On these Sundays, Bryan and his congregation sang as they marched in solemn pro-

6. "Letters of Hon. James Habersham, 1756–1775," *Collections*, 6:99; *Abstracts of Colonial Wills of the State of Georgia, 1733–1777*, 151–52. There was also a provision in Zouberguhler's will that all Negro children on the plantation had to be taught to read and receive instruction in the Christian religion. Those who showed inclination and talent to teach the gospel were to be manumitted and employed for that purpose.

7. Frazier, *Negro Church in America*, 23; James M. Simms, *the First Colored Baptist Church in North America* (Philadelphia: Lippincott, 1888), 21; H. Shelton Smith, *In His Image But . . . Racism in Southern Religion, 1780–1910* (Durham: Duke Univ. Press, 1972), 53; Woodson, *The History of the Negro Church* (Washington, D.C. 1921), 37, 38, 40–45; J. Leitch Wright, Jr., "Blacks in British East Florida," *Florida Historical Quarterly*, Bicentennial Issue 54 (Apr. 1976): 439.

Figure 24. A Baptism at Pin Point near the Montgomery River on the Outskirts of Savannah. (Georgia Historical Society Collection.)

cession while going to the Savannah River at the foot of what is now Fahm Street for the baptismal ceremony. Those baptized were immersed in the river. As they rose up from the water, the communicants standing on the bank sang some of the songs of Zion, such as "I Am Bound for the Promised Land."[8]

Whites became fearful of Bryan's influence over the blacks and sought to discourage the growth of his church. Those who patrolled the area, to prevent the slaves from attending church, now declared their passes to be invalid and whipped and jailed the church leaders. Andrew Bryan and his brother, Samson, were befriended by their owner. Jonathan Bryan, who had them released from jail and allowed them to worship in the barn on his plantation. By 1790 Andrew Bryan was a free man and, with the help of friends, purchased a lot upon which the original Bryan Street African Baptist Church was erected a few years later. This frame structure remained in use until 1873 when it was dismantled to make way for construction of the new church, a handsome brick and stucco building, neoclassical in style, which stands today as a testimony to the courage and determination of blacks to overcome their hardships and strife under slavery.[9] Other historic churches built and preserved by blacks that are in use today in the Savannah area include the First African Baptist Church, the Second African Baptist Church, and St. Stephen's Episcopal Church, which later became St. Matthews.

The historic Negro churches in Savannah are notable in Georgia in that they enjoyed an independent status, though under supervision of the whites and served by black ministers whom the whites had to ordain. They conducted their services according to their own essentially Afro-American religious expression. The tradition is evident today in services held at the Bryan Street Church and in the First and Second African Baptist churches. The choirs sway while singing such mindful hymns as "Marching to Zion" accompanied by syncopated organ music.[10]

The music and religion of the plantation slave expressed a folk Christianity that synthesized African religion and the newly acquired Christianity. The otherworldliness expressed in the songs

8. Simms, *First Colored Baptist Church*, 42.

9. Interview with Thelma Lee, historian for the church. Lee says the title in use today is First Bryan Missionary Baptist Church.

10. Observations made by the writer while attending special services at these churches. William Glover, director of the choir at Bryan Street Baptist Church, was most generous and helpful in allowing the writer and the artist, Leonora Quarterman, to view and take pictures of the interiors and exteriors of the churches.

depicts "the sorrow and suffering which came from serving in a strange land."[11] The great majority of slaves could not read, so they memorized the hymns and scriptures. During Andrew Bryan's church services, he or one of the members who could read recited the hymns, two lines of a stanza at a time, for the congregation to sing. This procedure continued until the hymn was completed.

Many of Bryan's communicants, born in Africa and knowing little English, learned to recite from memory, in a broken English or dialect, the hymns and passages from the Bible. This knowledge of the scriptures they disseminated on the plantations. The Negro spirituals, rooted in the scriptures and created on the plantations, are distinctly sorrowful. W.E.B. Du Bois calls them the "Sorrow Songs" in which the soul of the Negro slave spoke to all people. They are also the Negro folk song, "the rhythmic cry of the slave," and were created out of an emotional need for self-expression. Slaves spoke to the world in the spirituals, and these songs continue to be a great cultural gift of the Negro people.[12]

The spirituals have been preserved by descendants of those who composed them and are sung today on special occassions. The Second African Baptist Church, when celebrating its 173rd anniversary, sang these antebellum songs as well as postbellum songs that express hope and progress in a world in which racial discrimination is being overcome. The songs sung included "Nobody Knows the Trouble I've Had," "Every Time I Feel the Spirit," "Tis the Old Time Religion," "Steal Away to Jesus," "Great Day for the Righteous Marching," "When the Storms of Life are Raging," "Somebody's Knocking at Your Door," "O Freedom—Before I'd Be a Slave," "We Shall Overcome," "Keep a Inching Along," "We are Climbing Jacob's Ladder," "He's Got the Whole World in His Hands," and the Negro national anthem written by James Weldon Johnson, "Lift Every Voice and Sing."[13]

11. Gold R. Wilson, "Religion of the American Negro Slave: His Attitude Toward Life and Death," *Journal of Negro History* 8 (Jan. 1923): 41, 46. See also Lawrence W. Levine, *Black Culture and Black Consciousness: Afro-American Folk Thought from Slavery to Freedom* (New York: Oxford Univ. Press, 1977), 33–54; Albert J. Raboteau, *Slave Religion: The "Invisible Institution" in the Antebellum South* (New York: Oxford Univ. Press, 1978), 35–37, and all of ch. 5; Mechal Sobel, *Trabelin' On: The Slave Journey to an Afro-Baptist Faith* (Westport, Conn., Greenwood, 1979), 77–99.

12. Simms, *First Colored Baptist Church,* 43–44. William Edward Burghardt Du Bois, *the Souls of Black Folk* (Greenwich, Conn.: Fawcett, 1961), 181–82, 186.

13. Recordings made by the writer while attending a service at Second African Baptist Church, Dec. 1975. See M.F. Armstrong and Helen W. Ludlow, *Hampton*

Figure 25. The Bryan Street African Baptist Church. (Drawing by Leonora Quarterman.)

The Negro preacher exercised enormous influence and control over his communicants, and commanded respect from the white community. He often interceded to save a rebellious slave from such harsh punishments as confinement or whipping or from the dreadful punishment of being sold away by a trader, never to see his family and friends again. Andrew Bryan was accorded great respect in the white community and was often called for by the owner of an offending slave to reprimand the slave and use the powerful threat of excommunication from the church to have him conform. When Bryan died in 1812 at the age of ninety-six, he had accumulated a rather substantial estate. He is buried in the Negro section of Laurel Grove Cemetery, where many other free blacks and slaves were buried.[14]

In 1802 the Savannah River Association was formed to include Baptist churches in Georgia and South Carolina. The growth in numbers of churches caused this union to be dissolved by mutual agreement in 1818 so that separate associations might be formed within the respective states. Delegates from the Georgia churches now met together at Sunbury in Liberty County and organized the Sunbury Baptist Association. Dissension within the church body of the Bryan Street African Baptist Church prevented its sending delegates to the meeting at Sunbury, and it was not represented in the association. The other three Baptist churches in Savannah—First African Baptist, Second African Baptist, and the First Baptist (white)—were represented, as were the Ogeechee Baptist Church (black) and the Sunbury Baptist Church, which had a mixed membership.[15]

Members of Andrew Bryan's church created the First African

---

and Its Students (New York: Putnam's, 1874), which contains fifty plantation songs or Negro spirituals, plus plantation stories and a history of Hampton College, founded in Virginia by the Freedmen's Bureau. See also J.B.T. Marsh, *The Story of the Jubilee Singers: With Their Songs* (Boston: Houghton, Osgood, 1880), which contains many of the same spirituals. The Jubilee Singers were a group of students at Fisk Univ. (founded 1865) who sang before royalty in many countries. Their sucess was spectacular.

14. *Savannah Morning News*, July 28, 1975. Bryan's body was originally buried in the black cemetery located in Troup Ward on Habersham Street. His remains and those of other blacks were later removed to Laurel Grove Cemetery. The Savannah branch of the National Association for the Advancement of Colored People has recently sponsored a program to rejuvenate these gravesites.

15. Emanuel K. Love, *History of the First African Baptist Church* (Savannah: Morning News, 1888), 1–9. See also Donald G. Mathews, "Charles Colcock Jones and the Southern Evangelical Crusade to Form a Biracial Community," and Kenneth K. Bailey, "Protestantism and Afro-Americans in the Old South: Another Look," both in *Journal of Southern History* 41 (Aug., Nov. 1975): 299, 320, 451–72.

Baptist Church. According to two of its Negro ministers who later wrote histories of the church, it began in the same year, 1788, that Andrew Bryan's church was organized. The Second African Baptist Church was created in 1802 by the Savannah River Association out of the need to serve Negroes who lived on the east side of the city. For the inception of this church, free blacks purchased a lot on Greene Square and sponsored construction of a one-story frame structure. Henry Cunningham served as the pastor of this church for thirty-nine years; he died in 1842 at the age of eighty-three. During his pastorage the church was remodeled and enlarged when a second story was added. Runaway slaves were hidden in the basement of the church until they could escape by boat on the Savannah River with the help of a sympathizer. The much-remodeled handsome brick church that stands today is another fine example of the Negro heritage in Georgia. The Second African Baptist Church was the first of the Negro churches to install a baptismal pool. The pool, located in the floor of the pulpit is covered over when not in use.[16]

The white Baptists of Savannah completed their new brick church on Chippewa Square in 1852, leaving their old wooden building vacant on Franklin Square. In the same year the First African Baptist Church purchased this property from the whites for $1,500. Payment was required within six months. The church members, composed mostly of slaves, made many small contributions to help raise money to purchase the church property. It was these Negroes, with no help from the whites, who engaged in the fund-raising drive and accumulated sufficient funds for the payment. Purchase of the property occurred while Andrew Marshall was being censured by the Sunbury Baptist Association. In Savannah the respect and influence Marshall commanded among the total population—he often preached to whites as well as blacks—made it possible for him to continue as pastor.[17]

Marshall's good relations with whites and his influence and control over the 2,000 members of his church insured the whites against trouble from the slaves in Savannah. George Lewis, the Presbyterian minister from Scotland who visited Savannah in 1845, described Marshall as "a stout built man, with a white crispy

16. Mabel F. Lafar, "The Baptist Church of Savannah: History, Record, and Register" (typewritten), 1941, GHS; Edgar G. Thomas, *The First African Baptist Church of North America* (Savannah, 1925), 25–32.

17. Love, *History of the First African Baptist Church*, 8, 31–32; Thomas, *First African Baptist Church*, 47, 61–62, 72–74.

Figure 26. The First African Baptist Church. (Drawing by Leonora Quarterman.)

Figure 27. Detail of the Left Front Interior of the First African Baptist Church. (Drawing by Leonora Quarterman.)

Figure 28. The Second African Baptist Church. (Drawing by Leonora Quarterman.)

head of hair, shrewd expression of face, and little quick eyes." Lewis questioned "the effect of forbidding education to the coloured population of Georgia." Marshall explained with a smile, " 'I hope, sir, it has increased our appetite.' "[18] Marshall served as pastor of the First African Baptist Church from 1812 until his death in 1856 at the age of one hundred. The church, completed in 1859, stands today as another reminder of the historic value of black culture in Savannah.

St. Stephens Episcopal Church was founded in 1855 by Bishop Stephen Elliott. Prior to this time no provision had been made for the black Episcopalians in Savannah to have their own church. Elliott appointed the Reverend S.W. Kennerly to organize St. Stephens and to find a temporary place for the communicants to worship until a church could be erected. A free black proprietor in the bakery business offered the top floor over his store as a meeting place. Hymn books were donated, and a free Negro from Charleston, South Carolina, was employed to lead the music and direct the choir. Membership increased in the church, and a lot was purchased on Habersham Street facing Troup Square. A Unitarian church building was acquired from a white woman and moved to the lot. This charming neo-Gothic building, remodeled, became St. Stephens Episcopal Church, completed in 1860. Kennerly wrote of it, "The erection of our church has been indeed, and in trust, a work of faith; starting as it did from a private conversation at Sunday School over the bakery shop."[19]

18. As quoted in Lewis, *Impressions of America*, in Lane, ed., *Rambler*, 182; Sir Charles Lyell also described Marshall as "a gray-haired venerable looking man with a fine sonorous voice," in *A Second Visit to the United States*, 2:14.

19. J.S. Atwell, *A Brief Historical Sketch of St. Stephen's Parish* (New York: Church Book and Job Printing, 1874), 4, 6, 7, 9, 14, 21. Before the Civil War the wardens and vestry of St. Stephens were black but the rector was white. During the war black lay readers directed the services and after the war black rectors were appointed by the bishop. When Bishop Elliott died in 1866 and was buried in Laurel Grove Cemetery, his body was borne by ten black pallbearers from St. Stephens Church. In 1948 the black Episcopalians sold their church to white Baptists and built a new one in another section of the city, renaming it St. Matthews Episcopal Church; interview with Gustave H. Caution, rector of St. Matthews Episcopal Church until his retirement in 1969. St. Bartholomews, located at Burroughs in Chatham County, was also founded (1845) by Bishop Elliott as a mission church for slaves in the Ogeechee River area. For the activity of the Episcopal church among slaves in Georgia, see Stiles B. Lines, "Slaves and Churchmen: The Work of the Episcopal Church Among Southern Negroes, 1830–1860" (Ph.D. diss., Columbia Univ., 1960); see also "A Sketch of the Ogeechee Mission," *Southern Episcopalian*, 1 (Feb. 1855): 494–97. For a general work see Anne C. Loveland, *Southern Evangelicals and the Social Order, 1800–1860* (Baton Rouge: Louisiana State Univ. Press, 1980).

In 1826 the white Independent Presbyterian Church in Savannah organized and maintained two church Sunday schools for Negro children. One was located at the Second African Baptist Church on Greene Square on the east side of the city and the other, in the First African Baptist Church on Franklin Square on the west side. Lowel Mason, superintendent of the Sunday school at Independent Presbyterian Church, initiated the move to organize the two church schools. From 1826 to 1839 white teachers from the Presbyterian Church instructed the 150 to 200 black children who attended regularly. After 1839 the Negro churches maintained these two Sunday schools.[20]

In 1833 the Reverend Charles C. Jones visited the Sunday school at First African Baptist Church, and the following year the school adopted his *Catechism . . . for the Oral Instruction of Colored Persons.* The *Catechism,* with its convincing literary style, was designed to insure docility and servility of the slave while promising, in return for good behavior, the rewards of spiritual paradise in the world to come. Religion was, without doubt, the strongest of any emotional device to be used in the control of slaves. Passages in Jones's *Catechism* are loaded with psychological gimmicks: Servants must serve their masters faithfully "behind their backs and before their faces." Servants must not run away nor harbor runaways. The Apostle Paul did not harbor Onesimus, the runaway, but instead sent him, with a letter, back to his master. Masters must provide "good houses, comfortable clothing, wholesome and abundant food" for servants, "nurse them carefully in their sickness" and *"keep their families together."* Abraham, the first master mentioned in the Bible, had 318 servants whom he cared for in such a manner.[21]

As attested in the *Catechism,* the rewards for faithfulness, obedience, and servility were manifold. Slaves, as good Jonesian Christians, would become "The Lord's Freemen" in the kingdom

20. "Minutes of the First African Sabbath School, 1826–1835," MS, Independent Presbyterian Church, Savannah. Lowell Mason was also organist of Independent Presbyterian Church and composed such hymns as "From Greenland's Icy Mountains," and "Safely Through Another Week." The Independent Presbyterian Church, aside from sponsoring the Negro Sunday schools, had its own Negro members who worshiped with the whites in segregated pews in the balcony.

21. Charles C. Jones, *A Catechism of Scripture* . . . (Savannah, 1837), 127–31; Matthews, "Charles Colcock Jones and the Southern Evangelical Crusade," 305. Matthews suggests that Jones's missionary zeal was prompted by the "threat to the Southern social order created by the imperfect socialization of blacks."

Figure 29. St. Stephens Episcopal Church. (Drawing by Leonora Quarterman.)

of heaven. What were the rewards for slaves who did not conform? They were punished and eventually sold away from the plantation. Jones, who professed an abhorrence for the practice of separating slave families through sale to a trader, resorted to it in 1856 when he sold a father, mother, and their five children. These offenders had continued to be incorrigible, and there was "a limit to his patience."[22] Jones proved to be a typical owner who would not tolerate continued insubordination.

In the more rural areas of coastal Georgia blacks were members of the white churches and worshiped with the whites in segregated pews. The records of Pleasant Grove Church, located near Hinesville in Liberty County, list some thirty Negroes who were members between 1816 and 1832. Of these, twenty-three were baptized "into full connection," four were expelled "for not giving satisfaction to the society," and three died, one of whom was "free Jesse, an old man and full of day."[23] Blacks and whites worshiped together in the First Presbyterian Church at Darien in McIntosh County. This historic church was organized in 1736 by the Scotch Highlanders, who were opposed to the introduction of slavery in Georgia.

The First Presbyterian Church records cover the years 1824 to 1862. When Federal troops invaded the area in 1862, this church and most of the others around Darien were destroyed. Total membership in the First Presbyterian Church at that time was 120, 61 of whom were listed as Negroes. Joseph Williams, a free black born in the West Indies, converted many of these slaves and recommended them for membership in the church. Williams worked with the white members of the Presbyterian Session and acted as itinerant preacher, visiting the rice plantations to teach the gospel to those not yet converted to Christianity. He preached at Darien, Midway, and Ebenezer (not to be confused with Ebenezer on the Savannah River). The whites respected him and recommended that he be licensed; thus, he was paid a regular salary for his missionary work. Williams is buried near the Mid-

22. As quoted in Myers, ed., *Children of Pride*, 183–85, 309. See W.W. Hazzard, "On the General Management of a Plantation," *Southern Agriculturist* 4 (Apr. 1831): 352, where the slave foreman is reminded that "as a religious man . . . he should recollect that if he cannot be faithful to his earthly master who at all times is near him, providing food and all things for his use and comfort . . ., he cannot be faithful to his heavenly master whom he has never seen."

23. Minute Book, 1813–1832, Pleasant Grove Church, 31–53, MS, Department of Archives and History, Atlanta. There is no denomination shown in this manuscript.

way Presbyterian Church in Liberty County, though not in the Midway Cemetery, which was reserved for whites.[24]

Williams's evangelical work exemplifies the expertise and valuable role of the black preacher in the control of slaves. The slaves Sandy, Abram, Sarah, and Edmund "upon profession and examination, together with the recommendation of Joseph Williams, under whose teaching they had sat for the past year," were baptized, given communion, and received into the church in 1856. On another occasion, at the request of Williams, the church service was held at Harris Neck, north of Darien, where the white preacher, F.R. Goulding, baptized and extended membership to twenty slaves, one of whom, Lucy, had been expelled because of her "cold and backsliding state." During the service at Harris Neck "the Sacrament of the Lord's Supper was administered to a few whites and a large number of blacks." The church secretary wrote, "It is pleasant to record these events as some of the harvest fruits in the field mostly occupied by Joseph Williams." Whites as well as blacks were placed on probation or excommunicated from the church for misconduct, such as "back-biting," excessive drinking, fighting, swearing, or immorality.[25]

The First African Baptist Church in Darien, the largest black church in the community, was created by the Sunbury Baptist Association in 1822 as a church for whites. Like the Presbyterian Church, it had a large black membership and also was destroyed during the Civil War. After the war the black members purchased the property on which the church had stood and built a new church that reproduced the architectural style of the original. The church, an attractive frame structure, has a quiet dignity that reflects again the determination of blacks to preserve their heritage. In Camden County blacks and whites worshiped together in the Methodist Episcopal Church at St. Marys. Membership was about evenly divided, and many of the blacks were free persons. After the Civil War these blacks left the white church to organize their own Methodist Episcopal Church. Negro members of the

24. Records of the Darien Presbyterian Church, in possession of Bessie Lewis, McIntosh County. After the Civil War the blacks separated from the whites and built their own church.

25. Ibid. Another black church in Darien, quaint and picturesque, is St. Cyprians Episcopal Church. It was founded by Fanny Kemble's son-in-law, Dr. James Wentworth Leigh, and was built by blacks in the 1870s. It stands on the north bank of the Altamaha River overlooking what were originally the extensive rice fields of Pierce Butler. This church is served by the white rector of St. Andrews Episcopal Church in Darien.

white Baptist Church in St. Marys also separated to create their own First African Baptist Church.[26]

The Cathedral of St. John The Baptist, the Catholic church in Savannah, had a mixed membership before 1865. Church records indicate that a few of the persons baptized were free blacks and slaves. In 1811 a "free born mulatto girl" of Jekyll Island, whose sponsors were Poulain Du Bignon and his wife, Margaret, was baptized. The baptismal record, though veiled, implies a blood relationship between the girl and her sponsors—hence, the obvious interest in making her nonslave status a matter of record. Poulain Du Bignon died in 1825. His son, Henry Du Bignon, had four legitimate children by his wife, Amelia. These children and twenty-four of his slaves were baptized in 1836 on Jekyll Island by a priest from the Catholic church in Savannah. Charlotte, "a free colored person and illegitimate child of Henry Du Bignon" was also baptized at the same time.[27]

In the 1830s and 1840s southern churchmen launched a movement to create plantation missions to bring Christianity to the large majority of rural slaves who remained outside the reach of the institutional church. The plantation mission movement, centered in the Carolina and Georgia low country, eventually spread to all the slave states. Charles C. Jones was one of its leading proponents. Along with such prominent South Carolina planters as Charles Cotesworth Pinckney, Edward R. Laurens, and Whitemarsh B. Seabrook, Jones launched a promotional campaign that stressed the benefits of a Christian slave population. Through a network of correspondence, their campaign paid off: missionary societies and associations were founded throughout the South. Notable among them was the Liberty County Association, founded by Jones, who acted as a missionary for the association to catechize the slaves of coastal Georgia.[28]

The success of Jones's missionary work among rice plantation slaves may be attributed to his appointment of Negro preachers, exhorters, and watchmen. These appointees more meaningfully

26. Interview with Lillie Harris, June 1975, St. Marys, Camden County; interview with Georgia Williams, Mar. 1975, Darien, McIntosh County. Williams is a deacon of the First African Baptist Church; MSS in possession of Bessie Lewis, McIntosh County; records of St. Marys Methodist Episcopal Church, 1839–56, MSS, Department of Archives and History, Atlanta.

27. "Baptisms, Marriages, Deaths, 1816–38," MSS, Cathedral of St. John the Baptist, Savannah; Wylly, *These Memories*, 7–9.

28. Raboteau, *Slave Religion*, 152–55.

communicated Christianity than did white preachers, whose doctrine centered upon docility, obedience, and subservience to the white man's rules. Negro slave preachers had to be cautious and stress a doctrine approved by whites, but they understood the slaves' secret longings for freedom and their desires to sublimate emotionally through dancing, shouting, and singing—to escape temporarily the demands of plantation routine exacted under the slave regime.

Negro slaves were aware that whites used religion as a form of social control. They were encouraged to attend the services of the whites and to become members of their churches. They preferred, however, the less formal services held by members of their own race, at which they could assert themselves while singing and shouting to express their African religious forms and to seek relief from their oppression. The plantations of coastal Georgia provided praise houses at which slaves met to pray and sing on Sunday evenings and hold prayer meetings during the week. Joseph Le Conte wrote that every plantation had a praise house and that Negro and white preachers visited the plantations regularly to conduct services.[29] The praise house on Charles C. Jones's plantation was a "neat plastered building with belfry and bell."[30] The praise house on Edward J. Thomas's plantation was a retreat for the slaves where "shouting and singing were enjoyed, and strange doctrines preached."[31] Georgia Bryan Conrad described the services she attended in the praise house on her family's plantation:

> When we were at our summer house in Glynn we always attended the servants' meetings, which generally took place in the afternoon on Sunday, and Saturday and Sunday nights. The afternoon performance we always attended, lingering at the door of the house until we were invited to enter and take seats, which consisted of rough benches placed around the wall. How we envied those who took part in the active shouting and singing! With what bated breath we watched the constant movements, the circling around and around, the bending, the scraping, wondering which of our favorites would hold out the longest! The modern cake-walk is a travesty upon the old-time shouting Negro. One is an affectation; the other, the spontaneous outburst of a naturally religious spirit.[32]

Africanisms in religious forms were more nearly preserved by

29. *Autobiography of Joseph LeConte*, 13.
30. Mallard, *Plantation Life*, 104.
31. *Memoirs of a Southerner*, 11–12.
32. *Reminiscences*, 9.

Figure 30. A "Praise House" in Liberty County. (Drawing by Leonora Quarterman.)

Figure 31. Interior of the "Praise House." (Drawing by Leonora Quarterman.)

plantation slaves than by city slaves. The isolation of the plantation from contact with more sophisticated mores encouraged preservation. The ring shout, a religious dance in which African dance style patterns are retained, was performed regularly by rice plantation slaves, in the praise house or a slave house after the regular religious meeting had been held. The benches were pushed to the wall, and men, women, boys, and girls formed a ring in the middle of the floor, then began chanting and shuffling, always in a counterclockwise direction. There are a number of descriptions of the ring shout; one, recorded in 1867, describes it being performed at Port Royal, South Carolina.

> [They] begin just walking and by-and-by shuffling round, one after the other, in a ring. The foot is hardly taken from the floor, and the progression is mainly due to a jerking, hitching motion, which agitates the entire shoulder, and soon brings out streams of perspiration. Sometimes they dance silently, sometimes as they shuffle they sing. The chorus of the spiritual, and sometimes the song itself is also sung by the dancers. But most frequently a band, composed of some of the best singers and of tired shouters, stand at the side of the room to "base" the others, singing the body of the song and clapping their hands together or on their knees. Song and dance alike are extremely energetic, and often, when the shout lasts into the middle of the night, the monotonous thud, thud, thud of the feet prevents sleep within half a mile of the praise house. . . . It is not unlikely that this remarkable religious ceremony is a relic of some African dance. . . .[33]

If the owner deprived the slaves of evening prayer meetings, they met together secretly in a cabin or brush arbor to hold their services, at which they were careful not to sing and shout too loud. The Negro spiritual "Steal Away to Jesus" was originally composed and sung to inform neighbors in the slave community of a secret prayer meeting to be held. The traditional custom mentioned many times in slave narratives of turning the iron pot or wash tub upside down to muffle the noise at these secret meetings is identified as a West African religious form associated with the gods. The iron pot did not muffle the noise but symbolized the African gods who gave divine protection.[34] The custom of wor-

33. As quoted in Raboteau, *Slave Religion*, 70, 71. In Africa religious behavior is expressed by dancing, singing, and drumming. In the Christian tradition dancing in church is regarded as irreligious. The ring shout reconciles both principles; shuffling and stamping conform to African traditions and are not recognized as dancing—to cross one's feet is to dance. See 72n, in Raboteau.

34. George P. Rawick, *From Sundown to Sunup: The Making of the Black Community* (Westport, Conn., Greenwood, 1972), 40–43; interviews with former

shiping in brush arbors was an African tradition; the African ancestors of slaves reserved sacred groves for their religious meetings.[35] The religion expressed by plantation slaves retained many African traits that are visible today in more diluted forms in rural areas of the Georgia coast where exhorting, shouting, and singing, while keeping time with the body and feet to a syncopated beat, can still be seen at church meetings.

Negro slaves preferred their own form of religion, away from the view of whites, where they could express a ritualistic style of singing and dancing reminiscent of their African origins. This was especially true of plantation slaves, who had to stifle these expressions when attending the white man's church on Sunday mornings. Slaves preferred a Negro preacher, licensed or unlicensed, to conduct their services. Those along the Georgia coast had Negro preachers, ordained by a white preacher like Charles C. Jones, or chosen from among their own elite—skilled slaves and drivers—on the basis of leadership, oratorical skill, and respect from the slave community. One such preacher in coastal Georgia received this comment: "He drives the Negroes at cotton all the week, and Sundays he drives them at the Gospel."[36]

Eloquent exhortations, designed to encourage emotional response from those listening, were characteristic of the slave preacher's sermons. Fanny Kemble wept as she listened to a burial service delivered by London, the slave preacher on Pierce Butler's plantation: "London read parts of the funeral service from the prayer-book . . . . The words were rustic but there was nothing grotesque in either the matter or the manner . . . . This was one of the most striking religious ceremonies at which I ever assisted."[37] The slave preacher on a plantation in middle Georgia could not read; still, according to Louis Fowler, he preached "a powerful sermon. O Lawd! He am inspire from de Lawd and he preached from his heartfelt."[38]

Testimonials of former slaves illuminate the personality of the black preacher and his ability to stimulate his listeners spiritually. Clara Young's favorite slave preacher was Matthew Ewing: "He

---

slaves and their descendants along the Georgia coast and in Savannah. There are frequent references to brush arbors in slave narratives.

35. Donald R. Mathews, *Religion in the Old South* (Chicago: Univ. of Chicago Press, 1977), 211.

36. Mallard, *Plantation Life*, 104; Olmsted, *Journey in Seaboard Slave States*, 451.

37. Armstrong, *Fanny Kemble*, 228–29.

38. As quoted in Raboteau, *Slave Religion*, 234.

was a comely [Negro], black as night and he sure could read out of his hand. He never learned no real readin' and writin' but he sure knowed his Bible and would . . . make like he was readin' and preach de purtiest preachin' you ever heard." Anthony Dawson testified, "Mostly we had white preachers, but when we had a black preacher, that was heaven."[39]

Missionaries and reporters who came south during Reconstruction were impressed by the intellectual depth of the sermons delivered by black preachers. "What wonderful preachers these blacks are!" declared one missionary. A reporter with the Union army attended a church service conducted by a black preacher and was inspired by the beauty and persuasiveness of his oratory: "He held his rude audience with most perfect control; subdued them, excited them, and, in fact, did what he pleased with them!"[40] Slaves wanted to hear the black man's version of Christianity, not the white man's repetitious Christian dialogue that emphasized docility, honesty, and obedience to the white man's laws. The black preacher spoke to the slaves from the Bible and, when he could, delivered a religion of hope for freedom and a better way of life for those of his race. On the surface he had to preach a doctrine approved of by the slaveholding class; in more subtle and elusive ways he preached a doctrine that was Afro-American in essence and, in so doing, offered his communicants an opportunity for self-expression.

In the South generally, Negroes tended to join the Baptist and Methodist churches of the whites and worshiped with them in segregated pews. In smaller numbers they joined the Presbyterian, Episcopal, Lutheran, and Roman Catholic churches. Nonetheless, Negroes preferred their own churches and, had they been allowed, would have continued to participate in an independent church movement that developed late in the eighteenth century, as illustrated by the African Methodists of Charleston, South Carolina. They withdrew from the white Methodist church and ordained their own bishop and other church officials. Their action was disallowed by the whites, who forced the bishop to leave the state. Blacks who participated in the movement to create an independent church system were imprisoned. Negroes were

39. Yetman, *Life Under the "Peculiar Institution,"* 95, 335.

40. Raboteau, *Slave Religion*, 235–36. See Genovese, *Roll, Jordan, Roll*, 255–79, for the role of the black preacher in slavery.

gradually forced into a role of accommodation in the white churches throughout the South.[41]

Totally Negro Baptist churches, however, prevailed in coastal Georgia. The Sunbury Baptist Association in 1857 listed thirteen Negro church congregations out of a total of twenty-five affiliated churches. Total membership in these churches was 5,607; only 537 were white membes. The high percentage of Negroes in the total population of the coastal counties accounts for this ratio in some degree, but talented Negro Baptist religious leaders successfully prompted growth in membership.[42] The Negro slaves of coastal Georgia did enjoy a greater degree of religious freedom than could be seen in other sections of the South.

41. Woodson, *The Negro in Our History* (Washington, D.C.: Associated publishers, 1922), 225–27; Frazier, *Negro Church in America*, 25–28.

42. Bailey, "Protestantism and Afro-Americans in the Old South," 361; LaFar, "Baptist Church of Savannah." Within the statewide Georgia Baptist Convention, in addition to the Sunbury Baptist Association, there were two others: the Hephzibah Association and the Georgia Association. Neither of these compared favorably with the Sunbury Baptist Association in membership ratios of blacks to whites.

CHAPTER NINE

Slave Culture on the Georgia Coast

Basil Hall was favorably impressed with the slaves who transported him by canoe on the Altamaha River from Darien to St. Simon's Island. The canoe was pulled by five black oarsmen, "smart Negroes, merry fellows, and very happy looking, as indeed," Hall thought, were "most of their race, in spite of all their bondage." Hall was impressed by the beauty of their singing, which he likened to that of the Canadian voyageurs and the Bunder-boatmen of Bombay.[1] Contemporary literature is filled with references to the singing of slaves. Slaves sang while they worked and during their leisure hours. They spoke to the world through their songs, many of which they composed "with tongue in cheek" to express a double meaning. They could not express outwardly to whites their longings for freedom from bondage nor their hopelessness because of their conditions in bondage. The slave songs were the most meaningful and satisfying of all their expressions of sublimation in adjusting to the harsh realities of the slave system. The songs, African in origin, were a natural response that helped them contend with their enslavement in a new environment.

The dance songs, work songs, religious and burial chants of the Georgia coastal and Sea Island Negroes are rooted in their African musical heritage. Lydia Parrish studied the origins of these dances and songs, and found evidence of continuity of development of the dancing and singing of Bahamian and Sea Island Negroes. For example, the ring dance performed in the Bahamas

1. *Travels in North America*, 2:228.

called "Emma, You My Darlin' " and the accompanying tune are the same as the ring dance and tune performed and sung by Negro children on St. Simon's Island.[2]

Bishop Henry Benjamin Whipple visited the rice plantation of Duncan L. Clinch on the Satilla River in Camden County during Christmas, 1845. Whipple was fascinated with the "jollity and mirth of the black population." This was the season the slaves were given three days in which to celebrate. They danced and sang continuously, accompanied by the music of their own band. The instruments used consisted of three fiddles, two drums, two fifes, two triangles, and two tamborines. They sometimes performed on the front veranda of Clinch's plantation house and "aped the manners of the whites." On the last day of celebration they arrayed themselves in their best finery and paraded around the plantation, led by their "staff of officers," who were bedecked "with red sashes, mock epaulettes and goose quill feathers." They were collecting pocket money "by levying contributions from all the whites."[3]

Georgia Bryan Conrad recalled the singing of slaves as they rowed her, with her family, back and forth to Darien: "On these occasions the Negroes always sang to us, keeping time with their oars."[4] Edward J. Thomas remembered the "sweet chants" of his father's "people" on moonlight nights "when the young men and girls would meet to grind their corn around the handmills."[5] Charles Lyell visited Hopeton, the rice plantation of James Hamilton Couper on the Altamaha River, in 1845. Couper came down the river to meet Lyell at Darien "in a long canoe, hollowed out of the trunk of a single cypress, and rowed by six negroes, who were singing loudly, and keeping time to the strokes of their oars."[6]

Boat racing became a sport and social event in which slave crews from different plantations competed against each other. Owners and slaves viewed these races with great enthusiasm and placed bets on their favorite crews. The canoes used in these races

2. *Slave Songs of the Georgia Sea Islands*, 5–7. Parrish refers to a description of life on board a slave ship where men, women, and children, when allowed on deck, sang African melodies to the rhythm of an improvised beat, made on the bottom of a tub or tin kettle.

3. *Whipple's Southern Diary, 1843–44*, in Rose, ed., *Documentary History of Slavery*, 507–508.

4. *Reminiscences*, 6.

5. *Memoirs of a Southerner*, 12.

6. *A Second Visit to the United States*, 2:244–45.

were thirty to fifty feet long, hollowed out until the sides were no more than an inch thick. They were capable of traveling a mile or less in six minutes.[7] The boat races, or regattas, as they came to be called, were held at the various coastal cities, St. Marys, Frederica, Darien, Brunswick, and Savannah; they were exciting events and attracted large crowds. The men of the slave crews were skilled oarsmen and impressive in appearance. They wore white shirts and pantaloons with colorful turbans on their heads. At one such race, held on the Savannah River in 1838, which attracted thousands of black and white spectators, the crew of the *Star* wore blue turbans while the crew of the *Lizard* wore red.[8] The racing canoes were graceful boats, painted differently in exotic colors; as they glided through the inland waterways, rowed by their singing slave crews, traveling in groups to participate in a scheduled race, they created a most romantic scene. The winning crews were sometimes given awards. After a race held at St. Marys in 1835, Colonel Henry Du Bignon of Jekyll Island awarded Thomas Stafford's oarsmen $50 in prize money as they prepared to depart for Stafford's plantation on Cumberland Island.[9]

The marsh lands and islands of coastal Georgia abounded in small wild horses called "marsh tackies." These animals were frequently caught, penned, fed, tamed, and then used by blacks and whites. Edward J. Thomas and his slave friends, during their youth, rode these ponies. They "would bridle the devilish beasts, strap a saddle cloth on, and go bouncing and scampering over the plantation." This was thought to be a "magnificant sport for boys." The slaves of coastal Georgia often used these ponies to pull their wagons. It was not unusual on Sundays to see a cavalcade of horsedrawn wagons filled with slaves, traveling to attend the church services of the whites.[10] Georgia Bryan Conrad referred to these marsh tackies; she called them "horses, something like Shetland ponies." When these animals were used to pull a carryall that held eight or ten people, a team of six was generally required.[11]

Trustworthy slaves were given guns with which to shoot wild

7. Coulter, "Boating as a Sport in the Old South," *Georgia Historical Quarterly* 27 (Sept. 1943): 237.

8. Charles Rinaldo Floyd Diary, 1816–45, MS in possession of Bryce McAdoo Clagett, Bethesda, Md.

9. Ibid.

10. *Memoirs of a Southerner*, 11, 12.

11. *Reminiscences*, 13.

Figure 32. A Former Slave of Coastal Georgia Making a Casting Net. (Georgia Historical Society Collection.)

Figure 33. Uncle Ed McIver, a Former Slave of McIntosh County. (Photograph in possession of the author.)

game, animals, and crop-destroying birds. In the early nineteenth century, while the lower counties of coastal Georgia were in a frontier stage of development, the Creek Indians were a menace, making sporadic attacks upon outlying plantations. John R. Le Conte developed a plantation in McIntosh County soon after the Revolutionary War, built a stockade, and stored muskets therein as a defense against Indian raids; his slaves were instructed to seek shelter in the stockade and use the guns when Indians attacked; a force of several hundred did. They fought with bows and arrows and were no match for Le Conte's slaves, who had guns. When the skirmish ended and the Indians retreated, they captured and took with them three female slaves and Le Conte's trusted slave Samson. Several years later Samson escaped and returned to the plantation. The female slaves had become wives of the Indians.[12] Rebecca, a slave who was sold from Pierce Butler's plantation and taken to Wilcox County, Georgia, was later kidnapped by an Indian who "took her on his shoulders" to his village where she became his wife. She had fourteen children by him.[13]

During the War of 1812 British warships preyed upon coastal Georgia and occupied several of the islands, destroying property and enticing slaves away from plantations. Thomas Spalding, to prevent such an invasion of his plantation on Sapelo Island, secured guns and ammunition from the state government. He armed and drilled the slaves under direction of his slave foreman, Bu Allah. Because of the display of force shown by Spalding's slaves, the British fleet did not attack. Bu Allah was Moslem; this remarkable man kept a record of his plantation rules in Arabic. He prayed three times each day, facing east, on his sheepskin prayer rug. Bu Allah had twelve sons and seven daughters. When he died, his Koran and prayer rug were buried with him.[14]

Another remarkable Spalding slave was Betsy Beagle, called "Baba" by the Spalding children. She nursed most of the Spalding children and outlived both her master and mistress by almost a half century. When she died, she was buried in the slave cemetery on Sapelo, and this inscription was carved on her tombstone:

12. *Autobiography of Joseph LeConte*, 19–21.

13. Interview with George Williams, Darien, McIntosh County, Mar. 1975. Williams is a deacon of the historic First African Baptist Church at Darien. Rebecca was his great-aunt's niece.

14. Coulter, *Thomas Spalding*, 90; Wylly, *The Seed That Was Sown*, 52.

In memory of Betsy Beagle
Born July, 1796
Died Jan. 30, 1890
She was the faithful loving
Nurse of the Spalding children
for two generations
"My Baba"
May she rest as peacefully as the
Little heads she pillowed to sleep
on her bosom.[15]

When Africans arrived in America they were not taught English; they had to acquire a sufficient grasp of the language to understand orders, but then were left to themselves to communicate with one another in their vernacular tongue. The syntax or word construction of their African language was unlike that of the English. They retained this structure and blended with it English words in order to communicate in English. The result of the adaptation came to be known as the Gullah dialect. Gullah, which has rapidly disappeared in the last generation, is not mongrelized English but a creolized African language that resulted from a fusion of English and African words.[16]

Among scholars of linguistics who have made a determined study of the Gullah dialect, two schools of thought prevail concerning its origin. Mason Crum, Ambrose E. Gonzales, Guy B. Johnson, and Reed Smith trace its peculiarities to the Elizabethan and Jacobean English spoken by the lower classes (indentured servants) in colonial America, whose vocabularies were limited and markedly dialectal. Melville J. Herskovits, Lorenzo D. Turner, and the creolists John F. Szwed and William A. Stewart place the origin of Gullah and all black English today, when it deviates from the standard spoken English, back to the linguistic history of Africa. In 1941 Turner published the first in a series of articles in which he presented a scientific method for the study of African speech survivals. Along the coast and on the Sea Islands of Georgia and South Carolina, he discovered about thirty West African

15. Wylly, *The Seed That Was Sown,* 84. Baba is an African name found among the Muslim Hausa of Nigeria. See Mary F. Smith, *Baba of Karo: A Woman of the Muslim Hausa* (New Haven: Yale Univ. Press, 1981).

16. The word *Gullah* is thought to be derived from the word *Angola.* Many of the Georgia and Carolina slaves were brought from Angola, Africa. References to "Angola Negroes" may have been shortened to "Gola Negroes," then distorted into "Gullah Negroes." The Geechee dialect sometimes referred to is a synonym of the Gullah dialect.

languages. A sampling of these African words are *buckra*, meaning 'white man'; *cooter*, 'tortoise'; *goober*, 'peanut'; *gumbo*, 'okra'; *samba*, 'to dance'; *tabby*, as in tabby house; *tote*, 'to carry'; *voodoo*, 'charm' or 'witchcraft'; *yam*, sweet potato'.[17]

Some years ago Albert H. Stoddard of Savannah recorded the folk tales and songs of former slaves living on Daufuskie Island. Evidence of the preservation of African cultural forms and traditions is seen in the sentence structure of the literature and songs that Stoddard collected. The following selection is based upon the creation story. It illustrates the dialect spoken along the Georgia coast and the Negro's outward acceptance of Christianity in his new environment while holding to his African religious beliefs in the forces of good and evil:

> God dun mek de wul en e bin all kibber ober wid watuh en e bin dak, en God ain lub de dak so e tun roun en mek de sun, en de moon, en put de sta een de hebben, en e tinks e looks mo bettuh. Den e study bout all da watuh wuh duh cubber de yeart en e dig canal en ditch en quatah drain fuh dreen de watuh off en mek de lan git dry. Den e tak en wuk de lan en plant all kine uh seed en tree. Grass seed en wegetable seed en watmillion en all kine uh ting fuh de bittle fuh man en beas. Den God does wan somebody fuh ten de yeart en e tek en mek Adam out de yeart. En God put um fuh ten he gaden.
>
> When da June grass stat fuh grow fuh true de wuk git so hebby Adam ain bin able fuh ten de gaden en ten e self. So God tun roun en mek Adam fuh drop sleep en e tek one uh Adam leases rib en mek ooman. God gie she name Ebe, en gie she tuh Adam fuh mine e house en cook e bittle, en fuh help Adam een e wuk. . . . En fuh Adam en Ebe so bex God e mek dem ting fuh bodderation dem. De skeeter en de house fly, fuh woan let e horse stan still, en de san nat, en de anch, en de oul, en all dem ting fuh bodderation um God mek.[18]

Gullah is a unique language. One word may mean several unrelated things and several different words may have the same

17. Turner, "African Survivals in the New World," *Africanisms in the Gullah Dialect, With a Foreword by David DeCamp* (Chicago: Univ. of Chicago Press, 1949; rpt. Ann Arbor: Univ. of Michigan Press 1974), 6–11, 68. Turner's discovery was followed by a new school of linguists who popularized the subject of creolization. Two of these scholars, Joel L. Dillard and William A. Stewart, have developed a decreolization hypothesis and link it with black English today, calling it Gullah decreolized because of the influence of white English.

18. "Origin, Dialect, Beliefs, and Characteristics of the Negroes of the South Carolina and Georgia Coasts," *Georgia Historical Quarterly* 28 (Sept. 1944): 186–95.

meaning. The letter *e*, also the two letters, *um*, are used to mean 'he,' 'she,' 'it,' or 'they.' *E shum*, means 'he,' 'she,' or 'they have seen it.' The past tense is rendered here for emphasis. Running words together is characteristic of Gullah. The phrase "come to see him" or "her" is rendered *Comefushum*. The word *specify*, though clear in meaning, is used interchangeably. A Gullah-speaking Negro who tore his pants as he slipped on a log declared, "Muh britchus ain bin able fuh specify en e git all tay up."[19]

The Gullah songs of Daufuskie Island preserved by Stoddard and arranged for piano accompaniment by Elizabeth A. Norton of Savannah are a choice collection of unpublished material. Their real beauty is not fully appreciated except when being sung. They serve to illustrate the creative musical talent expressed by slaves. One song refers to the boats *Olympia, Tecumseh, Fish Hawk*, and *Sea Gull*, which were in use at the Stoddard plantation. Each plantation had its own boating crews, and one could tell from the songs sung by these crews which plantation the boatmen came from. Another song, "Poosh de Aak" (Push the Ark), was a work song expressing hope for relief from the drudgery of field labor. The song "When we Hear de Rocks A-rendin' " refers to the millenium or the second coming of Christ as predicted in Revelation 20:1–5 of the New Testament. This is a hoped-for period of joy, serenity, prosperity, and justice. The following selection from another song has a humorous touch. Grip is the name of the mule:

> Ah galloped ter see my Lucindy
> Das her jes as sho as you bawn
> But who am dat nigger dats wid her
> Come, Grip, les us pass em wid skawn
>
> But Grip shied at dat nigger's white beaber [beaver hat]
> En trowed me as flat as er rule
> Right down ter de foot of Lucindy
> En dats why I spizes er mule[20]

Animal stories told by Gullah slaves had their origins in Africa, where they were a favorite form of evening entertainment. They served as parables to illustrate a moral or religious lesson. Storytelling was an art often accompanied by pantomime (gestures and dancing), the beating of drums, and responses from the audience.

19. Ibid., 189–90.
20. Stoddard Collection, MSS, GHS.

In these stories, from which the Uncle Remus tales were taken, the smaller and physically weaker animals like the rabbit and the tortoise are cunning, guileful, mischievous, patient, and wise; they eventually outwit their opponents, the stronger animals. In the folk tale "Buh Partridge Out Hides Buh Rabbit," a lesson in patience and intelligence is upheld. The tale is allegorical—a veiled manifestation of the slave who outwits his superior.[21]

Negro literature in the form of autobiographies, letters, and speeches of slaves who escaped to freedom to record their experiences while in bondage, and WPA interviews made with former slaves are a rich source for knowledge of their attitudes. In their work songs and spirituals the slaves expressed underlying themes: hope for freedom, for a better day, for relief from the burden of forced labor, as well as subtle attitudes toward the owner and his treatment of them. Perhaps the most noticeable evidence of racial attitudes of blacks is shown in their tenacious struggle to preserve as much of African culture as they could and to transform it into a weapon to repel the worst aspects of the slave system. Their art, dance, folk literature, language, music, and social traditions all manifested, to one or another degree, their African origins.[22]

Blacks retained their cultural heritage in America as a means of survival in a world where white ideals were superimposed as a condition for acceptable behavior. Blacks took their enslavement stoically, though they never admitted inwardly that it was right or permanent. They practiced diplomacy and showed marked expertise in misleading whites with their use of parables and symbols. In their religion this was especially true. What often appeared to the white man as harmless religious sentiments and aspirations camouflaged quite different thoughts. The phrase sung in a spiritual "by and by I'm goin' ter lay down my heavy load" suggests the release at death from the burdensome routine of labor; to the slave singers it meant the possibility of escape into Ohio or Canada.[23]

Various conditions of slave life and attitudes of slaves toward

21. Ibid.

22. Turner, "African Survivals in the New World With Special Emphasis on the Arts," Robert V. Haynes, ed., *Blacks in White America Before 1865: Issues and Interpretations* (New York: David McKay, 1972), 63, 67.

23. Asa H. Gordon, *The Georgia Negro: A History* (Ann Arbor: Edward Brothers, 1933; rpt. Spartanburg: Reprint Company, 1972), 3, 21.

the owner are seen in the rhymes and songs they created to express their feelings. In the rhyme "Ration Day," slaves were aware that "Ole Mosser" could supply them with a better quality of food:

Dat ration day come once a week
Ole Mosser's rich as Gundy
But he gives us 'lasses all de week
An' buttermilk fer Sund'y

The threat held over slaves that they would be sold if they did not conform produced this rhyme:

Way down yon'er in Possum Trot
In Ole Miss'sip' whar de sun shines hot
Dere hain't no chickens an' de Niggers eats c'on
You hain't never see'd de lak since youse been bo'n
You'd better min' Mosser an' keep a stiff lip
So's you won't get sol' down to ole Miss'sip.

The promise of owners to liberate their slaves was not always carried out. Disillusionment is shown in the following lines:

Ole Mosser lakwise promise me
W'en he died, he'd set me free
But ole Mosser go an' make his Will
Fer to leave me a-plowing ol Beck still

Yes, my ole Mosser promise me
But 'his papers' didn' leave me free
A dose of pisen he'ped 'im along
May de Devil preach his funer'l song.

Slaves longed to be free and expressed these desires in many of their compositions:

But you know, Aunt Dinah's gettin' sorter ole
An' she's feared to go to Canada, caze it's so col',

or:

Uncle Jack, he want to git free
He find de way Norf by de moss on de tree
He cross dat river a-floatin' in a tub
Dem Patterollers give 'im a mighty close rub.[24]

Slaves' attitudes depended in part upon the treatment they received and the conditions under which they worked; even with the best treatment, they wanted to be free. They were generally submissive in the presence of whites, for such an image was required; nonetheless, they retained their rich cultural heritage,

24. Talley, "Negro Folk Rhymes," 86–89.

deliberately hiding it from the eyes of the white master. This heritage is expressed in their religion, folk tales, work songs, and rhymes. When they were freed, they rarely expressed real devotion to their former masters. What they had learned during their years in bondage were the arts of accommodation and sublimation—mechanisms necessary for survival in a world where the white man's power and ideology prevailed.

Of all the African traits retained by slaves, perhaps the family concept was the strongest. Family solidarity was derived from within the slave culture and was not dependent upon prescribed civil and religious norms. Over the years expanded slave kin and quasi-kin networks characterized slave family linkages that were tremendously significant in providing social security within the slave community. Within the family the young slave learned behavioral patterns and traditional values (quite different from those upheld by whites) that fostered self-esteem. The slave family was "far more than an owner-sponsored device designed to reproduce the labor force" and serve as a form of social control.[25] Traditionally, the family was monogomous, and though it was frequently broken through separation by sale, extended kinship helped to ease the heartbreak and trauma of such an experience. Family solidarity acted as a survival mechanism.

Slave marriages were not legally recognized, though owners respected the slave's desire in choosing a spouse to encourage the unity of the slave family as an institution. The owner was motivated by his consideration of humanity and his desire for social order—contented and happy slave families who would increase his slave population with their offspring. This increase he measured in dollars and cents.

Slave narratives are filled with references to the typical plantation slave marriage ceremony called "jumping the broomstick." The two slaves who agreed to live together jumped backward and forward over the broomstick held for them while their friends looked on. Choosing a mate from another plantation was discouraged, though slaves often preferred a spouse from an adjoining plantation. They always had to make known to the owner and

25. Herbert G. Gutman, *The Black Family in Slavery and Freedom, 1750–1925* (New York: Vintage, 1976), 261. See also John W. Blassingame, *The Slave Community: Plantation Life in the Antebellum South* (New York: Oxford Univ. Press, 1972), 79.

obtain his approval of the choice of a mate. The young slave Landcaster, "very tall and strong," lived on a plantation adjoining that of John Thomas in McIntosh County. Landcaster became enamored of, and asked permission to marry, Nelly. Thomas refused. "His objections availed but little, for love found a way and year by year Nelly's family grew larger."[26]

Some deviation from the broomstick marriage did occur on plantations when a black preacher, or a white, married the couple. House servants were more likely to have a wedding sponsored by the owner's family. Andrew Marshall, the prestigious black preacher of the First African Baptist Church in Savannah, frequently performed the marriage ceremony for slaves. Margaret, a house servant belonging to Georgia Bryan Conrad, and Boney Hazzard were married by Marshall in the parlor of the owner's house. "The bride was dressed in white with veil and orange blossoms complete" and the groom was dressed in black. After the ceremony a reception was held in the basement of Bryan's house for the newly married couple and all of their friends.[27] Jacob W. Frederick remembered the marriage of his nurse, Charity, to Handy. Frederick's father performed the ceremony:

> On the evening of the marriage, the broad raised walk from their quarter to our dwelling was brilliantly lighted with piles of lightwood knots at frequent intervals, on each side of the walk. The bridal couple was preceded by torch bearers whose long burning sticks dripped pitch. The couple was followed by all the quarter. . . . Father, from the back porch, impressively read the ritual that made them man and wife and assigned them a cabin in which to begin a new home.[28]

Many features of African culture, transformed by contact with European culture, are in evidence today among blacks of coastal Georgia. These are seen in their religious and social beliefs, in manners of speech, in the matriarchal concept of the family as an institution, in art, music, the dance, in beliefs of the hereafter, in voodoo, fetishism, or the practice of magic, and in funeral services. The shout or prayer house of slavery times where blacks sang and danced while worshiping together exists today.[29]

The anthropologist John F. Szwed, in speaking of creolization

26. Thomas, *Memoirs of a Southerner*, 27.
27. Conrad, *Reminiscences*, 16.
28. Gerald J. Smith, ed., "Reminiscences of the Civil War By J.W. Frederick," *Georgia Historical Quarterly* 59 (Supplement 1975): 159.

at the University of South Carolina in the spring of 1976, emphasized the fact that the music of the United States "went Negro" in the 1920s. In the creolization process, whites have also adopted the African dance style. The spirituals and church hymns sung by Negroes along the Georgia coast and in the southern United States have retained much that is African. Because of the call and response method used, these songs are similar to the song styles of West Africa.[30]

The singing and dancing of slaves was a cultural form they brought from Africa, where this expression accompanies many aspects of social life. Along the Georgia coast several African dances have been preserved. These are the buzzard lope, juba dis juba dat, and the ring shout. Other American dances of African origin are the black bottom, the Charleston, the rhumba, the tango, and the zamba. Plantation slaves made many of their musical instruments, which were similar to the ones used in Africa. Banjos, drums, gongs, rattlers, and triangles were some of the instruments made by slaves and played by them to accompany their singing and dancing.[31]

The artistic talents demonstrated by slaves in basket and cloth weaving and wood carving are African in origin. Allen Greene of Sapelo Island makes attractive baskets in various styles, sizes, and shapes. He sells them throughout the state. His grandfather made them for "mauster" in slavery times and taught Greene this art. The basket makers north of Charleston, South Carolina, are descendents of slaves from Africa who brought the art of weaving with them. The wood carvings shown in *Drums and Shadows,* the book of Gullah folklore, were done in the 1930s by Stick Daddy, a former slave. Ulysses Davis, whose wood carvings have been on

29. Observations made by the writer.

30. A program entitled "Society and Culture in South Carolina," Mar. 26, 27, in which Szwed, Franklin W. Knight, George Fredrickson, William A. Stewart, and Herbert G. Gutman participated. See Szwed, "Musical Adaptations Among Afro-Americans," *Journal of American Folklore* 72 (Apr. 1969): 115; observations made by the writer while attending services at the historic Negro churches in Savannah.

31. Parrish, *Slave Songs of the Georgia Sea Islands,* 65, 128–29, 160, 192; Blassingame, *Slave Community,* 30–32. Katie Underwood of Sapelo Island, whose mother was a slave of Thomas Spalding, described the isolation of Sea Island blacks. Those who remain preserve a soul-lifting culture: "story-telling through gesture and animal characters, a call-and-answer song style, a dialect mixing European and West African elements, and an attachment to cooperative societies." See Julius Lester, *To Be a Slave* (New York: Dial Press, 1968), for references to African dance styles performed by slaves in other southern states.

exhibition at the Telfair Academy of Arts and Sciences in Savannah, is a talented black Georgian whose works are exceptionally fine.[32] Robert Delegal, a slave of McIntosh County who was brought to the area illegally from Africa, made drums of deer skins, wove baskets, and did wooden carvings. His ears were pierced, he wore wooden earrings, and his African tribal marks were on his face and arms.[33]

The handsome wood carvings, wood paneling, and decorative plaster motifs (medallions, moldings) that served to beautify the interiors of the more pretentious plantation and townhouses of the slaveholding class were done with perfection and were a contribution of blacks. Slaves also forged the handsome wrought iron that adorned the exterior of the townhouses; this talent and the art of wood carving were brought from Africa.[34]

The custom of passing babies or small children over the casket of a deceased relative before burial is not unusual along the Georgia coast. The procedure is said to seal the spirit of the dead. The tradition is popular among black families. A funeral director, when asked about the custom, said that it is practiced rather frequently, some families preferring to uphold the custom in the funeral parlor and others at the cemetery. Though interpretation may vary, it is generally considered to mean that the spirit of the deceased will work no adverse effects on the survivor passed over the coffined body.[35]

Plantations had their own slave cemeteries, separate from the whites', located some distance from the slave quarters. Owners respected the wishes of slaves in allowing them to have funerals for their dead. These were sometimes held during the day; slaves were given time off from work for the ceremony. More often, the funerals were held at night. The technique of vascular injection embalming was not yet in use, and so the body had to be placed in a pine box and buried soon after death. The funeral ceremony

32. Interview with Allen Greene, Aug. 1975; the basket makers are located on Highway 17 at Mount Pleasant, about seven miles north of Charleston; *Savannah Morning News*, June 6, 1976.

33. Interview with Charlotte Delegal Pierce and Essie Spalding, Apr. 1975, McIntosh County.

34. On African art in the United States, see Robert Farris Thompson, *An Aesthetic of Coal: African Art and Culture in the New World* (New York: Random, 1981), and Szwed, ed., *Black America* (New York: Basic Books, 1970).

35. *Savannah Morning News*, Nov. 16, 1976; interview with Frank H. Bynes of Bynes-Royall Funeral Home.

might be delayed until a more convenient time.[36] Frederick Law Olmsted reported that slave funerals in Georgia were always at night: "They were very quaint and picturesque—all the negroes of the neighborhood marching in procession from the cabin of the deceased person to the grave, carrying lightwood torches, and singing hymns, in their sad, wailing, chanting manner."[37]

Frances Ann Kemble attended and described a slave funeral on Butler's Island. The dead slave in his coffin was brought out of the cabin while all the slaves from the plantation gathered around. The slave preacher presented the words of a hymn that they sang in unison; then they kneeled on the ground while the preacher exhorted about life, death, and immortality. After this brief ceremony they walked to the gravesite, holding lightwood torches and chanting a hymn while following the coffin held in the air by the pallbearers. An elderly slave read the funeral service and another told them the Bible story in the New Testament about the raising of Lazarus from the dead.[38]

The process of creolization continues today, as blacks and whites adapt cultural expressions from one another. These adaptations are noticeable in styles of wearing apparel, in food habits, especially in the South where both races continue to prefer the traditional foods of their forebears, in dancing and music, in the folk tales told to children, in the superstitious beliefs to which many unsophisticated groups of both races still cling, and in other less noticeable customs and practices.

On smaller plantations throughout the South, and these were in the majority, there was an informality of control and intimacy of relations between slaves and their masters; such informality offered an opportunity for slaves to share in the cultural heritage of the master class.[39] By comparison, the tidewater plantations of Georgia and South Carolina were large estates with extensive

36. When the slave died, his body was laid out on a "cooling board" approximately 24 inches wide and 7 feet long. Until rigor mortis set in, a piece of cloth was tied under the chin to the head to keep the mouth closed. Pennies were placed on the eyes to keep them closed, and salt was placed on the chest to discourage purging. When the body became stiff, it was wound in a sheet. This is the origin of the terminology in the prayers of blacks today when they say, "Lord, I thank thee for permitting me to rise this morning and that my bed was not my cooling board," or "that my cover was not a winding sheet."

37. *Journey in Seaboard Slave States,* 230.

38. *Records of Later Life* (New York: Henry Holt, 1882), 139–42.

39. Edgar T. Thompson, *Plantation Societies, Race Relations, and the South: The Regimentation of Populations* (Durham: Duke Univ. Press, 1975), 101–108.

slave populations. They were more formal and efficiently controlled, and there was less contact between the blacks and whites. Acculturation was less complete and these slave populations remained decidedly different from the slave populations in other parts of the South where plantations were smaller. These sociological differences are apparent in the ethos of rice plantation slaves, who retained their African cultural elements more completely than did slaves in other plantation settings in the Old South.

In evaluating all the cultural elements of coastal Georgia and the creolization process that has gone on since blacks and whites first populated the area, it is correct to say that whites have taken from blacks and blacks have taken from whites. They have created a cultural blending of the African and Anglo-American to form a distinct low country society in which the contributions and traditions of both may be seen. African cultural elements were more likely to survive where Negroes were in the majority and were isolated from the mainstream of Euro-American civilization, as they were on the coast and Sea Islands of Georgia and South Carolina. The isolation and size of the rice plantation provided greater room for black cultural development—greater opportunity for blacks to build upon their African heritage and to express their evolving Afro-American sensibility in work songs, folk tales, moral and religious beliefs and rites, mannerisms, words, culinary skills, and the arts. These cultural manifestations, developed even in slavery, remain evident today among their descendants along the Georgia coast.

CHAPTER TEN

Slave Resistance, Free Negroes, and Racial Attitudes in Coastal Georgia

Georgia modeled its slave laws on those of South Carolina. The Georgia slave code of 1755, entitled "An Act for the Better Ordering and Governing of Negroes and Other Slaves in this Province," with slight revision in 1770, remained in effect until after the American Revolution and served as a basis for the codes adopted during the nineteenth century. The colonial laws were designed to protect whites against all possibility that slaves would rise in rebellion to destroy them and their properties, and to insure servility and illiteracy among slaves.

The code defined a slave as "chattel personal," with status inherited from the condition of the mother. Fear of insurrection prompted the regulation that prohibited more than seven slaves to assemble or travel together off the plantation unless accompanied by a white. A slave rebellion in South Carolina in 1738 spread to Georgia when some of the insurgents crossed the Savannah River, murdering several whites and destroying their property. The Stono Rebellion in South Carolina the following year, in which twenty whites were murdered, made Georgians ever more fearful. There had to be insurance against such overt resistance.[1]

To prevent secret meetings that might result in plots of insurrection, slaves were not allowed to gather together in groups on the plantation, or to carry "wooden swords and other mischievous

1. *Colonial Records*, 9:232–36, 283–84; Wood, *Black Majority*, 308–326. See also John Hope Franklin, "Slavery and the Martial Law," *Journal of Negro History*

and dangerous weapons," or to have in their possession "drums, horns or other loud instruments which may call together or give sign or notice to one another of their wicked designs and purposes." Resisting interrogation by a white was a capital offense. The death penalty was also imposed on slaves convicted of arson, inciting insurrection, or willfully injuring or killing a white. Slaves, as personal property, had no status under the law and could not testify. They were entitled to a trial by a jury of two justices and not less than three freeholders. When the slave was declared guilty of a capital offense and condemned to die, the provincial treasury paid the owner his appraised value, not to exceed £50. This regulation was designed to discourage owners from concealing crimes of their slaves.[2]

It was unlawful for slaves to have firearms, except with permission of the owner, to kill game and animals from the woods on the plantation. Runaway slaves, when caught, were kept in jail under custody of the provost marshall until they were claimed by the owner; if they were not claimed within a certain period of time, they were sold at public auction. Slaves were not allowed to buy or sell merchandise or liquors without the owner's consent; the punishment for this offense was twenty lashes. Slaves were, however, allowed to sell and barter in the city when given a license by the owner, who classified the quality and quantity of the goods to be bartered.[3]

If the slave was absent from his place of abode without permission (a license, letter, pass, or ticket), he received twenty lashes. If he continued to be incorrigible, he was placed in irons or imprisoned. The colonial code presumably protected him against more harsh forms of punishment such as branding, castration, and mutilation of other body parts; however, advertisements in local newspapers describing runaways often referred to branding and mutilation of part of an ear or toe as a means of identification. If the slave was "beaten, bruised, maimed, or disabled" without cause

---

37 (Jan. 1952): 36–52; and William G. Suttles, Jr., "African Religious Survivals as Factors in American Slave Revolts," *Journal of Negro History* 56 (Apr. 1971): 91–104.

2. *Colonial Records*, 18: 102–103, 131. See A.E. Keir Nash, "Reason of Slavery: Understanding the Judicial Role in the Peculiar Institution," *Vanderbilt Law Review* 32 (Jan. 1979): 8–205. Nash summarizes existing interpretations of the law of slavery and finds them lacking. He then makes a three-state comparison (Georgia, Tennessee and Virginia) of judicial attitudes toward manumission.

3. *Colonial Records*, 18:118, 127–29, 130, 139–40.

by a white, the offender was fined 6 shillings (a small penalty). But the person found guilty of stealing slaves or killing a slave "in a sudden heat of passion" was fined £50. The owner was fined £3 if he neglected to provide adequate food and clothing for his slaves. The person who taught a slave to read and write was fined £15.[4] This provision of the law was not always enforced by whites.

The same restrictions under the law applied to free Negroes. The free Negro had to have a guardian, a white person who vouched for his status. If found guilty of harboring a runaway slave, he was fined 30 shillings for the first day and 3 shillings for each day thereafter that the runaway was harbored. If the free Negro could not pay the fine, he was sold as a slave at public auction. He could not testify in court, though he was entitled to the same trial as the slave. Regardless of the controls placed upon blacks, whether slave or free, they did engage in trade when licensed by the owner or guardian and were hired out or hired out their own time. Some were vendors buying and selling produce for the owner, and others were employed as porters, draymen, drivers of public carriages, and the like. In the case of Ishmael, who was licensed and employed during the day, at night he was "often seen playing the fiddle at tippling houses" on his own time.[5]

The slave code also provided for a patrol system that confined plantation slaves and restricted city slaves to a curfew regulation to get them off the streets before dark unless licensed, like firemen and night watchmen, for special employment. All white males between the ages of sixteen and sixty were subject to patrol duty from time to time. When patrolling an area, the white had to intercept any slave who was away from the plantation and make him show his pass. If the slave had no pass, he was dubbed a runaway, returned to the plantation, and given the usual whipping. The patrolman had to regularly visit each plantation within his district to search Negro houses for firearms and other weapons. In slave narratives, patrolmen are referred to as "patty-rollers," "patter-roses," or "paddle-rollers"; they often terrified slaves by "Negro hunting, Negro catching, Negro watching, and Negro whipping." Patrolling an area provided great sport for many youthful whites.[6]

4. Ibid., 106, 132–33, 136; *Georgia Gazette*, 1763–75, 1780–85.
5. *Colonial Records*, 18:137–38.
6. Ibid., 225–35; Slave Narratives; John B. Cade, "Out of the Mouths of Ex-

Slaves resisted and protested in many ways, most frequently by running away. Runaway slave notices, which usually described the fugitive, did not sterotype or stylize slave personality, as some studies have since done. Rather, they often portrayed slaves as aggressive and individualistic, with a wide variety in patterns of behavior. The problem of runaways plagued owners throughout the colonial era. The Spanish on the southern border continued until 1763 to entice slaves to escape to freedom. To thwart their escapes, the provincial government offered rewards for their capture: for an adult male slave, £12; for an adolescent, £5; for every scalp of a grown slave, £1.[7]

Advertisements for fugitive slaves inadvertently told of the slaves' capabilities, courage, intelligence, perceptiveness, and resourcefulness. More than three hundred such notices appeared in the *Georgia Gazette* for the period 1763 to 1776. The following are but a few phrases culled from the ads: "An artful plausible fellow who may pass for free; a tall slim likely young negro; a stout able negro man, speaks very good French and broken English; very artful and may probably endeavor to pass for a freeman; a fiddler who used to play the violin at the Assembly, is a very artful fellow, had large iron on each leg and remarkable scar on one knee occasioned by being shot; a short black Ebo Negro fellow named Nero, very artful and cunning with some of his country marks on his face; a Negro boy about 15 years of age, is sensible and speaks good English."[8]

Fugitive slaves were usually young, in their twenties and thirties, and spoke no English, having been purchased from slave traders who brought them directly from Africa. They came from Angola, Congo, Gambia, Guinea, and Dahomey. Descriptions given by owners who offered rewards for their return often referred to their African names along with their new names, also their cultural or "country" marks and any other peculiarities like filed teeth that might be helpful in identifying or locating them. Many were described as having a "yellowish cast" and as having had

---

Slaves," *Journal of Negro History* 20 (July 1935): 322–23.

7. *Colonial Records*, 18:137–38. The Altamaha River was the southern boundary of Georgia until 1763. For the resistance of slaves in South America and the Carribean, see Leonard E. Barrett, *Soul-Force: African Heritage in Afro-American Religion* (Garden City: Anchor Press, 1974), 57–93.

8. July 21, 1763; Sept. 3, 1766; Feb. 4, Dec. 23, 1767; Feb. 27, 1768; Jan. 25, 1769; May 23, 1770; Sept. 28, 1774.

smallpox. Often they had lost part of a finger, toe, or ear or had been branded with the initials of the owner: Ned, "a very well made fellow with his country marks on his face," was branded on the shoulder and had "lost part of one of his ears;" Perth "a short fellow with sharp teeth, [was] much marked in the body with his country marks and of a yellowish complexion"; Quamina, "very black, from Guinea," had the mark of his African origin on his face; Sameo, who could read and write, was good-looking, a good dancer, six feet tall, spoke very good English, and had "one of his toes lately cut next to his little toe." The owner, Philip Dell, offered five pistols for Sameo's return, a rather unusual reward.[9]

Free Negroes aided runaway slaves. A reward was offered for Primus "who may have been taken up by some of the black settlers who . . . frequently conceal runaway Negroes and work them in their own fields or change them in some of the Northern colonies for horses." The slave Sally and her two mulatto children, after having been sold at public auction to satisfy debts of the deceased owner, ran away from the new owner, who suspected that she and her children were being "concealed from him" and offered a reward of £5 for their return.[10] To help others identify the fugitive slave, one owner described the slave's clothing when offering a reward for his return. "Ranaway from Augusta, a negro fellow named Bain, about five feet high, well made, has a bold look, speaks good English, about 30 years of age. Had on a white negro cloth jacket, a blue cap, a spotted blue and white handkerchief about his head, a pair of white boots tied with Indian garters, shoes and buckles, and carried away a gun."[11]

The number of fugitives who escaped permanently or who were caught and returned to owners is not known. Some did escape to Florida, where isolated Negro villages within Seminole country were later reported: "The Negroes dwell in towns apart from the Indians and are the finest looking people I have ever seen. They dress and look pretty much like the Indians, each having a gun,

9. Ibid., May 30, 1765; July 2, 1766; Mar. 22, 1769; Feb. 1, May 24, 1775. During these years, white servants also ran away to escape the period of their indenture. Descriptions giving their ages, the clothing they were wearing and the articles they had stolen when they left indicate that they were motivated, like blacks, to be free, and to escape from the labor routine. They were from England, Holland, Ireland, and Scotland.

10. *Georgia Gazette,* June 21, 1763; June 28, 1764.

11. Ibid., June 28, 1764.

and hunting a portion of his time." Other slaves escaped to live with the Creek Indians or formed maroon societies, existing by hunting, fishing, stealing, and terrorizing white settlements.[12]

Maroon camps composed of fugitive slaves were located in Georgia, the Carolinas, Virginia, Louisiana, Florida, Mississippi, and Alabama. In Georgia, swampy areas along the Savannah River appear to have been favorite haunts for these black Robin Hoods. Governor James Habersham reported in 1771 that "a great number of fugitive Negroes had committed many robberies and insults" between Savannah and Ebenezer and that their numbers "might be expected to increase daily." A detachment of the Georgia militia was employed to destroy them and their camp.[13]

In 1772 maroons were again plundering, pillaging, and setting fire to property in Chatham County. A group of 300 Negroes who fought with the British during their occupation of Savannah chose to remain in Georgia when the British withdrew. Calling themselves the "King of England's" soldiers, they lived in a secluded encampment from which they performed raids and ravaged settlements, killing whites along both sides of the Savannah River. They were not subdued until 1786, when Georgia militiamen broke up their camp and killed many of their group.[14]

During the Revolutionary War slaves worked for the British as spies, guides, and informers. In the capture of Savannah, the aged

12. William Simmons, *Notices of East Florida* (Charleston, S.C., 1822; rpt. Gainesville: Univ. of Florida Press, 1973), 76; *Colonial Records*, 19:185, 501, 502. See Wright, "Blacks in British East Florida," for a good account of the blacks who lived in East Florida, not to be confused with those who lived among the Seminoles farther south.

13. Richard Price, ed., *Maroon Societies: Rebel Slave Communities in the Americas* (New York: Anchor Press, 1973), 152–53. At least fifty Negro maroon communities existed in the southern United States between 1672 and 1864; a few were not migratory, but built houses for themselves and their families, engaged in agriculture, and lived settled lives. *Colonial Records*, 12:146–47, 325–26. See Herbert Aptheker's two pioneering articles on maroons: "Notes on Slave Conspiracies in Confederate Mississippi," *Journal of Negro History* 29 (Jan. 1944): 75–79, and "Additional Data on American Maroons," ibid. 32 (Oct. 1947): 452–60. See also Aptheker, *Documentary History of the Negro People in the United States: From Colonial Times to the Founding of the NAACP in 1910* (New York: Citadel Press, 1969), for documentary sources on slave resistance.

14. Stevens, *History of Georgia*, 2:317, 376–78. It was natural that slaves who served with the Americans in the Revolutionary War should consider freedom as the reward for participation. During the siege of Savannah, those slaves who performed valuable service working in entrenchments in and around the city for the Americans were given arms. When the siege ended, they "grew bold and presumptious, and it was found no easy matter to check their insolence and reduce them to their proper obedience and position."

slave guide Quamino Dolley, contributing to the overwhelming defeat of the Americans, led British troops through swamp lands to stage a surprise attack upon the rear of the American position. Because of the help of slave guides, a British detachment at Beaufort, South Carolina under command of Colonel John Maitland reached Savannah undetected by the French, to reinforce General Prevost's position.

Blacks also performed valuable service for the British in Georgia as couriers. During the siege of Charleston the slaves Bristol and Harry frequently traveled from Savannah to Charleston and back, accompanying a British messenger carrying dispatches. They also aided the British by harassing Americans. Parties of slaves foraged, stealing livestock and food from plantations, and destroying crops and buildings.[15] The British withdrew from Savannah during the summer of 1782. Between July and December they evacuated 7,210 Negroes from Georgia; from Charleston, they evacuated 5,327.[16]

After the American Revolution the colonial laws to restrict slaves were reinforced and enlarged. Fear of the impact of the insurrectionary movement in Santo Domingo prompted the Georgia legislature in 1798 to pass a law against the importation of slaves from abroad or from any other state within the Union.[17] Before this law became effective slaves were imported in large numbers from Africa and from South Carolina to ease the labor shortage created by the disappearance, during the war, of thousands of slaves.

Slaves continued to resist bondage by running away. During

15. "Letters from Governor John Houstoun, Feb. 3, Aug. 20, 1778," Records of the Continental and Confederation Congresses, 1774–89, MSS, National Archives.

16. Quarles, *Negro in the American Revolution*, 144–45, 163, 167, 172. The following year (1783), with the Peace of Paris that recognized American independence, the British formally withdrew from New York City and 3,000 Negroes left with them. Most were taken to Jamaica and Canada. The total number of slaves who escaped during the American Revolution is not known. In 1781 the brilliant and popular General Nathanael Greene, now in command of the Continental Army in the South, proposed that Negroes from Georgia and South Carolina be enlisted to reinforce his army. Greene asked for four black regiments and a "corps of pioneers"; those making up the regiments would immediately be given their freedom and owners would be paid $1,000 for each enlisted slave; this proposal was not acceptable to Georgians and Carolinians, who were fearful of blacks' being armed. See "Letter to Governor John Rutledge, South Carolina, Dec. 9, 1781, MS, file 329, National Archives. As late as 1782 Timothy Pickering recommended that a company of Negro "Pioneers" be formed for the Continental Army in the South. See Records of the Continental and Confederate Congresses.

17. O.H. Prince, *Digest of the Laws of Georgia enacted Previous to 1837* (Athens, Ga., 1837), 559.

the years 1780 to 1798 the *Georgia Gazette* printed 446 notices that offered rewards for the capture of runaways. During these years slaves often escaped in groups, and the total number of fugitives rose to well above 800. Descriptions of these runaways show that prior to 1798 owners continued to brand slaves, to shackle them with irons, to mutilate them by cutting off part of a finger, toe, or ear, or by subjecting them to whippings that left permanent scars. As an example, Paris, who had lost a toe, and Anthony escaped from Charleston, changed their names, and hired themselves out in Savannah as free Negroes; Edinburgh, from Guinea, whose African name was Sula, was branded on the breast with the initials W.M.G.; George "a very tall straight limbed fellow," and Jack, "very black, with 14 lb. of iron on one of his legs," escaped from Samuel Stiles; a fugitive recently arrived from Angola had "a great many dog bites about his legs and thighs"; his native African marks were on his face above both eyes and on his left breast.[18]

Aaron, a slave about sixteen years old, had "lost all of the toes on one of his feet"; Quamina, about eighteen, was "marked by whipping on his back and thighs"; Harry, a skilled carpenter and an "artful fellow," was branded on one breast and had scars on his back and buttocks from whippings; Will, who spoke "good English," was "Virginia born and branded on the posteriors S S"; Aleck was branded on the right side with the initials S.B. A reward of £10 was offered for Will, a cooper who was "remarkable for being covered from his waist downwards with the marks of a severe correction given him in the West Indies for an attempt to murder."[19]

Most revealing is the evidence that in the nineteenth century a good number of fugitive slaves in coastal Georgia could read and write. A $10 reward was offered for Charles "of a yellow complexion and a very sensible young fellow" who wrote his own pass to escape to New York. A $50 reward was offered for George, a skilled carpenter, cabinet maker, boat and shoe maker, who "read pretty well" and had on his person $180 and a watch. Edward, the

18. *Georgia Gazette*, Feb. 26, Mar. 1, June 24, 1781; Sept. 25, 1784; July 24, 1786.

19. Ibid., Jan. 4, Oct. 11, Nov. 8, 1787; Aug. 25, 28, Oct. 3, 1788; Oct. 4, 1792; *Columbian Museum and Savannah Advertiser*, July 15, 1808. See Blassingame, *Slave Community*, 104–131, for the frequency of runaway notices in evaluating slave resistance. There is overwhelming evidence in newspaper advertisements referred to above of the slaves resistance to bondage and of their desire to be free.

slave son of two free Negroes, Rosa and Jack Simpson, who were literate, escaped from his owner by using a pass forged by his parents. A reward of $75 was offered for Tutt, the owner's carriage driver, who had written his own papers and was passing as a free person while working in Savannah. Abraham, who could read and write, had forged his pass and hired himself out. Peter, who escaped from a plantation in Bryan County, could read and write. Joe, a "very intelligent" slave, could read and write, and was known "to write his own pass." A $50 reward was offered for Ned, a carpenter by trade, who could read and write well, and had expressed a desire "to make his way North."[20]

Slaves resisted their bondage in other ways. They set fire to the owner's property, sometimes with intent to kill him and his family; they habitually stole from the owner, slowed down in their work, broke tools, injured mules, and resorted to pretense while feigning ignorance to outsmart the owner or overseer. Slaves on a plantation adjoining Georgia Bryan Conrad's destroyed a barn and other outbuildings by setting them on fire; this rebellious display caused them to be sold to a slave trader.[21] On Christmas Day in 1858 slaves set fire to Hugh Fraser Grant's barns and storage houses: "All my Barns, Machinery, Saw Mill etc. and 7000 Bushels Rice destroyed by fire occasioned by carelessness. My House also took fire from the half burned shingles. Commenced immediately to erect New Barns and contracted with Messr. Lachlison for entire new Machinery at $4000."[22]

On the Thomas plantation slaves periodically absconded, living in the woods in makeshift camps while stealing food and livestock from surrounding plantations: "The young negro men, getting tired of cultivating the fields, would at times *run away;* that is, they would leave their cabins and seek shelter in the neighboring woods or some isolated 'hammock,' which so abundantly are found about plantations on the seaboard." They "were always slyly abetted by those of their family at home." At another time, ten field hands on this plantation absconded "when the hot weather was the greatest and the grass began to race with the crops for existence." This display of rebelliousness caused the owner to lose part of his cotton crop. After two months of depredations in the neighborhood caused by these outlaws, the owner

20. *Daily Georgian*, Aug. 12, 1837; Oct. 29, Dec. 23, 1847; Jan. 15, 1849; *Daily Morning News*, May 31, 1852; Feb. 12, 1855; Feb. 22, 1858.

21. *Reminiscences*, 12.

22. House, ed., *Planter Management*, 127.

employed a man from Savannah with "trail hounds" to catch them; house servants kept these fugitives informed and they managed to elude the hounds. They did not return until December, at which time Thomas hired them out to a railroad company.[23]

Plantation law, and not state law, governed acts of insubordination. Whipping was the common form of punishment, though more harsh forms like branding, confinement in stocks, the use of leg irons, and sale were implemented when slaves refused to conform. The slave laws of Georgia became more restrictive during the nineteenth century.

A law of 1801 restricted manumission: owners could no longer free their slaves of their own volition. The slave could be declared free only be a special act of the legislature. This law was amended in 1815 to recognize manumission only when the owner stipulated in his will that the slave be freed and provided sufficient funds to have the slave removed to a free state. The slave who accumulated money to purchase his freedom had to have legislative approval to acquire his free status. The penal code of 1833 summarized the laws on slaves and free Negroes.[24] These laws reaffirmed the status of the slave and contained all of the earlier controls thought necessary to maintain a labor force and to insure against any possibility of Negro insurrections.

Although slaves resisted their bondage directly, most frequently by running away, they also resisted in more subtle ways like destroying property, stealing, slowing down on the job, hiding out as maroons, feigning illness, and creating their own *volksunde* to preserve their traditional customs, beliefs, dances, songs, and tales, often impregnating them with undetected allegory to express their hidden feelings of resentment and rebelliousness. As a former South Carolina slave explained, "De Buckruh hab scheme, en de nigger hab trick en ebery time de buckruh scheme once, de nigger trick twice."[25]

Slave rebellion along the Georgia coast occurred more frequently during the colonial era and immediately after the American Revolution than during the nineteenth century, especially

23. Thomas, *Memoirs of a Southerner*, 17–20.

24. Prince, *Digest of the Laws*, 456–57, 466, 795; T.R.R. Cobb, *Digest of the Statute Law in Force Prior to 1851* (Atlanta, 1851), 982; Slave Owner Affidavits, 1818–47; the owner who brought slaves into the state had to certify that they would be used only for labor on his lands. They were not to be sold, hired out, or transferred in any other way. The law against bringing slaves into Georgia was not enforced.

25. Heyward, *Seed From Madagascar*, 165.

after the Denmark Vesey slave conspiracy in South Carolina in 1822. As slave society matured along the Georgia coast, it introduced a more positive and sophisticated system of control. Religion was stressed and facilities for religious worship were provided; work routine became more efficient and humane; and maintenance and health care were improved. Owners, now more sensitive to the needs of their slaves, heeded recommendations made in contemporary journals for improved slave care. The rice planters improved their slaves' standard of living, which, by contemporary standards, seemed adequate and which compared favorably to that of laboring classes throughout the world. In consequence—and in the light of the ruthless suppression of the Vesey conspiracy—the slaves accommodated over the years, and their overt rebelliousness decreased.[26]

The diversity in individual owner attitudes, caused by variations in social and economic environments in rural and urban settings, was not reflected in civil laws and judicial interpretations concerning Negroes and their status as slaves or freemen. Generally, slave laws were relatively harsh in all of the North American provinces during the colonial era; became more liberal immediately after the American Revolutionary War; and then, as a result of changing economic trends after 1800, became less liberal, as the legal condition of the Negro deteriorated progressively.

Since the legal structure in Georgia, like that of the older plantation colonies to the north, was composed largely of English elements, Anglo-American laws and customs were imposed. In Alabama, Mississippi, Louisiana, and to a smaller degree, in Florida, where French-Spanish legal and religious elements were inherited, Anglo-American laws and customs were superimposed. The Gulf Coast states displayed, until the 1840s, a more liberal legal attitude toward Negroes than did Georgia and the older slave states.

In Georgia, for example, the law of 1801 forbade manumission except by legislative approval and aimed to discourage any increase in the free black population; this law was enacted in response to the movement of free mulattoes who migrated from Santo Domingo after the slave revolt of 1792 to settle in Savannah and Charleston. White residents resented these émigrés and ob-

26. See Genovese, "Rebelliousness and Docility in the Negro Slave: A Critique of the Elkins Thesis," *In Red and Black: Marxian Explorations in Southern and Afro-American History* (New York: Pantheon, 1968, rpt. Knoxville: Univ. of Tennessee Press, 1984), 73–101.

jected to their influx. Though the law forbade manumission of slaves by deed or will, in a long series of decisions made by the Georgia Supreme Court between 1818 and 1860, the state recognized extraterritorial manumission when the testator stipulated in his will that funds were provided to have the slave or slaves transported to a free state or territory to be emancipated. Slaves could not become free within the state of Georgia without special provision of the legislature.[27]

Free Negroes, like slaves, suffered from a legal and social order that demanded the perpetuation of their servile status to insure racial control. Free Negroes constituted only a small percentage of the total populations in all of the slave states, except Maryland. By 1810 almost one-quarter of Maryland's Negroes were free, and they numbered nearly 34,000; this was the largest free Negro population of any state in the nation. In Georgia free Negroes were centered at St. Marys, Savannah, and Augusta, where there was opportunity for employment. Regardless of the legal barriers imposed to discourage their population growth within the state, their numbers increased over the years, from 398 in 1790 to 3,500 in 1860, 2,004 of whom were mulattoes. Of the total slave population of 462,198 in 1860, 35,900 were mulattoes.[28]

Free Negroes were subject to Anglo-American legal devices and were not allowed to participate equally with whites in the exercise of civil and political liberties. They could own, inherit, and transmit property by will in Georgia and had certain rights and privileges equal to those of whites in courts of law, though they were denied other important ones. They could not serve on juries or in the militia, and their social privileges were restricted. Nonetheless, when they were allowed to compete with whites in the economy, they succeeded and amassed property.[29]

27. A.S. Clayton, *Compilation of the Laws of Georgia*, 27; De Caradeuc Papers, MSS, GHS; Berlin, *Slaves Without Masters: The Free Negro in the Antebellum South* (New York: Vintage, 1974), 35–36; Prince, *Digest of the Laws*, 455–57; Cobb, *Digest*, 982; Catterall, *Judicial Cases*, 3:12, 14, 19, 28, 38, 46, 61, 75, 98, 102. See Thad W. Tate, *The Negro in Eighteenth-Century Williamsburg* (Charlottesville: Univ. of Virginia Press, 1972), 91–99, for the evolution of the Negro's legal status from ordinary indentured servant to servant for life to slave, with development of the colonial "black codes" upon which Carolina's codes concerning slaves and free blacks were based; see A. Leon Higginbotham, Jr., *In the Matter of Color: Race and the American Legal Process, The Colonial Period* (New York: Oxford Univ. Press, 1978), 216–66.

28. *United States Census Returns*, 1790, 1860. Cohabitation of blacks and whites was one aspect of the creolization process that became apparent in the nineteenth century. See Berlin, *Slaves Without Masters*, 46–49.

29. Free Negroes who owned property in Florida could not legally will it to

Charles Odingsells, a free Negro of Chatham County, possessed considerable property. When he died in 1810, he owned three plantations and seventy-three slaves. To his wife, he left a plantation and sixteen slaves on Skidaway Island "to dispose of as she might think proper." He provided funds to have his faithful "Negro wench Hannah and her children and mother, Old Lucy," liberated, with approval of the state legislature. To Anthony Odingsells, another child of Hannah who was already free, Odingsells left his plantation and slaves on Little Warsaw Island with provision that the child be educated and maintained from the proceeds of the estate, which was to vest in him when he reached maturity. To his daughter, Mary Ann, Odingsells left the remainder of his estate, which included his plantation in Effingham County.[30] It is assumed that Anthony Odingsells was the son of Charles, though this is not confirmed. Anthony retained his property through the years; in 1860 he owned thirteen slaves and 2,000 acres of land on Little Warsaw Island.[31]

Susan Jackson, a free Negro of Savannah, owned slaves and real estate. Jackson developed a profitable pastry business and eventually owned twenty-three brick dwellings in Reynolds Ward; these served as rental units and pastry shops. When she died in 1860 her real estate was valued at $5,000; ten years later, it sold for $15,000.[32] Andrew Marshall, the noted Baptist preacher, owned

---

their heirs. George Kingsley, a free Negro of Haiti and son of Zephaniah Kingsley, a slave trader at Fort George Island near Jacksonville, Fl., owned considerable property in Florida. Kingsley was lost at sea while on a voyage traveling between Haiti and New York in 1846. Although he directed in his will that his property be divided between his wife and children, there was no provision under Florida law for this direction, and the mulatto heirs of Kingsley were denied the right to inherit his property. See a memorial sent to the General Assembly, dated Nov., 1847, as well as the will of George Kingsley, dated Nov. 21, 1846, MSS, Secretary of State's Office, Tallahassee.

30. Will Book E, 157–58, 240–47, Probate Records, Chatham County. The story of Solomon Perteet of Tuscaloosa County, Ala., is similar to that of Charles Odingsells. Over the years Perteet increased his holdings and became a leading figure in a community of free blacks. He was respected by blacks and whites in Tuscaloosa. When he died in 1863, his remains were buried in Tuscaloosa's white cemetery, Greenwood. Free blacks sometimes purchased slaves to help them gain their freedom; Perteet secured freedom for his slave wife and their children. See James B. Sellers, "Free Negroes of Tuscaloosa County Before the Thirteenth Amendment," *Alabama Review* 23 (Apr. 1970): 110–27; Joseph G. Tregle, Jr., "Early New Orleans Society: A Reappraisal," *Journal of Southern History* 18 (Feb. 1952): 20–35.

31. Estate of Anthony Odingsells, 1881, file 0-107, Probate Records, Chatham County. Odingsells died in 1878 at age ninety-four; his land on Warsaw Island was assessed at $2,000.

32. Will of Susan Jackson, file J-125, Chatham County: *Tax Digest for Chatham*

and operated a profitable drayage business; he employed free Negroes and Negro slaves, though he owned only one for a brief period. In 1824 Marshall's real estate was valued at $8,400; this value exceeded real estate values of many prosperous whites.[33]

Among the free Negroes who migrated to Savannah from Santo Domingo were Louis Mirault, Andrew Morel, and Joseph Dubergier. They were skilled tailors who catered to prominent Savannahians and gained some success in the business world. Mirault owned six slaves and real estate valued at $1,000 when he died in 1828; Morel owned two slaves and real estate valued at $1,600 when he died in 1850; Dubergier owned several slaves, though no real estate. Other free Negroes owned slaves: Prince Candy, a cooper, owned seven, and John Gibbon, a carpenter, owned five; both owned real estate.[34]

Julien Fromotin, born in Santo Domingo, migrated from Charleston to Savannah in 1818 and opened a school for Negro children. In 1829 a state law banned the teaching of reading and writing to Negroes; nonetheless, Formotin continued to keep his school open until the mid-1840s, though as an underground operation.[35] Similarly, James Porter, a free Negro from Charleston, opened a school of music for Negroes in Savannah in the 1850s; he offered courses in violin, piano, and voice, while secretively teaching them to read and write.[36] Mary Woodhouse, another free Negro, maintained a school for Negro children in Savannah. Susie King Taylor, who attended this school, described it:

County, 1847, 1855, and *Tax Digest for City of Savannah*, 1860, GHS.

33. *Tax Digest for City of Savannah*, 1824, 1827.

34. Ibid., 1824, 1827, 1837, 1848; Whittington B. Johnson, "Free Blacks in Antebellum Savannah: An Economic Profile," *Georgia Historical Quarterly* 64 (Winter 1980): 418–29.

35. Johnson, "Free Blacks in Antebellum Savannah," 425; Register of Free Persons of Color for the County of Chatham, 1826–35, 1828–47, 1837, 1849, 1863–64, 4 vols.; Register of Free Persons of Color, City of Savannah, 1817–29, 1860–73, 2 vols., GHS. Julien Fromotin appears only once in the City Register, 1817–29. He is listed as a carpenter; his age and place of nativity are not given. He is not listed in the Chatham County Registers. See Berlin, *Slaves Without Masters*, 305, where Julian Troumontaine, "a free Negro instructor of the Savannah African School, took his academy into hiding and continued to teach free negro children until he was caught fifteen years later." There is no Julian Troumontaine listed on the Chatham County register. Berlin's reference, no doubt, refers to Fromontin. See Joseph Frederick Waring, *Cerveau's Savannah* (Savannah: GHS, 1973), 67, for reference to Julien Fromontin, a "Santo Domingan freeman of color" who taught Negro children in Savannah with no interference until 1829.

36. Johnson, "Free Blacks in Antebellum Savannah," 425.

> My brother and I . . . were sent to a friend of my grandmother, Mrs. Woodhouse, a widow, to learn to read and write. She was a free woman and lived on Bay Lane . . . about half a mile from my house. We went every day about nine o'colock, with our books wrapped in paper to prevent the police or white persons from seeing them. We went in, one at a time, through the gate, into the L kitchen, which was the schoolroom. She had twenty-five or thirty children whom she taught, assisted by her daughter, Mary Jane. The neighbors would see us going in sometimes, but they supposed we were there learning trades, as it was the custom to give [slave] children a trade of some kind. After school we left the same way we entered, one by one, when we would go to a square, about a block from the school, and wait for each other.[37]

Matilda Beasley, a remarkable free Negro who lived in Savannah, also secretly maintained a school for black children, where she taught them to read and write. After the war she studied under the Franciscan nuns who came to Savannah during Reconstruction. She inherited considerable property from her husband, Abraham Beasley, and gave it to the Catholic church. The church sent her to England for her novitiate. Upon her return to Savannah, she spent the rest of her life working among her people; she died in 1903, greatly respected by the community. Mother Beasley, the first Negro nun in Georgia, established an orphanage for Negro children in Savannah.[38]

State laws and city ordinances concerning free Negroes in Georgia were designed to restrict job options and business choices, though mainly to discourage the presence of free Negroes within the state. The laws appear to have been loosely enforced in coastal Georgia, for free Negroes in Savannah and Chatham County succeeded in obtaining a measure of economic independence. They competed with whites in the work force, though they did not dominate any occupation. They worked as skilled laborers, barbers, draymen, seamstresses, tailors, and pastry cooks, and females were as prevalent as males. Apparently they encountered no real difficulties earning a living and shared

37. *Reminiscences of My Life in Camp With the 33rd United States Colored Troops Late South Carolina Volunteers* (Boston: published by the author, 1902; rpt. New York: Arno Press, 1968), 3, 5.

38. Interview with Veronica Arnold, a descendant of Mother Beasley. Mrs. Arnold told the writer that Abraham Beasley was a free mulatto who assisted a trader in selling slaves prior to the Civil War. During Reconstruction he owned fine race horses and a large amount of real estate. Taylor in *Reminiscences of My Life in Camp*, 54, mentioned a free Negro, Mrs. Mary Beasley, whose school she attended in Savannah in 1859 and 1860. It is not possible to determine that Mary was Matilda. Matilda's school was illegal and no records were kept.

Figure 34. Matilda Beasley, the First Black in Georgia to Become a Catholic Nun. (Georgia Historical Society Collection.)

in the prosperity of the 1820s and 1830s, purchasing homes and slaves. There were sixty-four free Negro homeowners in 1823, though the number increased only by one during the next twenty-five years; some lost their property during the depression of the 1840s but others became homeowners, and so the number remained approximately the same. The number of free Negro slaveholders declined between 1823 and 1855, from seventy to ten.[39]

The status of the free Negroes deteriorated after 1840. Their movements were restricted; they could live only in certain sections of cities and could engage only in occupations approved by whites. The presence of free blacks was thought to have a demoralizing effect upon slaves, as they were more knowledgeable and might pass information to plantation slaves and incite them to rebel. They were unwanted in Georgia and in all of the slave states. Southerners came to believe that the only successful means of removing the threat of free Negroes was to expel them from the southern states or change their status from freedom to slavery. Political action to remove the free Negro never matured, though restrictions became more severe during the decade preceding the Civil War.[40]

Racial amalgamation of the Anglo-American and Negro slave created a variety of social situations and emotional attitudes. White fathers, who felt a human attachment for their slave children, found ways to protect these offspring. The will of Daniel Ross, dated 1770, for example, provided that Sally, the mulatto daughter of his slave Phillis, be made free, that she be taught to read and write, and that she be "brought up in a decent and

39. *Tax Digest*, 1823, 1837, 1847, 1855. The number of free Negro homeowners in Savannah exceeded the number in Petersburg and Richmond, Va., though those cities each had twice the number of free Negro populations. See Johnson, "Free Blacks in Antebellum Savannah," 426. See Richard C. Wade, *Slavery in the Cities: The South, 1820–1860* (New York: Oxford Univ. Press, 1964).

40. L.Q.C. Lamar, *Compilation of the Laws of the State of Georgia* (Augusta: T.S. Hannon, 1821), 815, 820. See R.H. Clark, T.R.R. Cobb, and D. Irvin, *Code of Georgia* (Atlanta, 1861). In the historic section of Savannah there are a few houses still standing that were built for "free persons of color." One, which belonged to John Barlow, has recently been purchased for restoration. Today, black citizens in Savannah are tied historically with their past as they participate in the restoration movement to make known their contributions and past history in the area. See *Savannah Morning News*, Aug. 29, 1976, for mention of various historic houses that belonged to free Negroes prior to 1860. See Smith, *Slavery in Antebellum Florida*, 111–16, for restrictions against free Negroes in Florida.

industrious manner." Samuel Savory, whose will was dated 1771, granted freedom to his mulatto child, George Reeves Savory, and John Forbes, whose will was dated 1775, provided that Babet's mulatto daughter Dina "be given her freedom; also that 160 pounds sterling be held in trust for her by executors." Forbes also directed that "200 pounds sterling be given to Janet, a free negro girl residing at his house."[41]

A perusal of contemporary records, especially wills in which the individual provided for his mulatto offspring, verifies the frequency of cohabitation. Poulain Du Bignon of Jekyl Island directed that his "mulatto woman named Marie Therese and her Daughter Marguerette be made as free as the laws of the country" would allow and provided funds for "them to leave the state if necessary for their comfort." Du Bignon also left a legacy of $80 to be paid them annually, and a female slave for their use. He left the bulk of his estate to his "beloved wife, Marguerite Lesseur Du Bignon." The Du Bignon family were French émigrés and manifested a continental view with regard to miscegenation. The illegitimate mulatto children of Du Bignon's son, Henry, were baptized by the Roman Catholic priest and given free status by the church, though legally they were slaves.[42] Isham Spalding left his estate to his wife and daughter with provision that, should his daughter die without issue, her share of his estate vest in his two "natural children," Sally and Frank.[43]

Thomas Stafford, a wealthy cotton planter of Cumberland Island, sired four offspring by his slave mistress. Stafford, like other white fathers who felt affection and responsibility for their mulatto children, found ways to protect them from the stigma that attached to them as long as they were living in a slave state. He removed these children, Armand, Charles, Mary, and Medora, to New London, Connecticut, where they were maintained and provided with excellent educations and other cultural advantages. Stafford died in 1867 and left an extensive estate to his mulatto children and their descendants.[44] Another example of cohabita-

41. Bonds, Bills of Sale, Deeds of Gift, Powers of Attorney 1765–72, pp. 142–43, 523–24, Department of Archives and History, Atlanta; and Colonial Wills of Georgia, Book AA, pp. 148–49, Department of Archives and History, Atlanta.

42. Book D, Wills and Appraisements, 153–55, Probate Records, Glynn County; Cathedral of St. John the Baptist, MSS, Savannah; interview made by the writer with William Du Bignon, a mulatto grandson of Henry Du Bignon, Brunswick, Jan. 1975. This descendant died early in 1976 at the age of one hundred.

43. Wills Book A, 314, Probate Records, Chatham County.

44. Will Book C, 77–79, Probate Records, Camden County; interview with

Figure 35. Lavinia Tompkins. (Photograph in possession of the author.)

Figure 36. Her Descendants, the Harris Family of Camden County. (Photograph in possession of the author.)

tion involved Lavinia, the female slave of Lawrence Tompkins, for whom she bore a child, Matilda, in 1857. After the Civil War, Matilda Tompkins became supervisor of the Negro schools in Camden County.[45]

Owners, out of appreciation for faithful service or genuine devotion, freed certain slaves, left legacies for others, and directed that still others be sold at public auction. Joseph Bryan provided that his slave Peter be manumitted "in consideration of the many faithful service performed."[46] Isabella Mackay of Sapelo Island directed that her "negro woman, Justiana, on account of her fidelity," be given "four pounds sterling . . . per annum to be paid into her hands quarterly during her life."[47] The will of John Morel, dated 1802, made provision for his twelve-year-old mulatto slave Diana. Morel directed that she be emancipated and given $250, and that his wife care for Diana until she reached maturity. Josiah Tattnall freed his slave Bess, who had been a faithful nurse to all his children: "I leave her entire freedom and manumission from the time of my death, and it is my particular request that my executors do take the necessary steps under the law to place the said faithful negro woman, Bess, at her full liberty, free and unfettered by slavery, by which merit will receive its deserved reward."[48]

Mary Bullard, Cumberland Island, Oct. 1975. Stafford's children never knew their mother nor that she was Stafford's slave mistress. Stafford's wealth included investments in Connecticut, Massachusetts, New York, and Rhode Island. Many of Stafford's former slaves lived on Cumberland Island until fairly recently. Cumpsi, a former slave, nursed him while he was ill and dying. Stafford is buried in one of the old cemeteries on the island.

45. Matilda Tompkins married George Wright Harris, a white man, and had nine children by him, six of whom became educators. One of these children, Ola Harris, served in World War I and was cited for heroism and outstanding service. His widow resides in St. Marys; she has recently retired from the county school system. The descendants of Matilda Tompkins Harris are an accomplished and distinguished family. Several interviews were made with Mrs. Ola Harris during the summer of 1975. Mrs. Harris was born in Virginia. Her grandmother was white and her grandfather was a slave. See James Hugo Johnston, *Race Relations in Virginia and Miscegenation in the South, 1776–1860* (Amherst: Univ. of Massachusetts Press, 1970), for a source on racial attitudes. Johnston presents the complexities involved in race relations resulting from cohabitation. Sexual relations did not uniformly involve white men and black women, and genuine affection was often felt by both parties. Lifetime attachments, though, were never so frequent as was the practice of white males forcing helpless female slaves to have intercourse.

46. Will Book B, 131–34, Chatham County.

47. Will of Isabella MacKay, MS in possession of Bessie Lewis, Pine Harbor, McIntosh County.

48. Fols. 31, 107, Probate Records, Chatham County. These two wills are also recorded in Will Book D.

Raymond Demere, in appreciation for the loyalty displayed by two of his slaves, Joy and his wife, Rose, when they "buried and saved a large sum of specie with which they might have absconded and obtained their freedom," directed that they and their children be manumitted. These two slaves demonstrated their loyalty during the War of 1812, when British forces occupied St. Simons Island and many of Demere's slaves escaped to their lines. Joy, Rose, and their children were granted freedom by the Georgia legislature in 1830. Demere provided an annual income for their support, left them land and cattle, and directed that the eldest child, John, "be taught reading, writing, and arithmetic and be brought up and taught some mechanical profession."[49]

Though restrictions were placed upon manumission to discourage the increase of free Negroes within the state, the Georgia Supreme Court was rather liberal when extraterritorial emancipation was provided. But it denied the wishes of the testator when he unthinkingly allowed the wording of his will to mean domestic emancipation prior to foreign emancipation. In the case of *Drane vs. Beall,* the freedom of Thomas E. Beall's slaves was denied because he directed in his will, dated 1853, that they be freed and remain on his plantation for four years while the income from his estate accrued to defray costs for transporting them to California or Liberia. In a similar case, the will of Thomas Bivens was declared void because Bivens stipulated that his slaves be manumitted and removed to a free state after the death of his wife. Denial in this case hinged upon the interpretation that the moment Bivens's wife died the slaves would be free persons within the state of Georgia. By 1859 all post mortem manumissions of slaves by deed or will were prohibited under Georgia law.[50]

In 1854 the will of George M. Waters was upheld by the court, and thirty-seven of his slaves were delivered in Savannah to the American Colonization Society and sent to Liberia as free persons. Before they departed, each received new clothing and $100 in gold. Unprepared to sustain themselves in Liberia, they suffered great hardship. Thirty died within twelve months, and the remaining seven returned to the United States, first going to

49. Book D, Wills and Appraisements, 158–60, Probate Records, Glynn County; Cate, *Our Todays and Yesterdays,* 181–82.

50. Catterall, *Judicial Cases,* 3:52, 65, 183–84, 279–92. Alabama, Florida, and Mississippi granted manumission only upon removal from the state.

Philadelphia, then back to Georgia after the Civil War.[51] The slaves of Emily Tubman were sent to Liberia and made new and successful lives for themselves. Tubman was a southern philanthropist from Augusta, Georgia, and a supporter of the colonization movement; forty-two of her slaves were transported to freedom under sponsorship of the Maryland State Colonization Society. Tubman employed a missionary from the Protestant Episcopal Church to serve as sponsor in Liberia for these exiles and provided them with funds to maintain themselves while settling in a new land.[52]

Free Negroes, like slaves, had to accommodate and sublimate. By 1860 the total free Negro population in Georgia was 3,500. Most of these free Negroes lived in cities outside of the rice belt—Augusta, Macon, Milledgeville. The total free Negro population in coastal Georgia had decreased to 782—of this total, 725 were residents of Savannah and Chatham County; 54 were residents of Darien in McIntosh County; Bryan County had none; Camden, 1; Glynn 2; Liberty, none. With the exception of the record on Charles and Anthony Odingsells, who lived on Warsaw Island in Chatham County, there are no records of free negroes living in the plantation districts of the rice belt, nor on the Sea Islands. Free Negroes were tolerated in Savannah and apparently in Darien, though McIntosh court records were destroyed by Federal troops during the Civil War. Consequently, it can only be presumed that the free Negro residents in Darien, like those in Savannah, were skilled laborers and tradesmen.[53]

The foregoing discussion has centered upon slave resistance, racial attitudes, and the legal devices imposed by whites to insure effective control of Negroes. As slave society matured in the nineteenth century, slave resistance became less pronounced, for by now a more sophisticated system of control was in use: religion was stressed—slave preachers and facilities for preaching were provided within the slave community; owners were more sensi-

51. Scarborough, *Opposition to Slavery in Georgia,* 165–77; Catterall, *Judicial Cases,* 3:38, 46, 84.

52. James M. Gifford, "Emily Tubman and the African Colonization Movement in Georgia," *Georgia Historical Quarterly* 59 (Spring 1975): 16, 19, 20. In 1943 and again in 1951, the grandson of two of the Tubman slaves who emigrated to Liberia from Georgia was elected president of the Republic of Liberia. He is William Vaccanarat Shadrack Tubman.

53. *United States Census Returns.* See Appendix A, Tables A-5 and A-6, of this study for population growth of whites, Negro slaves, and free Negroes in the rice belt counties and the whole state from 1800 to 1860.

tive to the needs of their bondsmen and provided better health care, food, and maintenance; work demands were more realistic and punishments less severe. Albeit the legal condition of Negroes, slave and free, deteriorated progressively after 1800 as a result of changing economic trends, the lifestyle of slaves gradually improved as owners became more concerned with their welfare. This concern was motivated by a desire "to render them profitable," and it worked to the benefit of both masters and slaves.

While it is generally true that owners were primarily concerned with a profitable return from their investments in slaves, racial attitudes of individual owners were frequently motivated by feelings of affection and appreciation; this was especially true in low country Georgia, where owners' rather liberal disposition toward their bondsmen is expressed in their correspondence, in legacies provided in their wills for favorite slaves, or their desires that certain slaves be freed, have lifetime annuities, or that their offspring be taught to read and write. The slaves of coastal Georgia fared better, in some ways, than their counterparts in other areas of the plantation South.

CONCLUSION

The tidewater experiment in rice planting along the Georgia coast proved to be a productive and profitable enterprise. The introduction of slavery in 1750 and the new administrative policy introduced by crown officials in 1752 sparked an unprecedented economic growth that culminated in the creation of an extensive plantation system based upon capitalistic enterprise similar to the great plantation-slave units of South Carolina and the West Indies. On the eve of the American Revolution these units stretched all along the Georgia coast, where there were lands suitable for growing rice. During the Revolutionary War the rice plantations fell into disrepair. After the war they were slowly rehabilitated and once again became thriving units, to reach a "springtime" in production and prosperity for owners by 1860.

Tidewater rice plantations were unique among the plantations of the Old South—they were limited geographically to suitable areas of swamp land on the Atlantic Coast where fresh water river tides were available for irrigating crops. They were fewer, more isolated, more specialized, and, since their labor-management needs were greater, contained larger slave populations than plantations producing cotton, sugar, or tobacco. The successful production of rice required managerial efficiency and the implementation of an intricate system of irrigation. Owners and slaves contributed to the success of rice culture in Georgia; their talents and expertise emerged in the steady increase in production over the years.

The task system of labor used on rice and Sea Island cotton plantations on the Atlantic Coast was also unique—only on these plantations was the task system a general practice for labor assignments. When the daily task was completed, the slave had free time to fish and hunt, tend a garden plot, engage in some other form of activity, or relax, whereas the slave in other plantation belts throughout the South worked under the gang system from sunrise to sunset and had little time to engage in personal pursuits. The slaves of coastal Georgia were well cared for—their housing, food, and clothing were adequate, as was their medical care, by contemporary standards. Their masters were of that elite class of slaveholders whose esprit de corps determined the treatment of their "people"; this treatment was generally less harsh than slave treatment in other areas of the Old South.

Evidence indicates that tidewater culture was, indeed, separate and distinct from other plantation cultures. The standard of slave life on the Georgia coast was superior to the standard provided on inland plantations. Slave diet, with the accessible supplements that were consumed, was varied, palatable, and nutritious (blacks and whites today consume basically the same foods they did in slavery times). Slave houses were of good construction and contained adequate footage to accommodate, comfortably, a family of five (the average number of slaves per house, as shown on the unpublished census rolls for 1860), and slave families were recognized and family stability was encouraged. Health care was superior to the health care accorded slaves on smaller plantations—substantial hospitals were maintained to provide for and treat ill slaves, and pregnant women were cared for during their confinement and delivery of their offspring. Medical care was administered by a physician whose services were retained by the owner.

The rice planter, though a local absentee much of the time, was concerned with the welfare of his slaves. He made regular visits to the plantation and conferred with his overseer and/or slave foreman (drivers and others in command) to know the condition and needs of his slave community, as well as the progress of his crops. There were mutual feelings of trust and respect between the owner and these middlemen. There was also a close bond between the owner and his house servants. Over and over again, documentary evidence (contemporary wills and correspondence) reveals the favored position of the house servant and the special affection owners felt for this group of slaves. Frequently, house servants were provided for in the owner's will with modest annuities and stipulations that they be cared for while in life, or that funds be provided to send them to a free state to be set free.

Owners expressed genuine appreciation of this select group of slaves for long and faithful service and a desire to perpetuate the slave's favored position. Owners also expressed concern for their mulatto offspring: they were often emotionally involved and felt a moral obligation to protect these children from the stigma of their creole status; the offspring was favored by the owner and, at his death, as a beneficiary of his estate, was provided with funds for extraterritorial manumission, or to learn a trade, or have a stipulated income.

Life for the rice plantation slaves was not static; they enjoyed some mobility. A slave had the use of a gun to shoot wild game and animals; a boat to gather oysters, fish, and cast for shrimp; a garden plot to grow green vegetables and raise chickens. Slaves sold surplus produce and, from the proceeds, accumulated small amounts of cash. Slaves engaged in a fair amount of social activity on the plantation—church and prayer meetings head the list. The slave was also a mariner, making the canoes and boats for use on the inland waterways of coastal Georgia. Slaves' expertise, talent, and participation in boat racing developed this sport into a coastal institution.

The conclusions that the standard of slave life was superior to the standard on inland plantations is not meant to gloss over the fact that slavery was evil—any system that defines persons as property and denies them the basic right to be free cannot be justified. The critical moral point is not whether slave life in coastal Georgia, in terms of physical well-being, was less harsh than in other areas of the South, but that the slave system, by controlling the individual's life, denied him the basic right to human dignity. That the Negro slave retained human dignity and overcame the dehumanizing process of the slave system is a most singular achievement.

The distinctive characteristics of rice plantations offered opportunities for slaves to contain and preserve a more undiluted African cultural behavior than was possible in other plantation communities. This African ethos, though blended with white cultural patterns, is the ingredient that identifies tidewater culture. It was the slaves of coastal Georgia who created a tidewater culture out of a wilderness—their labor and talent made possible the growth of a plantation society that waxed rich from their efforts. Urban slaves also made a notable cultural contribution to the total area; their historically valuable churches stand today as evidence of their determination to overcome the degradation imposed by slavery. Their tenacious adherence to their religious beliefs and determined efforts to create and maintain their own church bodies are manifested in their historic churches. Today, more than ever, blacks in coastal Georgia are aware of their heritage and have enthusiastically supported local organizations that are resurrecting their heritage from the past.

APPENDIX A

Agricultural and Population Statistics for Low Country Georgia

Table A-1. Agricultural Statistics for the Lower Piedmont, the Coastal Strip, and the Whole State, 1860

	Lower Piedmont	*Coastal Strip*	*Whole State*
Inhabitants			
Per square mile	28.0	31.0	18.0
Percentage white	38.4	44.0	56.0
Percentage free black	0.3	1.9	0.3
Percentage Negro slave	61.3	54.0	43.7
Number of slaves per slaveholder	13.3	14.4	11.2
Percentage of slaveholders with 10 or more slaves	41.8	31.0	33.8
Number of slaves per farm	15.1	50.7	8.6
Percentage of land improved	45.1	8.3	21.5
Per farm	24.7	95.0	19.6
Improved acres per inhabitant	10.4	1.7	7.6
Average acres per farm	515.0	885.0	430.0
Average improved acres per farm	256.0	161.0	130.0
Average value of land and buildings per farm	$3,760	$11,000	$2,535
Average value of implements and machinery per farm	$178	$415	$111

SOURCE: Roland M. Harper, "Development of Agriculture in Upper Georgia from 1850 to 1880," *Georgia Historical Quarterly* 6 (Mar. 1922): 18; Harper, "Development of Agriculture in Lower Georgia from 1850 to 1880," ibid. (June 1922): 115. In these two articles Harper has traced the development of agriculture for each region in Georgia by means of census statistics. The regions not included in the table above are the Appalachian Valley, Blue Ridge, and Upper Piedmont in upper Georgia; the Sand Hills, Blue Marl, Red Hills, Red Lime Lands, Sandy Lime Sink, Rolling Wire Grass, Hammock Belt, and Flat Pine Lands in lower Georgia. These regions, uninviting from an economic point of view, were mostly areas of small farms with predominently white populations. The Lower Piedmont lies just north of the fall line that divides upper and lower Georgia; the coast strip, which includes the Sea Islands, needs no identification.

Table A-2. Barrels of Rice Exported from Charleston and Savannah, 1755–1773

Year	Charleston	Savannah	Total
1755	92,210	2,299	94,509
1756	72,230	2,997	75,227
1757	62,985	2,998	65,983
1758	64,337	2,371	66,708
1759	53,782	3,603	57,385
1760	64,652	3,283	67,935
1761	96,270	4,666	100,936
1762	84,760	6,509	91,269
1763	102,671	7,702	110,373
1764	110,216	9,690	119,906
1765	96,644	12,224	108,868
1766	—	14,257	—
1767	118,279	11,281	129,560
1768	124,829	17,773	142,602
1769	—	16,740	—
1770–71	130,500	22,129	152,629
1772	—	25,232	—
1773	112,469	23,540	136,009

SOURCE: The figures compiled are from Lewis C. Gray, *History of Agriculture in the Southern United States to 1860*, 2 vols. (Washington, D.C.: Carnegie Institute, 1933), 2:1022. Cf. Alexander Hewatt, *An Historical Account of the Rise and Progress of the Colonies of South Carolina and Georgia*, 2 vols. (London: Alexander Donaldson, 1769), 2:267. Note the discrepancy in figures for rice shipped from Georgia in 1763; Hewatt lists 7,500 barrels shipped; Gray lists 7,702.

Table A-3. Quantities and Prices of Rice Shipped from the United States, 1712–1860

Year	Quantity (1,000 lbs.)	Price (cts. per lb.)	Year	Quantity (1,000 lbs.)	Price (cts. per lb.)
1712–16 (average)	3,144	—	1764	53,646	2.5
1717	3,187	—	1767	68,267	2.2
1718	3,190	—	1768	67,234	2.2
1719	5,444	2.2	1769	76,294	2.2
1721	8,752	1.0	1770	76,511	3.4
1724	7,094	—	1771	70,000	3.4
1725	9,212	—	1772	68,078	3.4
1726	10,754	—	1773	62,538	—
1727	11,962	—	1782	12,112	—
1728	12,954	—	1783	30,987	—
1729	16,689	—	1784	31,857	—
1730	19,744	1.4	1785	32,929	—
1731	18,534	—	1786	32,598	—
1732	25,363	—	1788	50,000	—
1733	15,162	—	1789	60,507	2.9
1734	22,866	—	1790	74,136	2.6
1735	26,485	—	1791	85,057	2.3
1736	21,413	2.9	1792	80,767	2.9
1737	17,162	—	1793	69,892	2.7
1738	35,742	1.9	1794	83,116	3.5
1739	45,555	2.4	1795	78,623	5.9
1740	40,447	2.7	1796	36,067	—
1741	23,098	—	1797	75,146	—
1742	36,708	1.9	1798	66,359	—
1743	40,389	1.3	1799	67,234	—
1744	29,814	0.9	1800	56,920	—
1745	27,051	0.9	1801	47,893	—
1746	27,073	2.2	1802	49,103	5.0
1747	27,566	1.6	1803	47,031	4.9
1748	20,517	1.9	1804	34,098	5.0
1749	24,111	—	1805	61,576	4.3
1750	30,806	1.8	1806	56,815	4.2
1751	39,217	3.4	1807	5,537	4.0
1752	17,761	2.2	1808	70,144	3.0
1753	52,341	1.7	1809	78,805	3.3
1754	48,389	1.9	1810	71,615	3.3
1758	25,942	—	1811	46,314	3.1
1759	30,403	2.2	1812	72,506	4.1
1760	52,342	1.8	1813	6,886	3.3
1761	43,592	1.5	1814	77,549	3.6
1762	50,530	2.4	1815	82,706	4.3
1763	50,921	2.4	1816	47,578	5.0

Table A-3 (Continued)

Year	Quantity (1,000 lbs.)	Price (cts. per lb.)	Year	Quantity (1,000 lbs.)	Price (cts. per lb.)
1817	52,909	6.1	1839	60,996	3.2
1818	45,914	4.6	1840	60,970	3.3
1819	42,998	3.9	1841	68,770	2.8
1820	52,933	2.8	1842	64,060	2.6
1821	53,253	3.0	1843	80,829	2.7
1822	60,819	3.0	1844	71,173	3.0
1823	67,937	2.8	1845	74,404	3.5
1824	58,209	3.3	1846	86,656	4.2
1825	66,638	2.9	1847	60,242	3.9
1826	80,111	2.9	1848	77,317	3.3
1827	105,011	2.5	1849	76,241	3.5
1828	102,982	2.4	1850	63,354	3.4
1829	78,418	2.5	1851	71,840	3.4
1830	69,910	3.0	1852	40,624	4.1
1831	72,196	3.0	1853	63,073	4.2
1832	86,498	3.2	1854	39,422	4.3
1833	73,132	2.9	1855	67,616	3.5
1834	66,511	3.3	1856	68,323	3.4
1835	127,790	2.0	1857	58,122	3.2
1836	63,650	4.0	1858	77,070	2.9
1837	42,629	4.4	1859	81,633	3.2
1838	55,992	4.4	1860	43,512	3.2

SOURCE: Lewis C. Gray, *History of Agriculture in the Southern United States*, 2 vols. (Washington, D.C.: Carnegie Institute, 1933), 2:1030.

Table A-4. Population Figures by Counties in 1790

District	*County*	*Total Population*	*Whites*	*Negro Slaves*	*Free Negroes*
Lower	Camden	305	221	70	14
	Glynn	413	193	215	5
	Liberty	5,355	1,303	4,025	27
	Chatham	10,769	2,456	8,201	112
	Effingham	2,424	1,674	750	—
Middle	Richmond	11,317	7,162	4,116	39
	Burke	9,467	7,064	2.392	11
	Washington	4,552	3,856	694	2
Upper	Wilkes	31,500	24,052	7,268	180
	Franklin	1,041	885	156	—
	Greene	5,405	4,020	1,377	8
Total		82,548	52,886	29,264	398

SOURCE: *A Century of Population Growth from the First Census of the United States to the Twelfth, 1790–1900* (Washington, D.C.: Bureau of the Census, 1909). Free Negroes were centered in Chatham and Wilkes counties.

Table A-5. Population Growth in the Rice Coast Counties from 1800 to 1860

County	Year	Total Population	White	Negro Slave	Free Negro
Bryan	1800	2,836	528	2,306	2
	1810	2,827	557	2,264	6
	1820	3,021	759	2,238	24
	1830	3,149	733	2,402	14
	1840	3,182	751	2,407	24
	1850	3,424	1,164	2,245	15
	1860	4,015	1,636	2,379	—
Camden	1800	1,681	936	735	10
	1810	3,941	1,207	2,687	47
	1820	4,342	1,621	2,669	52
	1830	4,578	1,492	3,052	34
	1840	6,075	1,958	4,065	52
	1850	6,319	2,069	4,246	4
	1860	5,420	1,276	4,143	1
Chatham	1800	12,946	3,890	9,049	7
	1810	13,540	3,214	9,748	578
	1820	14,737	4,569	9,542	626
	1830	14,127	4,649	9,052	426
	1840	18,801	8,613	9,542	646
	1850	23,901	9,152	14,018	731
	1860	31,043	15,511	14,807	725
Glynn	1800	1,874	779	1,092	3
	1810	3,417	564	2,845	8
	1820	3,418	643	2,760	15
	1830	4,567	597	3,968	2
	1840	5,302	643	4,644	15
	1850	4,933	696	4,232	5
	1860	3,889	1,048	2,839	2
Liberty	1800	5,313	1,346	3,940	27
	1810	6,228	1,352	4,808	68
	1820	6,695	1,641	5,037	17
	1830	7,233	1,609	5,602	22
	1840	7,241	1,641	5,583	17
	1850	7,926	2,002	5,908	16
	1860	8,367	2,284	6,083	—
McIntosh	1800	2,660	831	1,819	10
	1810	3,739	761	2,957	21
	1820	5,129	1,343	3,715	71
	1830	4,998	1,204	3,685	109
	1840	5,360	1,366	3,923	71
	1850	6,027	1,326	4,629	72
	1860	5,546	1,429	4,063	54

SOURCE: *United States Census Returns*, 1800–1860. From 1800 to 1860 the rice coast counties continued to have a greater percentage of Negro slaves to total population than the cotton belt counties.

Table A-6. Population Growth of Georgia from 1800 to 1860

Year	*Total Population*	*White*	*Negro Slave*	*Free Negro*
1800	162,101	101,678	59,404	1,019
1810	252,433	145,414	105,218	1,801
1820	340,983	189,566	149,654	1,763
1830	516,823	296,806	217,531	2,486
1840	691,392	407,695	280,944	2,753
1850	906,185	521,572	381,682	2,931
1860	1,057,286	591,550	462,236	3,500

SOURCE: *United States Census Returns*, 1800–1860.

APPENDIX B

Noted Rice Planters of Coastal Georgia

CHATHAM COUNTY

Representative of those individuals in the Ogeechee River District of Chatham County who specialized in rice planting on a profitable scale were George W. Anderson, Langdon Cheves and his son Dr. John R. Cheves, Ralph E. Elliott, Stephen Habersham, Arthur Heyward, John W. Houston, and Francis Henry McLeod. Anderson owned 129 slaves, 1,200 acres of land, and in 1860 his yield was 176,000 pounds of rice and 8,000 pounds of Sea Island cotton. John R. Cheves owned 234 slaves and Grove Point Plantation, a 1,500-acre tract valued at $200,000. His rice yield in 1860 was 176,800 pounds; the yield from Langdon Cheves's plantation was 1,644,000 pounds. Elliott owned 232 slaves, 1,500 acres, and his rice fields produced 2,080,000 pounds in 1860. Habersham owned 181 slaves and Heyward, 352; their rice yields were comparable to that of their neighbors. The Ogeechee River District was inhabited by a small clique of slaveholding planters from South Carolina and a preponderance of Negro slaves. The pattern of migration from the tidewater region of South Carolina that began in the eighteenth century was accelerated in the nineteenth as the sons and relatives of the rice magnates of that state made claim to swamp lands suitable for rice culture along the Georgia coast.[1]

1. Unpublished Census Returns, 1830, 1840, 1850, 1860. When planters died intestate or when they left wills directing how their estates were to be managed, administrators or executors for these estates made accountings regularly in probate record books. These sources, listing estate inventories and appraisals, together

In the Savannah River District of Chatham County, William H. Gibbons, George P. Harrison, Charles Manigault, Mitchell King, James F. Potter, John F. Tucker, Zachariah M. Winkler, Dr. James P. Screven and his sons George B. and Thomas P. were representative of those planters who owned from 100 to 300 slaves (Gibbons and Potter owned more) and whose rice fields, like those along the Ogeechee River, produced large yields. At White Bluff, on the Montgomery River but still within the Savannah District, Robert Habersham owned two plantations, 213 slaves, and, for the year 1860, realized from his fields 1,404,000 pounds of rice. Chatham County had become an area of centralized wealth.[2]

In 1833 Louis Manigault purchased Gowrie, a 300-acre tract on the Savannah River in Chatham County, for his son Charles. The records kept by Charles serve to illustrate the initial cost of investment and estimated rates of return on capital invested in the operation of a rice plantation. The initial cost was $40,000 and included 220 acres in rice fields, 80 acres of unimproved land, 50 slaves, and a rice mill. The rice fields were valued at $70 per acre, the uncleared land at $37, the mill at $7,500, and the slaves at an average of $300 each. Manigault's annual expense for the first six years of operating Gowrie averaged $2,000. The annual cost of maintaining each grown hand was $21. This expense, when itemized, included 52 pecks of corn at $13; winter and summer clothing, $7; and shoes, $1. The cost of salt, molasses, and meat provided at intervals, plus medical expenses and the annual salary of an overseer, were not given.[3]

Annual production on Gowrie increased between 1833 and 1839; for the year 1838, on 193 acres worked by 35 hands, the yield of 578 barrels of rice was sold for $13,872. Other income was received from small rice and rice flour, as well as from 200 bushels of peas, making the total gross income for the year $15,239. By 1855 Manigault owned an adjoining plantation, East Hermitage, which he operated along with Gowrie as a consolidated unit. By now his rice fields and slave force had doubled; plantation ex-

---

with deed records, tax books, unpublished census returns, and limited information gathered from descendents, have been examined to determine methods of operation and profitability involved in production. The records of a goodly number of the rice plantations under consideration have been used to reinforce information taken from the census returns.

2. Unpublished Census Returns, 1850, 1860.

3. Manigault Plantation Records; see also Clifton, ed., *Life and Labor on Argyle Island.* Clifton's introduction to Manigault's plantation records is exceptionally good and stands up to the introduction done by Easterby, ed., *The South Carolina Rice Plantation.*

penses had increased accordingly. The rice crop of 1857, consisting of 21,326 bushels, was marketed between November 1857 and April 1858 in five shipments, grossing $16,979. After marketing costs were deducted, the net income from the crop was $12,965, and, after plantation expenses of $4,918 were debited, the net proceeds from Gowrie and East Hermitage amounted to $8,047. The Manigault family plantation records of rice planting on the Savannah River show average annual return on capital invested to have been 12 percent from 1833 to 1839 and 12.2 percent from 1856 to 1861, despite losses from deaths of slaves during cholera epidemics, inefficient management by overseers, and damage to rice crops caused by excessive flooding from a freshet in 1852 and a hurricane in 1854.[4]

The financial career of James P. Screven of Chatham County also illustrates how earnings appreciated over the years following initial investment in land and slaves for use in the production of rice. In 1843 Screven purchased Brewton Hill, a 200-acre tract of choice rice fields on the Savannah River. The purchase price of $14,000 included all improvements and machinery on the plantation and was negotiated while prices were depressed, the economy having not yet fully recovered from the Panic of 1837. Screven's assets at this time are not known; he had retired from his profession as a physician to devote more time to his planting interests. When he died in 1859, he owned two rice plantations, a cotton plantation on Wilmington Island near Savannah, 266 slaves, two rice mills, city property, which included the Savannah Steam Rice Mill, and an impressive amount of stock in various banks and railroads. His total assets were appraised at $688,545. The 200 acres of Brewton Hill had appreciated from $14,000 to $40,000 over a period of fifteen years. The 44 slaves on this unit were valued at $29,985, and plantation machinery, at $13,170. The 473 acres of rice fields under operation as a separate unit were valued at $70,000, and the 173 slaves on this unit, at $98,293.[5] The

4. Manigault Plantation Records; Clifton, ed., *Life and Labor*. See also Phillips, *American Negro Slavery*, 254–57, and *Plantation and Frontier Documents, 1649–1863* (Cleveland: Clark, 1909), 31–33; Flanders, *Plantation Slavery in Georgia*, 104–117; Starobin, *Industrial Slavery*, 152; Govan, "Was Plantation Slavery Profitable?" 513–35, as well as in Harold D. Woodman, ed., *Slavery and the Southern Economy* (New York: Harcourt, Brace and World, 1966), 63–64, for references to the profitability involved from rice production on Manigault's two units on the Savannah River. Phillips was the first to use these records but did not evaluate earnings to interpret percentages on annual income to show profitability.

5. Deed Records, Book 3A, p. 300, Inventories and Appraisements, Book L, 1858–61, pp. 96–104, Chatham County; *Savannah Morning News*, Oct. 5, 1858;

estates of William Gibbons, Mitchell King, Henry McAlpin, James and Thomas N. Potter compared favorably in size and value with Screven's.[6]

BRYAN COUNTY

A relatively small area of Bryan County extends along the Atlantic coast, and lands suitable for growing rice were limited, though by 1860 there were seven units sufficiently productive on the south side of the Ogeechee River, which divides Bryan and Chatham counties, to be classified as rice plantations. The owners of these units were Richard J. Arnold, Eliza C. Clay, Ralph E. Elliott, whose holdings in Chatham County have already been mentioned, John P. Hines, Joseph L. McAllister, James M. Middleton, William Patterson, as well as Charles W. and William M. Rogers. Arnold owned 195 slaves; Clay, 230; McAllister, 271; and Middleton, 180; the others owned between 75 and 150. With the exception of Charles W. Rogers, whose plantation produced Sea Island cotton, these individuals realized annual yields in rice of from 100,000 to 600,000 pounds.[7]

LIBERTY COUNTY

In Liberty County there were no extensive river systems with surrounding swamp lands to be utilized for growing rice. The lack of available swamp lands caused the planters of Liberty County to produce smaller quantities of rice than their neighbors along the coast and considerably more of cotton. The labor-management needs in growing cotton were not so great and the average ownership in slaves was less, though some Liberty County citizens owned more than 100 and a few, like Nathanial Varnedoe and

---

Charles C. Jones, Jr., *History of Savannah, Georgia* (Syracuse, N.Y., 1890), 438–39.

6. Inventories and Appraisements, Book K, 1850–56, pp. 37–40, 59–60, 94–99, Book M, N, 1861–68, pp. 111–73, Will Book J, 1862–69, pp. 15–27, Chatham County.

7. Unpublished Census Returns, 1850, 1860; Inventory and Appraisements, Book L, 1858–61, pp. 158–60, Chatham County.

George W. Walthour, owned more than 200. Walthour was the largest property owner in Liberty County; in 1850 his rice yield was 195,000 pounds, and his Sea Island cotton, 45,000. Rice, at an average of 3 cents per pound, and Sea Island cotton at 30 cents, reflected a gross return of $19,350. Walthour's estate had 300 slaves in 1860, but we do not have statistics for staples produced. Representative of other Liberty County planters whose estates produced both staples were John B. Barnard, Charlton Hines, John and Joseph Le Conte, Thomas Mallard, Thomas Quarterman, John P. Stevens and his sons Henry and William, George W. Waldburg and his brother Jacob Waldburg. Waldburg's plantation on St. Catherines Island was notable for the abundance and quality of Sea Island cotton grown there.[8]

MC INTOSH COUNTY

The extensive watersheds of the Altamaha and Satilla rivers and their surrounding low country made possible the creation of large rice plantations in McIntosh, Glynn, and Camden counties. Rice was the staple produced almost exclusively in this area, though Sea Island cotton was grown in great quantities on Sapelo, St. Simons, Jekyll, and Cumberland islands. Illustrative of the larger rice plantations developed in McIntosh County were those belonging to Jacob Barrett, Pierce Butler (whose holdings are listed under the estate of John P. Butler), D.M. and E.W. Dunwody, Thomas W. Foseman, William R. Gignilliat, Thomas S. Mallard, Charles W. and R.L. Morris, P.M. Nightingale, R.B. Rhett, and Thomas Spalding. With the exception of Spalding, whose plantation on Sapelo Island produced cotton and sugar cane and whose slaves numbered 252, these individuals produced rice, realizing an average of from 300,000 to 700,000 pounds annually between 1850 and 1860. Two of them, Pierce Butler and P.M. Nightingale,

8. Unpublished Census Returns, 1850, 1860; *United States Census Returns*, 1840, 1850, 1860. Estate inventories among records of the counties involved in this study list cotton shipments in pounds, indicating the price per pound for which the cotton was sold. Sea Island cotton, because of its superior quality and the limited amount that could be grown for the world market, continued throughout the antebellum era to bring good prices, ranging from 15 to 30 cents per pound and by 1860, escalating to as high as $1 and more per pound. See Smith, *Slavery in Antebellum Florida*, 151–52.

had yields of more than 1 million pounds. Butler owned 505 slaves and Nightingale, 170.[9]

GLYNN COUNTY

In Glynn County, Francis P. Corbin, James Hamilton Couper, George C. Dent, Hugh Fraser Grant, T. Pinckney Huger, Daniel H.B. Troup and James R. Troup exemplify the affluent rice planters of lower Georgia whose estates were comparable in size and production to those in McIntosh County. Though Francis P. Corbin is not listed in the census rolls for 1850, his harvested rice amounted to 1,137,000 pounds in 1860, the largest yield in Glynn County for that year; he and Richard Corbin each owned 235 slaves. Mallory P. King, Thomas Butler King, and John and Henry Du Bignon of Jekyll Island were prominent cotton planters among the slaveholders of Glynn County.[10]

James Hamilton Couper managed, but did not own, two plantations in Glynn County: Hopeton, a rice plantation on the Altamaha River in which he inherited a half-interest; and Hamilton, a cotton plantation on St. Simons Island. Couper was named executor for the estate of James Hamilton of Philadelphia, and these two plantations constituted a portion of that estate. The annual accountings kept by Couper from 1827 to 1852 while directing the operations of Hopeton and Hamilton reflect earnings fairly typical among those of large scale. The year 1833 may be used to illustrate earnings. For that year, capital investment was $302,617; net income from the sale of rice, sugar, molasses, and cotton was $22,016; operating expense was $10,937, leaving a profit of $11,079, representing interest earning at 3.6 percent. Couper absorbed this profit by debiting against the estate his salary of $8,589 as manager for the two plantations, as well as his commission of $2,490 as executor for handling the accounts. Operating costs included Couper's living expenses, maintenance for slaves, and partial payment on the rice mill at Hopeton; a meager $1,630 was forwarded to Philadelphia for distribution among the heirs. In 1840 Couper sold his interest in Hopeton to the Hamilton estate

9. Unpublished Census Returns, 1850, 1860.
10. Ibid.

but continued to manage the two plantations until 1852 at a salary ranging from $5,000 to $6,000 annually. He also continued to deduct, as an expense from income, maintenance costs for himself and his family to support his extravagant way of life.[11]

Hopeton Plantation was equipped with an elaborate outlay of machinery for manufacturing sugar and milling rice. One of Couper's first large expenditures as manager of Hopeton was to purchase machinery for a sugar mill that he ordered from England at a cost of $22,444. The manufacture of sugar was not so profitable as rice, and Couper, like other planters of the Altamaha delta, gradually converted cane fields into rice fields, as these low-lying stream beds suitable for growing sugar cane were adaptable and desirable for growing rice. By the 1830s sugar cane had lost its significance as a staple crop in lower Georgia. Under Couper's management, Hopeton Plantation appreciated in value slightly more than 20 percent between 1827 and 1852, from $274,000 to $349,475.[12]

Despite the glowing descriptions of the illustrious James Hamilton Couper made by contemporary writers and twentieth-century novelists, court records reveal that he owned neither Hopeton nor Hamilton Plantations, though he did inherit a half-interest in Hopeton that later reverted to the estate. He did direct the operations of the two plantations successfully but diverted much of the profit to his own interest. He was undoubtedly ingenious and skillful in coping with the complexities involved in cultivating rice. He traveled to Holland as early as 1825 to observe the diking system there in order to introduce improved methods of tidal flow irrigation at Hopeton. He was an ardent horticulturist and keenly interested in the natural sciences. J.D. Legare, editor

11. Wills and Appraisements, Book D, 171–83, 295, 305; Record of Wills, Appraisements, Book E, 222–40, Glynn County. Couper's annual accountings are also contained in the Southern Historical Collection, University of North Carolina, under the title James Hamilton Couper Plantation Records, 1818–1854. Other papers in this collection include a plantation journal, dated 1839–54, of similar accounts; crop records from 1818 to 1831 for cotton, rice, sugar cane, corn, and peas; and "Notes on Agricultural and Rural Economy" containing extracts from agricultural journals, information from friends, and notes on Couper's personal experiences.

12. Wills and Appraisements; the unpublished census rolls for 1850 show Couper's ownership in slaves to be 112. See Wills and Appraisements, Book D, 171–83, Glynn County, for the will and inventory of James Hamilton, dated 1829. The inventory lists 125 slaves on Hamilton Plantation, 101 on Cabbage Bluff, 37 on Nodings Point, and 390 on Hopeton. The total value of the slave property at this time was $154,477. There are no slave listings in the James Hamilton Couper Collection at the University of North Carolina.

of the *Southern Agriculturist,* visited Hopeton in 1832 and was greatly impressed with the systematic and efficient operation of this plantation.[13]

CAMDEN COUNTY

A natural setting along the Satilla River, which divides Camden and Glynn counties, and along the St. Marys River, the southernmost boundary of coastal Georgia, made possible the development of extensive plantations in the tidewater lands of Camden County. The sixteen rice plantations under operation in this county compared favorably with those along the Altamaha, Ogeechee, and Savannah rivers; some were larger. The aggregate figure for rice produced in Camden County increased from 6,400,940 pounds in 1850 to 10,330,068 in 1860, making Camden County second only to Chatham in rice production. Stephen King and George Owens (deceased) had the largest holdings in the county. Their rice fields produced, respectively, 1,933,768 and 2,400,000 pounds in 1860. King owned 311 slaves and Owens, 256. Owens's personal property was appraised at $254,000 in 1856; of this amount, $170,000 represented the value of 340 slaves. His other assets included bonds and stocks worth $40,000; 10,000 bushels of rice, $9,000; cash on deposit with a local bank, $25,000; "furniture, flats, wines, horses, and stock," $10,000. The value of his land is not known. Other rice planters in Camden County worthy of mention were F.M. Adams, John Bailey, Duncan L. Clinch, J.B. Guerrard, L.W. Hazelhurst, George Lang, E.A. Riley, and J.J. Ryals.[14]

13. Record of Wills, Appraisements, Book E, 222–40, Glynn County; Caroline Couper Lovell, *The Golden Isles of Georgia* (Boston: Little, Brown, 1939), 214–15, 230–31, 262.

14. Unpublished Census Returns, 1850, 1860; Inventories and Appraisements, Book K, 1850–56, p. 310, Chatham County.

BIBLIOGRAPHY

UNPUBLISHED SOURCES

Manuscripts

Arnold-Screven Papers, 1827–45. Plantation journals, diaries, and letterbooks of John Screven and the family of Joseph Bryan, Chatham County, Georgia. MSS, series E, 3419, Southern Historical Collection, Univ. of North Carolina, Chapel Hill.

Blake, Daniel Papers, 1831–33. Certain of these papers refer to machinery for rice mills. MSS, series 72, item 4, Georgia Historical Society, Savannah.

Bonds, Bills of Sale, Deeds of Gift, Powers of Attorney, 1765–72. MSS, Department of Archives and History, Atlanta.

Camden County: Estate Accounts, Book C; Inventory and Appraisements of Estates; Minutes of the Court of Ordinary; Reports on Estates and Administrations, Will Books B, C.

Cathedral of St. John the Baptist. MSS, Savannah.

Chatham County: Deed Records; Estate Accounts; Inventories and Appraisements; Record of Wills.

Christ Episcopal Church Records. Parish Registers, 1820–65. MSS, Georgia Historical Society, Savannah.

Colonial Wills of Georgia, Book AA. MSS, Department of Archives and History, Atlanta.

Couper, James Hamilton. Plantation Records, 1818–1854. MSS, Southern Historical Collection, Univ. of North Carolina, Chapel Hill.

Cummings, Wallace Papers, 1852–63. Records of sales of slaves.

MSS, series 189. Georgia Historical Society, Savannah.

DeCaradeuc Papers, 1751–1909. One item, consisting of seven pages, refers to the slave insurrection in Santo Domingo. MSS, series 207. Georgia Historical Society, Savannah.

First Baptist Church, 1800–1946, Chatham County. MSS, Department of Archives and History, Atlanta.

First Presbyterian Church, 1822–69, McIntosh County. MSS, Department of Archives and History, Atlanta.

Floyd, Charles Rinaldo Diary, 1816–45. In possession of Bryce McAdoo Clagett, Bethesda, Md. Floyd, a son of General John Floyd, was a resident and slaveholder of Camden County.

Floyd, James Boog Papers, 1820–1930. In possession of Sarah Smith Floyd, Savannah. Among them are the records of General John Floyd, planter of Camden County.

Floyd, Marmaduke H. "Certain Tabby Ruins on the Georgia Coast, 1935." In possession of Picot de Beoufillet Floyd, Clearwater, Fla.

Fraser, Couper Family Papers, 1810–84. Certain items are bills of sales of slaves. MSS, series 265. Georgia Historical Society, Savannah.

Georgia General Assembly, 1785, Savannah. MS, National Archives, Washington, D.C.

Glynn County: Deed Books; Inventories and Appraisals of Estates; Record of Wills.

Granger, Mary Collection (typewritten). Georgia Historical Society, Savannah.

Greene, Nathaniel Letter, Dec. 9, 1781. Greene speaks of the possibility of using Negro troops in a plan to force the enemy to evacuate Charleston, S.C. MS, file 329, National Archives, Washington, D.C.

Habersham, Robert, and James Papers, 1806, 1823. These letters pertain to seedling cotton and rice. MSS, series 342. Georgia Historical Society, Savannah.

Houstoun, John, Letter (n.d.). Refers to the loss of an overseer. Colonial Dames of America Collection, MS, Series H81J62. Georgia Historical Society, Savannah.

Independent Presbyterian Church Records, 1826–87, Chatham County. MSS, Department of Archives and History, Atlanta.

Jackson, W.E. "The Siege and Capture of Fort Pulaski, Cockspur Island, Georgia, 1951" (typewritten). U.S. Department of the Interior, National Park Service, Fort Pulaski.

Jones, Charles Colcock Papers. Special Collections Division, Tulane Univ. Library, New Orleans.

King, Thomas Butler Papers, 1763–1925. King was a planter of St. Simons Island in Glynn County. Certain papers pertain to the management of his plantation and slaves. MSS, series D, 1252. Southern Historical Collection, Univ. of North Carolina, Chapel Hill.

King, Thomas Butler Papers, 1835–39. Some of these letters refer to crops and money matters. MSS, series 464. Georgia Historical Society, Savannah.

Kollock Papers, 1799–1850. MSS, Colonial Dames of America Collection. Georgia Historical Society, Savannah.

Kollock Plantation Books, 1837–61. Daily records of three plantations of George J. Kollock, containing slave records: sick lists, punishments, supplies issued, cotton production records, and other information. MSS, 407. Southern Historical Collection, Univ. of North Carolina, Chapel Hill.

Lafar, Mabel F. "The Baptist Church of Savannah: History, Record, and Register" (typewritten). 1941. Georgia Historical Society, Savannah.

Leake, Richard Plantation Account Book, 1785–1801. Colonial Dames of America Collection, MS, L47R38. Georgia Historical Society, Savannah.

"Letters from Governor John Houstoun, Feb. 3, Aug. 20, 1778." MSS, Letters of the Continental and Confederation Congresses, 1774–89, National Archives, Washington, D.C.

Lewis, Bessie, Papers. MSS, Pine Harbor, McIntosh County.

Liberty County: Deed Records (Probate Records are boxed).

Manigault, Louis, Papers, 1834–56. Letters to overseers and to members of the Charles Manigault family. MSS, Duke Univ., Durham.

Manigault, Louis, Plantation Records, 1845–76. Journals for Gowrie and East Hermitage rice plantations on the Savannah River (typewritten). Georgia Historical Society, Savannah.

Mackey and Stiles Family Papers, 1741–1915. Correspondence of the Mackeys for the period before 1865 relates to illness of family and slaves. Certain volumes include mercantile accounts and plantation records in Chatham County. Series A, 470. MSS, Southern Historical Collection, Univ. of North Carolina, Chapel Hill.

Mackey, McQueen, Couper Papers, 1810–37. These include the

purchase of a plantation, business and family correspondence, and listings of slaves named in a settlement. Colonial Dames of America Collection. MSS, series 3. Georgia Historical Society, Savannah.

McIntosh County: Deed Records; Record of Wills (rerecorded).

Methodist Episcopal Church, 1788–1864, Camden County. MSS, Department of Archives and History, Atlanta.

Methodist Episcopal Church Records, 1848, Chatham County. MS, Department of Archives and History, Atlanta.

Methodist Episcopal Church, 1815–35, Liberty County. MS, Department of Archives and History, Atlanta.

Minute Book, 1813–1832, Pleasant Grove Church. Department of Archives and History, Atlanta.

Minutes of the Board of Health, 1828–32. MSS, Georgia Historical Society, Savannah.

Minutes of the First African Sabbath School, 1826–1835. MSS, Independent Presbyterian Church, Savannah.

Potter, James Papers, 1828–31. This is a journal for Argyle Plantation (rice) on the Savannah River. MS, Series 630. Georgia Historical Society, Savannah.

Records of the Continental and Confederation Congresses, 1774–89. MSS, National Archives, Washington, D.C.

Records of the Darien Presbyterian Church. In possession of Bessie Lewis, McIntosh County

Records of the Federal District Court, Savannah. Microfilm Records Center, East Point, Georgia.

Records of the Governor of Georgia, 1760–71, 1773–76. Register of Colonial Grants, Department of Archives and History, Atlanta.

Register of Free Persons of Color, City of Savannah, 1817–29, 1860–73. 2 vols. Georgia Historical Society, Savannah.

Register of Free Persons of Color for the County of Chatham, 1826–35, 1828–47, 1837–49, 1863–64. 4 vols. Georgia Historical Society, Savannah.

Register of Free Persons of Color, 1813–43, Camden County. MSS, Department of Archives and History, Atlanta.

St. Stephens Episcopal Church, 1856–1913, Chatham County. MSS, Department of Archives and History, Atlanta.

Schroder Collection, 1850–1890. Folders 1, 2, and 3 are records of slave hirings. MSS, series 719. Georgia Historical Society, Savannah.

Slave Narratives, A Folk History of Slavery in the United States from Interviews with Former Slaves (typewritten). Federal Writers' Project, 1936–38, Library of Congress, Washington, D.C., 1941.

Slave Owner Affidavits, 1818–47, Camden County. MSS, Department of Archives and History, Atlanta.

Stiles, Samuel Papers, 1783–1803. This account book is for provisions from Stiles's plantation for the French and American armies during the siege of Savannah. MS, Colonial Dames of America Collection, file D164. Georgia Historical Society, Savannah.

Stoddard, Albert H. Collection. MSS, Georgia Historical Society, Savannah.

Tucker, F. Bland. "Christ Church and the Negro, 1750–1860" (typewritten). In possession of Dr. Tucker, Rector Emeritus, Christ Episcopal Church, Savannah.

Unpublished Census Returns: Agriculture, Slave Rolls, Social Statistics, 1850, 1860. MSS, Duke Univ. Library, Durham.

War Department Collection of Revolutionary War Records. MSS, National Archives, Washington, D.C.

Will Books, A–AA, B, C, E, 1754–1817, Chatham County. MSS, Department of Archives and History, Atlanta.

Young, Rogers W. Records relating to the labor of slaves in the construction of Fort Pulaski (typewritten). United States Department of the Interior. National Park Service, Fort Pulaski, Chatham County.

Theses

Byrne, William A. "The Burden and Heat of the Day: Slavery and Servitude in Savannah, 1733–1865." Ph.D. diss., Florida State Univ., 1979.

Coon, David LeRoy. "The Development of Market Agriculture in South Carolina, 1670–1785." Ph.D. diss., Univ. of Illinois, 1972.

Gifford, James M. "The African Colonization Movement in Georgia, 1817–1860." Ph.D. diss., Univ. of Georgia, 1976.

Lines, Stiles B. "Slaves and Churchmen: The Work of the Episcopal Church Among Southern Negroes, 1830–1860." Ph.D. diss., Columbia Univ., 1960.

Mohr, Clarence L. "Georgia Blacks During Secession and Civil War." Ph.D. diss., Univ. of Georgia, 1975.

Newton, Reginald A. "Health Care on Georgia Plantations, 1830–1865." Thesis, Atlanta Univ., 1976.

Tafelski, Robert L. "Slavery in the Interior Cities of Georgia, 1820–1860." Ph.D. diss., Univ. of Georgia, 1977.

Washington, Austin D. "The Free Negro in Savannah Before the Civil War." Ph.D. diss., Pennsylvania State Univ., 1975.

PRINTED SOURCES

Public Records

Abstracts of Colonial Wills of the State of Georgia, 1733–77. Atlanta: Colonial Dames of America, 1962 (for the Department of Archives and History).

Acts passed by the Colonial Assembly of Georgia, 1755–74. Printed in Candler and Knight, eds., *Colonial Records of the State of Georgia* (q.v.), vols. 18, 19.

Acts passed by the General Assembly of the State of Georgia 1778–1865. Department of Archives and History, Atlanta.

Bancroft, Joseph, *Census of the City of Savannah, together with Statistics relating to the trade, commerce, mechanical arts and health of the same; with historical notices, and a list of the incorporated companies and charitable societies; to which is added a Commercial Director of the principal mercantile houses, manufacturers, mechanics, professions, together with particulars respecting the railroads, steamers, packets, etc., connected with the city.* Savannah, 1848.

Candler, Allen D., and Lucian Lamar Knight, eds., *Colonial Records of the State of Georgia.* 26 vols. Atlanta, 1904–1916.

City of Savannah Peddler's Licenses. 1861.

Clark, R.H., T.R.R. Cobb, and D. Irvin. *Code of Georgia.* Atlanta, 1861.

Clatyon, A.S. *A Compilation of the Laws of Georgia Enacted Between 1800 and 1810.* Augusta, 1813.

Cobb, T.R.R. *Digest of the Statute Law in Force Prior to 1851.* Atlanta, 1851.

Directory for the City of Savannah. 1859.

Duncan, W. *Tabulated Mortuary Record of the City of Savannah from January 1, 1854 to December 31, 1869.* Savannah, 1870.

Lamar, L.Q.C., *Compilation of the Laws of the State of Georgia.* Augusta: T.S. Hannon, 1821.

Marbury, H., and W.H. Crawford. *A Compilation of the Laws of Georgia from 1755 to 1800.* Savannah, 1802.

Mayor's Annual Report. Savannah, 1861.

Prince, O.H. *Digest of the Laws of Georgia enacted previous to 1837.* Athens, 1837.

Records of the Commons House of Assembly, 1770–1773. In Candler and Knight, eds. *Colonial Records* (q.v.)

Register of Colonial Grants. Atlanta: Department of Archives and History.

Revolutionary Records of the State of Georgia. 3 vols. In Candler and Knight, eds. (q.v.).

Society for the Propagation of the Gospel in Foreign Parts, 20 vols. London: E. Owen, Printer, 1744–63.

Tax Digest for Chatham County, 1874–75. Georgia Historical Society, Savannah.

Tax Digest for City of Savannah, 1824, 1827, 1837, 1848. Georgia Historical Society, Savannah.

Watkins, George. *A Compilation of the Laws of Georgia,* 1802.

Watkins, Robert, and George Watkins, eds. *Digest of the Laws of the State of Georgia.* Philadelphia, 1800.

Wilson, Edward G. *A Digest of all the ordinances of the City of Savannah and various laws of the State of Georgia, relative to said city, which were in force 1st January 1858.* Savannah, 1858.

Statistical Collections

Affleck's Southern Rural Almanac. Washington, Miss., 1854.

Agriculture of the United States in 1860, Compiled from the Original Returns of the Eight Census. Washington, D.C., 1854.

Blair, Ruth, ed., *Some Early Tax Digests.* Atlanta: Georgia Department of Archives and History, 1926.

A Century of Population Growth from the First Census of the United States to the Twelfth, 1790–1900. Washington, D.C.: Bureau of the Census, 1909.

De Bow, J.D.B., *Compendium of the Seventh Census.* Washington, D.C., 1854.

———. *Industrial Resources of the Southern and Western States.* 3 vols. New Orleans, 1852.

Fifth Census or Enumeration of the Inhabitants of the United States. Washington, D.C.: Duff Green, 1832.

Georgia, Statistics of, an abstract of the State of Georgia compiled from the census of 1850. Milledgeville, 1851.

Historical Statistics of the United States; Colonial Times to 1957. Washington, D.C.: Bureau of the Census, 1960.

Holmes, George K. *Rice Crop of the United States.* Washington, D.C.: United States Department of Agriculture, Bureau of Statistics, Circular 34, 1912.

Manufactures of the United States in 1860; compiled from the Original Returns of the Eighth Census Under the Direction of the Secretary of the Interior. Washington, D.C.: Government Printing Office, 1865.

Report on the American Rice Industry. Savannah: Morning News Printing House, 1888.

Sixth Census or Enumeration of the Inhabitants of the United States. Washington, D.C.: Blair and Rives, 1841.

United States Census Returns. 1790–1860.

White, George M. *Statistics of the State of Georgia.* Savannah, 1849.

Newspapers

Augusta Chronicle, 1796–99, 1800–32, 1838–39, 1840–41.

Augusta Courier, 1827–28.

Augusta Herald, 1800–1806, 1812, 1815, 1817, 1821.

Columbian Museum and Savannah Advertiser, 1796–1810.

Columbian Sentinel, 1806–1807, 1809 (Augusta).

Constitutionalist, 1825–27, 1829, 1834–41 (Augusta).

Daily Georgian, 1819 (Savannah).

Daily Morning News, 1859–62 (Savannah).

Darien Gazette, 1820–21, 1824–25.

Evening Journal, 1854 (Savannah).

Federal Union, 1830–65 (Milledgeville).

Floridian and Journal, 1850–60 (Tallahassee).

Georgia Gazette, 1763–76, 1785–1802 (Savannah).

Georgian, 1818–54 (Savannah).

Royal Georgia Gazette, 1781 (Savannah).

Savannah Morning News, 1975–76.

Savannah Republican, 1807–1813, 1825, 1840–41, 1850–52, 1860.

Savannah Weekly Republican, 1847–49.

Bibliography

Contemporary Periodicals

African Repository. 34 vols. Washington, D.C., 1825–92.
American Agriculturist. New York: Saxton and Miles, 1850–59.
American Cotton Planter. Montgomery, Ala., 1853–60.
Cotton Planter and Soil of the South. Columbus, Ga., 1858–60.
De Bow's Commercial Review. New Orleans, 1846–70.
Farmers' Register. Shellbanks and Petersburg, Va., 1833–42.
Niles' Weekly Register. Baltimore, 1811–49.
Savannah Journal of Medicine, 1859–60.
Savannah Medical and Surgical Journal, 1837–58.
Southern Agriculturist. Charleston, S.C., 1828–46.
Southern Christian Advocate. Charleston, S.C., 1858–59.
Southern Cultivator. Augusta, Ga., 1853–60.
Southern Episcopalian, 1855–60.
Transactions of the Medical Society of the State of Georgia, 1853.

Travel Accounts

Adams, Nehemiah. *South-Side View of Slavery; or Three Months at the South in 1854.* Boston, 1854.

Bartram, John. *Diary of a Journal Through the Carolinas, Georgia, and Florida, 1765–66.* Rpt. Philadelphia: American Philosophical Society, 1942.

Bartram, William. *Travels in Georgia and Florida, 1773–74.* Rpt. Philadelphia: American Philosophical Society, 1942.

Bremer, Frederika. *The Homes of the New World and Impressions of America.* Trans. Mary Howitt. 2 vols. New York: Harper, 1853.

Buckingham, James S. *The Slave States of America.* 3 vols. London: Fisher, 1842.

Featherstonhaugh, George W. *Excursion Through the Slave States From Washington on the Potomac to the Frontier of Mexico, 1834–1835.* 2 vols. London: Harper, 1844.

Hall, Basil. *Travels in North America in the Years 1827 and 1828.* 3 vols. Philadelphia, 1829.

Hundley, D.R. *Social Relations in our Southern States.* New York: Henry B. Price, 1860.

Lane, Mills, ed. *The Rambler in Georgia.* Savannah: Beehive Press, 1973.

Lewis, George. *Impressions of America.* Edinburgh, 1845.

Lyell, Sir Charles. *A Second Visit to the United States of America.* 2 vols. New York, 1850.

Olmsted, Frederick Law. *A Journey in the Seaboard Slave States,* in Mills Lane, ed., *The Rambler in Georgia.* Rpt. Savannah: Beehive Press, 1973.

Power, Tyrone. *Impressions of America.* 2 vols. London, 1836.

Robinson, Solon, Pioneer and Agriculturist, ed. Herbert Q. Keller. 2 vols. Indianapolis: Indiana Historical Bureau, 1936.

Singleton, Arthur (pseud., Knight, Henry Cogswell). *Letters From the South and West.* Boston: Richardson and Lord, 1824.

Books

Abbott, W.W. *The Royal Governors of Georgia, 1754–1775.* Chapel Hill: Univ. of North Carolina Press, 1959.

Aptheker, Herbert, ed. *A Documentary History of the Negro People in the United States: From Colonial Times to the Founding of the NAACP in 1910.* New York: Citadel Press, 1969.

Armstrong, M.F., and Helen W. Ludlow. *Hampton and Its Students.* New York: Putnam's, 1874.

Armstrong, Margaret. *Fanny Kemble, A Passionate Victorian.* New York: Macmillan, 1938.

Atwell, J.S. *A Brief Historical Sketch of St. Stephen's Parish, Savannah, Ga.* New York: Church Book and Job Printing, 1874.

Bancroft, Frederic. *Slave Trading in the Old South.* New York: Frederick Ungar, 1931.

Banks, Enoch M. *The Economics of Land Tenure in Georgia.* New York: Columbia Univ. Press, 1905.

Barrett, Leonard E. *Soul-Force: African Heritage in Afro-American Religion.* Garden City: Anchor Press, 1974.

Berlin, Ira. *Slaves Without Masters: The Free Negro in the Antebellum South.* New York: Vintage, 1974.

Blassingame, John W. *The Slave Community: Plantation Life in the Antebellum South.* New York: Oxford Univ. Press, 1972.

Boles, John B. *Black Southerners, 1619–1869.* Lexington: Univ. Press of Kentucky, 1983.

Boney, F.N., ed. *Slave Life in Georgia: A Narrative of the Life, Sufferings, and Escape of John Brown, A Fugitive Slave.* Savannah: Beehive Press, 1972.

Bonner, James C. *A History of Georgia Agriculture, 1732–1860.* Athens: Univ. of Georgia Press, 1964.

Botkin, B.A., ed. *Lay My Burden Down.* Chicago: Univ. of Chicago Press, 1945.

Breeden, James O., ed. *Advice Among Masters: The Ideal in Slave Management in the Old South.* Westport, Conn., Greenwood Press, 1980.

Breen, T.H., and Stephen Innes. *"Myne Owne Ground": Race and Freedom on Virginia's Eastern Shore, 1640–1676.* New York: Oxford Univ. Press, 1980.

Burke, Emily. *Pleasure and Pain: Reminiscences of Georgia in the 1840s.* Introduction by Felicity Calhoun. Rpt. Savannah: Beehive Press, 1978.

Carman, Harry J., ed. *American Husbandry Containing an Account of the Soil, Climate, Production, and Agriculture of the British Colonies in North America and the West Indies With Observations on the Advantages and Disadvantages of Settling in them, Compared with Great Britain and Ireland. by an American.* 2 vols. London: J. Bew, 1775. Rpt. New York: Columbia Univ. Press, 1939.

Cate, Margaret Davis. *Early Days of Coastal Georgia.* New York: Gallery Press, 1955.

———. *Our Todays and Yesterdays: A Story of Brunswick and the Coastal Islands.* Brunswick, Ga.: Glover Brothers, 1930.

Catterall, Helen, ed. *Judicial Cases Concerning American Negro Slavery and the Negro.* 5 vols. Washington, D.C., 1926–37.

Clifton, James M., ed. with an introduction. *Life and Labor on Argyle Island: Letters and Documents of a Savannah River Plantation, 1833–1867.* Savannah: Beehive Press, 1978.

Clinton, Catherine. *The Plantation Mistress: Woman's World in the Old South.* New York: Pantheon, 1982.

Cohen, David W., and Jack P. Green, eds. *Neither Slave nor Free: The Freedmen of African Descent in the Slave Societies of the New World.* Baltimore: Johns Hopkins Univ. Press, 1972.

Coleman, Kenneth. *The American Revolution in Georgia, 1763–1789.* Athens: Univ. of Georgia Press, 1958.

———, ed. *A History of Georgia.* Athens: Univ. of Georgia Press, 1977.

Collections of the Georgia Historical Society. 6 vols. Savannah, 1870–80.

Conrad, Georgia Bryan. *Reminiscences of a Southern Woman*. Rpt. Hampton, Va.: Hampton Institute Press, n.d.

Coulter, E. Merton. *Thomas Spalding of Sapelo*. Baton Rouge: Louisiana State Univ. Press, 1940.

Crary, Catherine S., ed. *The Price of Loyalty: Tory Writings from the Revolutionary Era*. New York: McGraw-Hill, 1973.

Crum, Mason. *Gullah: Negro Life in the Carolina Sea Islands*. Durham: Duke Univ. Press, 1940.

David, Paul A., Herbert G. Gutman, Richard Sutch, Peter Temin, Gavin Wright, with introduction by Kenneth M. Stampp. *Reckoning With Slavery: A Critical Study in the Quantitative History of American Negro Slavery*. New York: Oxford Univ. Press, 1976.

Davis, Arthur P. and Saunders Redding. *Cavalcade: Negro American Writing From 1760 to the Present*. Boston: Houghton Mifflin, 1971.

Davis, Charles S. *The Cotton Kingdom in Alabama*. Montgomery: Alabama State Department of Archives and History, 1939.

DeBraham, John G.W. *History of the Province of Georgia, With Map of Original Survey*. Wormsloe edition, 1849.

Degler, Carl N. *Neither Black Nor White: Slavery and Race Relations in Brazil and the United States*. New York: Macmillan, 1971.

Doar, David. *Rice and Rice Planting in the South Carolina Low Country*. Charleston: Charleston Museum, 1936.

Donnan, Elizabeth, ed. *Documents Illustrative of the History of the Slave Trade to America*. 4 vols. Washington, D.C.: Carnegie Institution of Washington, 1930–35.

Drums and Shadows: Survival Studies Among the Georgia Coastal Negroes. Georgia Writers' Project. Athens: Univ. of Georgia Press, 1940.

Du Bois, William Edward Burghardt, ed. *The Negro American Family*. Atlanta: Atlanta Univ. Press, 1908; rpt. Westport, Conn.: Negro Universities Press, 1971.

———. *The Souls of Black Folk*. Greenwich, Conn.: Fawcett, 1961.

Easterby, J.H., ed. *The South Carolina Rice Plantation as Revealed in the Papers of Robert F.W. Allston*. Chicago: Univ. of Chicago Press, 1945.

Engerman, Stanley L., and Eugene D. Genovese, eds. *Race and*

Slavery in the Western Hemisphere: Quantative Studies. Princeton: Princeton Univ. Press, 1975.

Escott, Paul D. *Slavery Remembered: A Record of Twentieth Century Slave Narratives.* Chapel Hill: Univ. of North Carolina Press, 1979.

Finkelman, Paul. *An Imperfect Union: Slavery, Federalism and Comity.* Chapel Hill: Univ. of North Carolina Press, 1981.

Flanders, Ralph B. *Plantation Slavery in Georgia.* Chapel Hill: Univ. of North Carolina Press, 1933.

Fogel, Robert W., and Stanley L. Engerman. *Time on the Cross: The Economics of American Negro Slavery.* Boston: Little, Brown, 1974.

Foner, Philip S. *Business and Slavery: The New York Merchants and the Irrepressible Conflict.* Chapel Hill: Univ. of North Carolina Press, 1941.

Frazier, E. Franklin. *The Negro Church in America.* New York: Schocken, 1964.

Gamble, Thomas, Jr. *History of the Municipal Government of Savannah.* Savannah, 1910.

Genovese, Eugene D. *From Rebellion to Revolution: Afro-American Slave Revolts in the Making of the Modern World.* Baton Rouge: Louisiana State Univ. Press, 1979.

———. *In Red and Black: Marxian Explorations in Southern and Afro-American History.* New York: Pantheon Books, 1968; rpt. Knoxville: Univ. of Tennessee Press, 1984.

———. *Roll, Jordan, Roll: The World the Slaves Made.* New York: Pantheon, 1974.

Gilmore, Al-Tony, ed. *Revisiting Blassingame's The Slave Community: The Scholars Respond.* Westport, Conn.: Greenwood Press, 1978.

Gonzales, Ambrose E. *The Black Border: Gullah Stories of the Carolina Coast.* Columbia, S.C.: State Company, 1922.

Gordon, Asa H. *The Georgia Negro: A History.* Ann Arbor: Edwards Brothers, 1933; rpt. Spartanburg, S.C.: Reprint Company, 1972.

Goveia, Elsa V. *Slave Society in the British Leeward Islands at the End of the Eighteenth Century.* New Haven: Yale Univ. Press, 1965.

Granger, Mary, ed. *Savannah River Plantations.* Savannah Writers' Project. Savannah: Georgia Historical Society, 1947; rpt. Spartanburg, S.C.: Reprint Company, 1972.

Gray, Lewis C. *History of Agriculture in the Southern United*

States to 1860. 2 vols. Washington, D.C.: Carnegie Institute, 1933.

Gutman, Herbert G. *The Black Family in Slavery and Freedom, 1750–1925*. New York: Vintage, 1976.

Hall, Gwendolyn Midlo. *Social Control in Slave Plantation Societies. A Comparison of St. Dominque and Cuba*. Baltimore: Johns Hopkins Univ. Press, 1971.

Hamer, Philip M., George C. Rogers, Jr., David R. Chestnutt, Peggy J. Clark, eds. *The Papers of Henry Laurens*. 3 vols. Columbia: Univ. of South Carolina Press, 1976.

Handler, Jerome S. *The Unappropriated People: Freedmen in the Slave Society of Barbados*. Baltimore: Johns Hopkins Univ. Press, 1974.

Hardee, Charles Seton Henry. *Reminiscences and Recollections of Old Savannah*. Savannah, 1926.

Harden, William. *Recollections of a Long and Satisfactory Life*. Savannah: Review Printing, 1934.

Haynes, Robert V., ed. *Blacks in White America Before 1865: Issues and Interpretations*. New York: David McKay, 1972.

Heath, Milton S. *Constructive Liberalism; the Role of the State in Georgia to 1860*. Cambridge, Mass.: Harvard Univ. Press, 1945.

Herskovits, Melville J. *The Myth of the Negro Past*. New York: Harper, 1941.

Hewatt, Alexander. *An Historical Account of the Rise and Progress of the Colonies of South Carolina and Georgia*. 2 vols. London: Alexander Donaldson, 1769.

Heyward, Duncan Clinch. *Seed From Madagascar*. Chapel Hill: Univ. of North Carolina Press, 1937; rpt. Spartanburg, S.C.: Reprint Company, 1972.

Higginbotham, A. Leon, Jr. *In the Matter of Color: Race and the American Legal Process, The Colonial Period*. New York: Oxford Univ. Press, 1978.

Hilliard, Sam Bowers. *Hog Meat and Hoecake: Food Supply in the Old South, 1840–1860*. Carbondale: Southern Illinois Univ. Press, 1972.

Hindus, Michael Stephen. *Prison and Plantation: Crime, Justice, and Authority in Massachusetts and South Carolina, 1767–1878*. Chapel Hill: Univ. of North Carolina Press, 1980.

House, Albert V., ed. *Planter Management and Capitalism in Antebellum Georgia: The Journal of Hugh Fraser Grant, Rice Grower*. New York: Columbia Univ. Press, 1954.

Hughes, Langston, and Arna Bontemps, eds. *The Poetry of the Negro, 1746–1970.* New York: Doubleday, 1970.

Johnson, Guy B. *Folk Culture on St. Helena Island, South Carolina.* Chapel Hill: Univ. of North Carolina Press, 1930.

Johnston, Edith Duncan. *The Houstouns of Georgia.* Athens: Univ. of Georgia Press, 1950.

Johnston, James Hugo. *Race Relations in Virginia and Miscegenation in the South, 1776–1860.* Amherst: Univ. of Massachusetts Press, 1970.

Jones, Charles C., Jr. *The Dead Towns of Georgia.* In *Collections of the Georgia Historical Society,* vol. 4. Savannah: Morning News, 1878.

———. *The Religious Instruction of the Negro.* Princeton: O'Harte, 1832.

Jones, Charles C., Jr. *The Dead Towns of Georgia. In Collections of the Georgia Historical Society,* vol. 4. Savannah: Morning News, 1878.

———. *History of Savannah, Georgia.* Syracuse, N.Y., 1890.

———. *Negro Myths from the Georgia Coast.* Columbia: Univ. of South Carolina Press, 1925.

Kemble, Frances Anne. *Journal of a Residence on a Georgia Plantation, 1838–1839.* New York: Harper, 1863.

———. *Records of Later Life.* New York: Henry Holt, 1882.

Kiple, Kenneth F., and Virginia Himmelsteib King. *Another Dimension to the Black Diaspora: Disease, Diet, Racism.* New York: Cambridge Univ. Press, 1981.

Klein, Herbert S. *The Middle Passage: Comparative Study in the Atlantic Slave Trade.* Princeton: Princeton Univ. Press, 1978.

———. *Slavery in the Americas.* Chicago: Univ. of Chicago Press, 1967.

Knight, Franklin W. *Slave Society in Cuba During the Nineteenth Century.* Madison: Univ. of Wisconsin Press, 1970.

Lawson, Dennis T. *No Heir to Take Its Place: The Story of Rice Planting in Georgetown County, South Carolina.* Georgetown: Rice Museum, 1972.

Leconte, Joseph. *Autobiography of Joseph LeConte,* ed. William D. Armes. New York: D. Appleton, 1903.

Leigh, Frances Butler. *Ten Years on a Georgia Plantation.* London: R. Bentley, 1883.

Lester, Julius. *To Be a Slave.* New York: Dial Press, 1968.

Levine, Lawrence W. *Black Culture and Black Consciousness: Afro-American Folk Thought from Slavery to Freedom.* New

York: Oxford Univ. Press, 1977.

Littlefield, Daniel C. *Rice and Slaves: Ethnicity and the Slave Trade in Colonial South Carolina.* Baton Rouge: Louisiana State Univ. Press, 1981.

Litwack, Leon F. *North of Slavery: The Negro in the Free States, 1790–1860.* Chicago: Univ. of Chicago Press, 1961.

Love, Emanuel K. *History of the First African Baptist Church.* Savannah: Morning News, 1888.

Loveland, Anne C. *Southern Evangelicals and the Social Order, 1800–1860.* Baton Rouge: Louisiana State Univ. Press, 1980.

Lovell, Caroline Couper. *The Golden Isles of Georgia.* Boston: Little, Brown, 1939.

M'Call, Hugh. *The History of Georgia, Containing Brief Sketches of the Most Remarkable Events up to the Present Day.* 2 vols. Savannah, 1811–16.

McLendon, Samuel G. *History of the Public Domain in Georgia.* Atlanta, 1924.

Mallard, R.Q. *Plantation Life Before Emancipation.* Richmond, Va.: Whittet and Shepperson, 1892.

Marsh, J.B.T. *The Story of the Jubilee Singers: With Their Songs.* Boston: Houghton, Osgood, 1880.

Mathews, Donald R. *Religion in the Old South.* Chicago: Univ. of Chicago Press, 1977.

Matthews, Essie Collins. *Aunt Phebe, Uncle Tom, and Others: Character Studies Among the Old Slaves of the South Fifty Years After.* Columbus, Ohio, 1915.

Menn, Joseph Karl. *The Large Slaveholders of the Deep South, 1860.* Ph.D. diss. 2 vols., Univ. of Texas, 1964. Ann Arbor: Univ. Microfilms, 1972.

Mullin, Gerald W. *Flight and Rebellion: Slave Resistance in Eighteenth-Century Virginia.* New York: Oxford Univ. Press, 1972.

Myers, Robert Manson, ed. *The Children of Pride: A True Story of Georgia and the Civil War.* New Haven: Yale Univ. Press, 1972.

Northup, Solomon. *Twelve Years a Slave,* ed. Sue Eakin, Joseph Logsdon. Rpt. Baton Rouge: Louisiana State Univ. Press, 1972.

Owens, Leslie Howard. *This Species of Property: Slave Life and Culture in the Old South.* New York: Oxford Univ. Press, 1976.

Parker, William N., ed. *Structure of the Cotton Economy of the*

Antebellum South. Washington, D.C.: Agricultural History Society, 1970.

Parrish, Lydia. *Slave Songs of the Georgia Sea Islands*. New York: Creative Age Press, 1942.

Patterson, Orlando. *The Sociology of Slavery: An Analysis of the Origins, Development, and Structure of Negro Slave Society in Jamaica*. Cranbury, N.J.: Associated Univ. Presses, 1969.

Perdue, Charles L., Jr., Thomas E. Barden, Robert K. Phillips, eds. *Weevils in the Wheat: Interviews With Virginia Ex-Slaves*. Charlottesville: Univ. Press of Virginia, 1976.

Perdue, Theda. *Slavery and the Evolution of Cherokee Society, 1540–1866*. Knoxville: Univ. of Tennessee Press, 1979.

Perkerson, Medora Field. *White Columns of Georgia*. New York: Rinehart, 1952.

Phillips, Ulrich B. *American Negro Slavery*. New York: D. Appleton, 1918.

———, ed. *Plantation and Frontier Documents, 1649–1863*, 2 vols. Cleveland: Clark, 1909

Pinckney, Elise, ed. *The Letterbook of Eliza Lucas Pinckney, 1739–1762*. Chapel Hill: Univ. of North Carolina Press, 1972.

Postell, William D. *The Health of Slaves on Southern Plantations*. Baton Rouge: Louisiana State Univ. Press, 1951.

Price, Richard, ed. *Maroon Societies: Rebel Slave Communities in the Americas*. New York: Anchor Press, 1973.

Quarles, Benjamin. *The Negro in the American Revolution*. Chapel Hill: Univ. of North Carolina Press, 1961.

Raboteau, Albert J. *Slave Religion: The "Invisible Institution" in the Antebellum South*. New York: Oxford Univ. Press, 1978.

Ragatz, Lowell Joseph. *The Fall of the Planter Class in the British Caribbean, 1763–1833*. New York: American Historical Assoc., 1928; rpt. New York: Octagon Books, 1963.

Range, Willard. *A Century of Georgia Agriculture*. Athens: Univ. of Georgia Press, 1954.

Rawick, George P. *From Sundown to Sunup: The Making of the Black Community*. Westport, Conn.: Greenwood Press, 1972.

Redding, J.H. *Life and Times of Jonathan Bryan, 1708–1788*. Waycross, Ga., 1901.

Rogers, George C., Jr., David R. Chestnutt, and Peggy J. Clark, eds. *The Papers of Henry Laurens*. 7 vols. Columbia: Univ. of South Carolina Press, 1979.

Rose, Willie Lee, ed. *A Documentary History of Slavery in North America*. New York: Oxford Univ. Press, 1976.

Ruffin, Edmund. *Agricultural Survey of South Carolina*. Columbia, S.C., 1843.

Russel, Robert R. *Economic Aspects of Southern Sectionalism, 1840–1861*. Urbana: Univ. of Illinois Press, 1924.

Savitt, Todd L. *Medicine and Slavery: The Diseases and Health Care of Blacks in Antebellum Virginia*. Chicago: Univ. of Illinois Press, 1978.

Scarborough, Ruth. *The Opposition to Slavery in Georgia Prior to 1860*. Nashville: George Peabody College for Teachers, 1933; rpt. New York: Negro Universities Press, 1968.

Scarborough, William K. *The Overseer: Plantation Management in the Old South*. Baton Rouge: Louisiana State Univ. Press, 1966.

Scott, Anne Firor. *The Southern Lady: From Pedestal to Politics, 1830–1930*. Chicago: Univ. of Chicago Press, 1970.

Sellers, James B. *Slavery in Alabama*. University, Ala.: Univ. of Alabama Press, 1950.

Sheridan, Richard B. *Sugar and Slavery: An Economic History of the British West Indies, 1623–1775*. Baltimore: Johns Hopkins Univ. Press, 1973.

Shryock, Richard H., ed. *Letters of Richard D. Arnold, M.D., 1808–1876*. Durham, N.C.: Duke Univ. Press, 1929.

Simmons, William. *Notices of East Florida*. Charleston, S.C., 1822; rpt. Gainesville: Univ. of Florida Press, 1973.

Simms, James M. *The First Colored Baptist Church in North America*. Philadelphia: Lippincott, 1888.

Simpson, George Eaton. *Black Religions in the New World*. New York: Columbia Univ. Press, 1978.

Smith, H. Shelton. *In His Image, But . . . Racism in Southern Religion, 1780–1910*. Durham, N.C.: Duke Univ. Press, 1972.

Smith, Julia Floyd. *Slavery and Plantation Growth in Antebellum Florida, 1821–1860*. Gainesville: Univ. of Florida Press, 1973.

Smith, Mary F. *Baba of Karo: A Woman of the Muslim Hausa*. New Haven: Yale Univ. Press, 1981.

Sobel, Mechal. *Trabelin' On: The Slave Journey to an Afro-Baptist Faith*. Westport, Conn.: Greenwood Press, 1979.

Stampp, Kenneth M. *The Peculiar Institution: Slavery in the Ante-Bellum South*. New York: Vintage, 1956.

Starobin, Robert S., ed. *Blacks in Bondage: Letters of American Slaves*. New York: New Viewpoints, 1974.

———. *Industrial Slavery in the Old South.* New York: Oxford Univ. Press, 1970.

Steel, Edward M. *T. Butler King of Georgia.* Athens: Univ. of Georgia Press, 1964.

Stevens, William B. *A History of Georgia.* 2 vols. New York: E.O. Jenkins, 1847; rpt. Savannah: Beehive Press, 1972.

Stoddard, Albert H. *Buh Partridge Out Hides Buh Rabbitt.* Savannah: E.L. Roberts, 1939.

Swan, Dale Evans. *The Structure and Profitability of the Antebellum Rice Industry, 1859.* Ph.D. diss., Univ. of North Carolina, 1972. New York: Arno Press, 1975.

Sydnor, Charles S. *Slavery in Mississippi.* New York: Appleton, 1933.

Szwed, John F., ed. *Black America.* New York: Basic Books, 1970.

Tailfer, Patrick, et al. *A True and Historical Narrative of the Colony of Georgia, in America, From the First Settlement Thereof Until the Present Period . . . .* Charleston, S.C., 1741.

Tannenbaum, Frank. *Slave and Citizen.* New York: Knopf, 1946.

Tate, Thad W. *The Negro in Eighteenth-Century Williamsburg.* Charlottesville: Univ. of Virginia Press, 1972.

Taylor, Joe Gray. *Negro Slavery in Louisiana.* Baton Rouge: Louisiana Historical Association, 1963.

Taylor, Susie King. *Reminiscences of My Life in Camp With the 33rd United States Colored Troops Late South Carolina Volunteers.* Boston: published by the author, 1902; rpt. New York: Arno Press, 1968.

Thomas, Edgar G. *The First African Baptist Church of North America.* Savannah, 1925.

Thomas, Edward J. *Memoirs of a Southerner, 1840–1923.* Savannah, 1923.

Thompson, Edgar T. *Plantation Societies, Race Relations, and the South: The Regimentation of Populations.* Durham, N.C.: Duke Univ. Press, 1975.

Thompson, Robert Farris. *An Aesthetic of Coal: African Art and Culture in the New World.* New York: Random House, 1981.

Turner, Lorenzo D. *Africanisms in the Gullah Dialect, With a Foreword by David DeCamp.* Chicago: Univ. of Chicago Press, 1949; rpt. Ann Arbor: Univ. of Michigan Press, 1974.

Tushnet, Mark V. *The American Law of Slavery, 1810–1860: Considerations of Humanity and Interest.* Princeton: Princeton Univ. Press, 1981.

Van Deburg, William L. *The Slave Drivers: Black Agricultural Labor Supervisors in the Antebellum South.* Westport, Conn.: Greenwood Press, 1979.

Vanstory, Burnette. *Georgia's Land of the Golden Isles.* Athens: Univ. of Georgia Press, 1956.

Wade, Richard C. *Slavery in the Cities: The South, 1820–1860.* New York: Oxford Univ. Press, 1964.

Walton, Gary M., and James F. Shepherd. *The Economic Rise of Early America.* New York: Cambridge Univ. Press, 1979.

Waring, Joseph Frederick. *Cerveau's Savannah.* Savannah: Georgia Historical Society, 1973.

Whartenby, Franklee Gilbert. *Land and Labor Productivity in United States Cotton Production, 1800–1840.* New York: Arno Press, 1977.

What Became of the Slaves on a Georgia Plantation? Great Auction Sale of Slaves at Savannah, Georgia, March 2nd and 3rd, 1859. A Sequel to Mrs. Kemble's Journal. N.p.: American Anti-Slavery Society, n.d.

Wood, Peter H. *Black Majority: Negroes in Colonial South Carolina From 1670 Through the Stono Rebellion.* New York: Knopf, 1974.

Woodman, Harold D., ed. *Slavery and the Southern Economy.* New York: Harcourt, Brace and World, 1966.

Woodson, Carter G. *The Education of the Negro Prior to 1861.* Washington, D.C., 1919.

———. *The History of the Negro Church.* Washington, D.C., 1921.

———. *The Negro in Our History.* Washington, D.C.: Associated Publishers, 1922.

Wylly, Charles Spalding. *The Seed That Was Sown in the Colony of Georgia: The Harvest and the Aftermath, 1740–1870.* New York: Neale, 1910.

———. *These Memories.* Brunswick, Ga.: Glover Brothers, n.d.

Yetman, Norman R., ed. *Life Under the "Peculiar Institution": Selections From the Slave Narrative Collection.* New York: Holt, Rinehart and Winston, 1970.

Articles

Allston, R.F.W. "Essay on Sea Coast Crops." *De Bow's Review* 16 (June 1851): 589–615.

Aptheker, Herbert. "Additional Data on American Maroons." *Journal of Negro History* 32 (Oct. 1947): 452–60.

———. "Notes on Slave Conspiracies in Confederate Mississippi." *Journal of Negro History* 29 (Jan. 1944): 75–79.

Arnow, Isaac F. "History of St. Marys and Camden County, Georgia." *Camden County Tribune,* 1950–53.

Atherton, Lewis E. "The Problem of Credit Rating in the Ante-Bellum South." *Journal of Southern History* 12 (Nov. 1946): 534–56.

Bailey, Kenneth K. "Protestantism and Afro-Americans in the Old South: Another Look." *Journal of Southern History* 41 (Nov. 1975): 451–72.

Bascom, William R. "Acculturation Among the Gullah Negroes." *American Anthropolgist* (Jan.–Mar. 1941): 43–50.

Bassett, Victor H. "Plantation Medicine." *Journal of the Medical Association of Georgia* 20 (Mar. 1940): 112–22.

Bennett, John. "Gullah: A Negro Patois." *South Atlantic Quarterly* 7 (Oct. 1908): 332–47.

Berlin, Ira. "Time, Space, and the Evolution of Afro-American Society in British Mainland North America." *American Historical Review* 85 (Feb. 1980): 44–78.

Cade, John B. "Out of the Mouths of Ex-Slaves." *Journal of Negro History* 20 (July 1935): 294–337.

Conrad, Alfred H., and John R. Meyer. "The Economics of Slavery in the Ante-Bellum South." *Journal of Political Economy* 56 (Apr. 1958): 95–122.

Coulter, E. Merton. "Boating as a Sport in the Old South." *Georgia Historical Quarterly* 27 (Sept. 1943): 231–47.

Crow, Jeffrey J. "Slave Rebelliousness and Social Conflict in North Carolina, 1775 to 1802." *William and Mary Quarterly* 37 (Jan. 1980): 79–102.

Donnan, Elizabeth. "The Slave Trade into South Carolina Before the Revolution." *American Historical Review* 33 (Oct. –July 1927–28): 804–828.

Doran, Michael F. "Negro Slaves of the Five Civilized Tribes." *Annals of the Association of American Geographers* 68 (Sept. 1978): 335–50.

Escott, Paul D. "The Context of Freedom: Georgia's Slaves During the Civil War." *Georgia Historical Quarterly* 58 (Spring 1974): 79–101.

Fant, H.B. "The Labor Policy of the Trustees for Establishing the

Colony of Georgia in America." *Georgia Historical Quarterly* 16 (Mar. 1932): 1–16.

Flanigan, Daniel J. "Criminal Procedure in Slave Trials in the Antebellum South." *Journal of Southern History* 40 (Nov. 1974): 536–64.

Floyd, General John. "On the Cultivation and Preparation of Indigo." *Southern Agriculturist* 2 (Mar. 1829): 105–107, 154–62.

Franklin, John Hope. "Slavery and the Martial Law." *Journal of Negro History* 37 (Jan. 1952): 36–52.

Genovese, Eugene D. "The Medical and Insurance Costs of Slaveholding in the Cotton Belt." *Journal of Negro History* 45 (July 1960): 141–55.

"Georgia's Baby Catchin Grannies." *Georgia Department of Archives and History Newsletter*, Atlanta (Aug. 1980).

Gifford, James M. "Emily Tubman and the African Colonization Movement in Georgia." *Georgia Historical Quarterly* 59 (Spring 1975): 10–24.

Govan, Thomas P. "Was Plantation Slavery Profitable?" *Journal of Southern History* 8 (Nov. 1942): 513–35.

Harper, Roland M. "Development of Agriculture in Lower Georgia from 1850 to 1880." *Georgia Historical Quarterly* 6 (June 1922): 107–128.

———. "Development of Agriculture in Upper Georgia from 1850 to 1880." *Georgia Historical Quarterly* 6 (Mar. 1922): 18–26.

Hazzard, W.W. "On the General Management of a Plantation." *Southern Agriculturist* 4 (Apr. 1831): 352–53.

Hertzler, James R. "Slavery in the Yearly Sermons (1731–1750) Before the Georgia Trustees." *Georgia Historical Quarterly* 59 (Supplement 1975): 118–26.

House, Albert V. "Labor-Management Problems on Georgia Rice Plantations, 1840–1860." *Agricultural History* 28 (Oct. 1954): 149–55.

Johnson, Michael P. "Planters and Patriarchy: Charleston, 1800–1860." *Journal of Southern History* 46 (Feb. 1980): 45–72.

Johnson, Whittington B. "Free Blacks in Antebellum Savannah: An Economic Profile." *Georgia Historical Quarterly* 64 (Winter 1980): 418–29.

Jones, J. Ralph. "Portraits of Georgia Slaves." *Georgia Review* 21 (Spring 1967): 130.

Jordan, Weymouth T. "Plantation Medicine in the Old South." *Alabama Review* 3 (Apr. 1950): 83–107.

King, Roswell. "On the Management of the Butler Estate." *Southern Agriculturist* 1 (Sept. 1828): 523–29.

Kiple, Kenneth F., and Virginia H. Kiple. "Black Tongue and Black Men: Pellagra and Slavery in the Antebellum South." *Journal of Southern History* 43 (Aug. 1977): 411–28.

———. "Slave Child Mortality: Some Nutritional Answers to a Perennial Puzzle." *Journal of Social History* 10 (July 1977): 284–309.

Kollock, Susan M., ed. "Letters of the Kollock and Allied Families, 1826–1884." *Georgia Historical Quarterly* 34 (June 1950): 126–31.

Lawrence, James B. "Religious Education of the Negro in the Colony of Georgia." *Georgia Historical Quarterly* 14 (Mar. 1930): 43–57.

Littlefield, Daniel C. "Plantations, Paternalism, and Profitability: Factors Affecting African Demography in the Old British Empire." *Journal of Southern History* 46 (May 1981): 167–82.

"Management of a Southern Plantation." *De Bow's Review* 22 (Jan. 1857): 38–44.

Mathews, Donald G. "Charles Colcock Jones and the Southern Evangelical Crusade to Form a Biracial Community." *Journal of Southern History* 41 (Aug. 1975): 299–320.

May, Philip S. "Zephaniah Kingsley, Non-Conformist, 1765–1843." *Florida Historical Quarterly* 23 (Oct. 1945): 145–59.

Morgan, Philip D. "Work and Culture: The Task System and the World of Low Country Blacks." *William and Mary Quarterly* 39 (Oct. 1982): 563–99.

Morris, Richard B. "The Measure of Bondage in the Slave States." *Mississippi Valley Historical Review* 41 (Sept. 1954): 219–40.

Nash, A.E. Keir. "Reason of Slavery: Understanding the Judicial Role in the Peculiar Institution." *Vanderbilt Law Review* 32 (Jan. 1979): 8–205.

Olmsted, C.H. "Savannah in the '40's." *Georgia Historical Quarterly* 1 (Sept. 1917): 243–52.

"Rules on Rice Estate of P.C. Weston." *De Bow's Review* 22 (Jan. 1857): 38–44.

Sellers, James B. "Free Negroes of Tuscaloosa County Before the Thirteenth Amendment." *Alabama Review* 23 (Apr. 1970): 110–27.

Shryock, Richard H. "Medical Practice in the Old South." *South Atlantic Quarterly* 29 (Apr. 1930): 160–78.

"A Sketch of the Ogeechee Mission." *Southern Episcopalian* 1

(Feb. 1855): 494–97.

Smith, Gerald J., ed. "Reminiscences of the Civil War by J.W. Frederick." *Georgia Historical Quarterly* 59 (Supplement 1975): 154–59.

Smith, Julia F. "Racial Attitudes in the Old Southwest." *Americanization of the Gulf Coast, 1803–1850* 2 (1972): 68–77.

Smith, Reed. "Gullah." *Bulletin of the Univ. of South Carolina* 190 (Nov. 1926): 7–43.

Spalding, Phinizy. "Some Sermons Before the Trustees of Colonial Georgia." *Georgia Historical Quarterly* 57 (Fall 1973): 332–46.

Steel, Edward M.J. "Flush Times in Brunswick, Georgia, in the 1830's." *Georgia Historical Quarterly* 39 (Sept. 1955): 231–38.

Stoddard, Albert H. "Origins, Dialect, Beliefs, and Characteristics of the Negroes of the South Carolina and Georgia Coasts." *Georgia Historical Quarterly* 28 (Sept. 1944): 185–95.

Swann, Ann Caldwell. "Landgrants to Georgia Women, 1755–1775." *Georgia Historical Quarterly* 61 (Spring 1977): 23–33.

Sydnor, Charles S. "The Southerner and the Laws." *Journal of Southern History* 6 (Feb. 1940): 3–23.

Szwed, John F. "Musical Adaptations Among Afro-Americans." *Journal of American Folklore* 72 (Apr. 1969): 115–25.

Talley, Thomas W. "Negro Folk Rhymes, Wise and Otherwise, with a Study." Review by E.C.M. *Georgia Historical Quarterly* 6 (Mar. 1922): 86–89.

Tankersley, Allen P. "Midway District: A Study of Puritanism in Colonial Georgia." *Georgia Historical Quarterly* 32 (Mar. 1948): 149–57.

Tregle, Joseph G., Jr. "Early New Orleans Society: A Reappraisal." *Journal of Southern History* 18 (Feb. 1952): 20–35.

Twyman, Robert W. "The Clay Eater: A New Look at an Old Southern Enigma." *Journal of Southern History* 37 (Aug. 1971): 439–48.

Waring, Joseph I. "Colonial Medicine in Georgia and South Carolina." *Georgia Historical Quarterly* 59 (Supplement 1975): 141–59.

Weaver, Herbert. "Foreigners in Ante-Bellum Savannah." *Georgia Historical Quarterly* 37 (Mar. 1953): 1–17.

Williams, Edwin L., Jr. "Negro Slavery in Florida." *Florida Historical Quarterly* 27 (Oct. 1949): 93–110, and 28 (Jan. 1950): 180–204.

Wilms, Douglas C. "The Development of Rice Culture in 18th Century Georgia." *Southeastern Geographer* 12 (May 1972): 45–57.

Wilson, Gold R. "The Religion of the American Negro Slave; His Attitude Toward Life and Death." *Journal of Negro History* 8 (Jan. 1923): 41–71.

Wood, Betty C. "Thomas Stephens and the Introduction of Black Slavery in Georgia." *Georgia Historical Quarterly* 58 (Spring 1974): 24–40.

Wood, Peter H. "People's Medicine in the Early South." *Southern Exposure* (Summer 1978): 50–53.

Woodman, Harold D. "The Profitability of Slavery: A Historical Perennial." *Journal of Southern History* 29 (Aug. 1963): 303–325.

Wright, J. Leitch, Jr. "Blacks in British East Florida." *Florida Historical Quarterly*, Bicentennial Issue 54 (Apr. 1976): 425–42.

INDEX

The author gratefully acknowledges the assistance of Julius Ariail, Director, Georgia Southern Library, in preparation of the Index.

Abraham (Biblical Character) 154
Adams, F.M. 226
African Methodist Church 164
Alabama 104, 107, 137, 193, 204
—Camps of Runaway Slaves 188
Alexander, Charles 114
Allah, Bu 171
Allen, George W. 105
Allston, Robert F.W. 4
Altamaha River 15, 21, 23, 25, 27, 35–36, 41, 43, 55, 62, 98, 113–14, 157, 166–67, 186, 223–26
American Colonization Society 204
American Revolution 15, 23, 26–27, 34–35, 40–41, 71, 81, 143, 171, 183, 192; Armed Bands of Runaway Slaves 188; Effect on Land Tenure 29–31, 43; Effect on Rice Plantations 29, 207; Effect on Slave Population 98, 189, French Army 189; Loyalists 28, 30–31, 99, 101; Slave Assistance to British Forces 188–89; Slave Regiments in American Forces 189
Amino Acids 114
Anderson, George W. 219
Anglican Church: *See* Episcopal Church
Angola 97, 100, 172, 186, 190
Antigua 93, 96
Argyle Island 67, 110
Argyle Plantation 54, 67
Arkansas 104
Arnold, Richard D. 132, 136–37
Arnold, Richard J. 66, 222
Arnold, Veronica 197
Associates of Dr. Bray 141
Atlantic Ocean 15, 37
Augusta, Ga. 22, 24, 72, 187, 194, 205; Port Activity 78

Bahamas 166
Bailey, John 226
Baltimore, Md. 88
Bance Island (Africa) 100
Bancroft, Goodwin, and Dawson (Factorage House) 87
Banks 76, 81, 88, 221, 226
Baptist Church 143, 145–46, 148, 157–58, 164–65, 195
Barbados 68, 93
Barlow, John 199
Barnard, John B. 223
Barrel Staves 22
Barrett, Jacob 223
Bartram, John 21
Bartram, William 21
Beagle, Betsy 171–72
Beall, Thomas E. 204
Beasley, Abraham 197

Beasley, Mary 197
Beasley, Matilda 197
Beaufort, S.C. 189
Beaverskins 23
Beech Tree Plantation 40
Beef 24, 113, 115, 117–18
Bellamy, William 88
Belvin, James W. 6
Bendix and Company (Factorage House) 78
Beth Abram Plantation 142
Bethesda Orphanage (Savannah, Ga.) 19
Beverly-Berwick Plantation 106
Bivens, Thomas 204
Blake, Daniel 34–35
Bobolinks 50
Bonaventure Plantation 105
Bonner, James C.
Bordeaux, France 88
Boston, Mass. 88
Brampton Plantation 26, 143
Brandy 116, 119
Bremer, Frederika 118
Brewton, Miles 26–27
Brewton Hill Plantation 221
Broughton Island 27
Brunswick, Ga. 78, 168
Brunswick and Altamaha Canal 60
Bryan, Andrew 143, 145–46, 148–49
Bryan, Joe: *See* Bryan, Joseph
Bryan, Jonathan 26, 81, 143, 145
Bryan, Joseph 81, 107, 203
Bryan, Sampson 145
Bryan County, Ga. 28, 32, 37, 40, 66, 105, 132, 191, 205, 222
Bryan Street African Baptist Church (Savannah, Ga.) 145, 148
Bullard, Mary 122, 203
Bulloch, William 31
Bunting, Isaac 88
Burke, Emily 72–73
Burke County, Ga. 6, 143
Burroughs, Ga. 153
Butler, John P. 223
Butler, Pierce 69, 105, 117, 126, 157, 163, 171, 223–24; Large Sale of Slaves 107–108
Butler's Island 126, 181
Butter 84

Cabbage 84, 116
Caig and Company (Factorage House) 78
Calabar 97
California 204
Camden County, Ga. 28, 32, 35, 37, 55, 85, 102, 105, 157, 167, 203, 205, 223, 226
Canada 175
Canals 60, 85
Candy, Prince 196
Canoochee River 25
Cape Fear River 9
Capers, William 65, 72
Carnegie, Thomas 122
Carnochan, William 121
Carswell, John 6
Catechism . . . for the Oral Instruction of Colored Persons 154, 156
Cathedral of St. John The Baptist (Savannah, Ga.) 158
Caution, Gustave H. 153
Census of 1790 32
Census of 1850 9, 36, 42, 104, 137, 223
Census of 1860 36, 104, 121, 208
Charleston, S.C. 23, 27, 31, 34, 69, 85, 87–88, 94, 96, 101, 110, 153, 164, 179, 189–90, 193, 196; As Residence of Absentee Plantation Owners 7; Factorage Houses 78, 86; Slave Port of Entry 24
Chatham County, Ga. 28, 31–32, 37, 55, 67–68, 85, 102–103, 105, 110, 116, 136, 153, 188, 195, 197, 205, 219–22
Cherokee Indians 23
Cherry Hill Plantation 66, 116, 119
Cheves, John R. 219
Cheves, Langdon 219
Chicken Pox 139
Chickens 113, 116, 118, 122, 209
Chippewa Square (Savannah, Ga.) 149
Cholera 40, 60, 139, 221

Christ Episcopal Church (Savannah, Ga.) 141–42
Church of England: *See* Episcopal Church
Civil War 27, 61, 77, 87, 156–57, 164, 197, 199, 205
Clay, Eliza C. 222
Clay, Joseph 29, 98–99
Clifton, James M. 3
Clinch, Duncan L. 35–36, 167, 226
Clinch County, Ga. 102
Clinkscales and Boozer (Factorage House) 107
Cockspur Island 60
Coffee 46, 113
Colerain Plantation 34, 54, 109
Collards 116
Colonial Assembly 37
Commission Merchants: *See* Factors
Concord (Slave Ship) 96
Condy, Jeremiah 99
Confiscation Acts of 1778 and 1780 30
Congo, The 186
Congo River 100
Congregational Church 104
Connecticut 203
Conrad, Georgia Bryan 113–14, 121, 159, 167–68, 178, 191
Cook, Jim 103–104
Cook, Williford and Company (Factorage House) 106
Corbin, Francis P. 224
Corbin, Richard 224
Corn 6, 23–24, 40, 66, 81, 113–14, 116–17, 119, 220
Cornmeal 113–14, 117, 126, 167
Cotton 3, 6, 30, 66, 74, 76–78, 81, 84–85, 87, 99–100, 105, 191, 207, 223–24
Cotton Gins 57
Cotton Plantations 8–9, 37, 42, 45, 57, 61, 65, 72–73, 126, 130, 132–33, 163, 191, 200, 207, 221–22; Land Value 6; Return on Capital 43
Cotton Production 36, 57; Annual Yield 6, 37, 219, 223; Crop
Cotton Production *(cont.)* Prices 223; Marketing Costs 87–88; Transportation to Market 86
Couper, James Hamilton 57, 71, 86–88, 117, 119, 133, 167, 224–25
Couper, Mary Ann 110
Cowes, Isle of Wight 78
Cowper, Basil 30
Creek Indians 23, 29, 171, 188
Crum, Mason 172
Cumberland Island 101, 122, 168, 200, 203, 223
Cumberland River 122
Cunningham, Henry 149
Curacoa 94

Dahomey 186
Daily Morning News 108
Darien, Ga. 19, 40, 78, 86–87, 101, 104, 121, 156–57, 166–68, 205
Daufuskie Island 173–74
Davenport, Isaiah 59
Davis, Ulysses 179–80
Dawson, Anthony 164
Dearborn, Mich. 122
Debraham, John G.W. 27, 98
Deerskins 22–24
Delegal, Robert 180
Dell, Philip 187
Demere, Raymond 86–87, 116, 119, 139, 204
Dent, George C. 224
Dew, Thomas R. 103
Dillard, Joel L. 173
Distilleries 121
Doar, David 4
Dolley, Quamino 189
Dorchester Academy 104
Drakies Plantation 34
Drums And Shadows 179
Dubergier, Joseph 196
Du Bignon, Amelia 158
Du Bignon, Charlotte 158
Du Bignon, Henry 158, 168, 200, 224
Du Bignon, John 224
Du Bignon, Marguerite Lesseur 158, 200

Du Bignon, Poulain 121, 158, 200
Du Bignon, William 200
Dublin Plantation 116, 119
Du Bois, W.E.B. 146
Ducks 116
Dunwody, D.M. 223
Dunwody, E.W. 223

East Hermitage Plantation 34, 67, 220–21
Easterby, J.H. 4
Ebenezer, Ga. 19, 24, 156, 188
Effingham County, Ga. 32, 195
Eggs 116, 118
Elbert, Samuel 29, 31
Elizafield Plantation 35, 41–42, 67
Elliott, Ralph E. 5, 40, 219, 222
Elliott, Stephen 34, 153
Emperor (Slave Ship) 96
England 7, 94–96, 98, 141–42, 171, 187, 225
Episcopal Church 141–42, 145, 153, 157, 164, 205
Evelyn Plantation 41–42
Ewell, James 132–33, 138
Ewen and Bolton (Factorage House) 96
Ewing, Matthew 163–64
Exports 22–24

Factorage Houses 25–26, 37, 76; Commissions 87–88; Extending Credit to Planters 76–77; Method of Settling Accounts with Planters 77; Services to Plantation Executors 81, 84; Shipping of Rice Flour 85; Slave Trade 95–96; Stock of General Merchandise 78, 81
Factorage System 76; Benefits for Planters 89; Dependence on Northern Credit 76–77; Detrimental Effects on Southern Economy 88–89
Factors 76–77, 81, 85–86
Fahm Street (Savannah, Ga.) 145
Farley, Joseph 30
Female Orphan Asylum (Savannah, Ga.) 73
Fernandina, Fla. 101
First African Baptist Church (Darien, Ga.) 157, 171
First African Baptist Church (St. Marys, Ga.) 158
First African Baptist Church (Savannah, Ga.) 145, 148–49, 153–54, 178
First Baptist Church (Savannah, Ga.) 148
First Bryan Missionary Baptist Church: *See* Bryan Street African Baptist Church
First Presbyterian Church (Darien, Ga.)156
Fish 113, 116–17, 119
Fish Hawk (Boat) 174
Flanders, Ralph B. 3
Florida 4, 18, 23, 98, 101, 104, 187, 193–95, 204; Camps of Runaway Slaves 188; Indigo Production 28; Land Available for Rice Industry 9
Floyd, John 121
Forbes, John 200
Ford, Henry 122
Ford Museum 122
Forrest, James 105
Fort George Island 101, 195
Fort McAllister, Ga. 37
Fort Pulaski, Ga. 59–60
Foseman, Thomas W. 223
Fowler, Louis 163
France 98, 132
Franciscan Nuns 197
Franklin County, Ga. 6
Frankin Square (Savannah, Ga.) 149, 154
Fraser, John A. 34
Frederica, Ga. 168
Frederick, Jacob W. 178
Frederickson, George 179
Free Negroes 36, 58, 153, 158, 190–93, 196, 200, 205; As Teachers 196–97; Assistance to Runaway Slaves 187; Business Occupations 197; Legal Rights 185, 194–95,

Free Negroes *(cont.)*
197, 199
Freedmen's Bureau 101
Fromotin, Julien 196
Fur Trade 24

Gambia 94, 96, 186
George Ballie and Company (Factorage House) 96
Georgetown, S.C. 34
Georgetown County, S.C. 21
Georgia: As Royal Province 22, 24–25; Camps of Runaway Slaves 188; Colonization Program 17–18; Cotton Industry 6; Expanding Plantation Economy 98; Fear of Slave Rebellions 18; Fertility of Rice Lands 9–10; Indigo Production 28; Land Available for Rice Industry 10, 15, 20, 36, 44, 98; Military Frontier for South Carolina 18; Plantation Belts 9; Population 32, 36; Rice Industry 3, 5, 7, 20; Slave Codes 183, 192, 194, 197, 204, 206; Slave Mortality 137; Slave Population 95, 98, 104–105, 141; Sources of Slaves 19, 94–95; Southern Boundary Extended to St. Mary's River 98
Georgia Association (Baptist Church) 165
Georgia Baptist Convention 165
Georgia Gazette 96, 99, 186, 190
Georgia Infirmary (Savannah, Ga.) 133
Georgia Medical Society 130, 139
Georgia Militia 188
Gibbon, John 196
Gibbons, William H. 220, 222
Gibson, Robert S. 84
Gignilliat, William R. 35, 223
Glover, William 145
Glynn County, Ga. 28, 32, 35, 37, 40–41, 55, 67, 69, 71, 85, 87, 101, 105, 107, 117, 119, 139, 159, 205, 223–24, 226
Gonzales, Ambrose E. 172
Goulding, F.R. 157
Gourdin Matthiessen and Company (Factorage House) 86
Govan, Thomas P. 3
Gowrie Plantation 34, 50, 55, 57, 67, 72, 220–21
Graham, John 20–21, 25–26, 30, 99
Granada 94
Grant, Charles 35, 41, 101
Grant, Hugh Fraser 35, 41–43, 65, 67, 191, 224
Grant, Robert 35, 41
Grantly Plantation: *See* Elizafield Plantation
Grapes 84
Gray, Lewis C. 3
Great Britain: *See* England
Greene, Allen 179
Greene, Nathanael 30–31, 189
Greene Square (Savannah, Ga.) 149, 154
Gross, John B. 66
Grove Point Plantation 126, 219
Guadaloupe 93
Guerard, Peter 84
Guerrand, J.B. 226
Guinea 186–87, 190
Gullah: *See* Slaves-Gullah Dialect
Gutman, Herbert G. 179

H. Meinhard and Company (Factorage House) 107
Habersham, James 19–20, 26, 29, 31, 99, 188
Habersham, John 29
Habersham, Joseph 29
Habersham, Robert 220
Habersham, Stephen 219
Habersham Street (Savannah, Ga.) 148, 153
Haiti 99, 195
Hall, Basil 61, 130, 166
Hamburg, Germany 88
Hamilton, James 86, 224
Hamilton Plantation 86–87, 117, 119, 224–25
Hammond, James H. 72

Harris, Francis 20, 26, 37
Harris, Francis Henry 40
Harris, George Wright 203
Harris, Mary Goodall 40
Harris, Ola 203
Harris Neck, Ga. 101–102, 157
Harris Neck Wildlife Refuge 101
Harrison, George P. 220
Haupt, John 106
Hazelhurst, L.W. 226
Hazelhurst, Robert 35
Hazzard, Boney 178
Hazzard, William H. 35
Hemp Plantations 9
Hepzibah Association (Baptist Church) 165
Herb, George 84
Hermitage Plantation 42, 55, 122, 136
Herskovits, Melville J. 172
Heyward, Arthur 34, 219
Heyward, Duncan Clinch, 4, 36, 71
Heyward, Louisa Blake 35
Heyward, Nathanial 36
Hides 84
Hines, Charlton 223
Hines, John P. 222
Hinesville, Ga. 156
Hogs 84, 113, 116, 119
Holland 132, 187, 225
Hookworm Disease 138
Hopeton (Schooner) 87
Hopeton Plantation 55, 71, 86–87, 117, 119, 139, 167, 224–26
House, Albert V. 3
Houston, George 58–59
Houston, John W. 219
Houston County, Ga. 6
Houstoun, Priscilla 109
Howe, Ashe 106
Huger, T. Pinckney 35, 224
Hume, James 30
Hunter, Pressman and Company (Factorage House) 78

Indentured Servants 17–18, 187, 194
Independent Presbyterian Church (Savannah, Ga.) 154
Indians 17, 24; Frontier Skirmishes 171; Harboring Slave Runaways 187–88; Land Treaties 23, 28; *see also* Cherokee Indians, Creek Indians, Seminole Indians
Indigo 20–23, 99, 143; Annual Production 28; Crop Prices 28
Ingliss and Hall (Factorage House) 96
Ireland 8, 60, 187
Irish Laborers 60
Isle of Delos (Africa) 99
Italy 141

Jackson, James 31
Jackson, Susan 195
Jacksonville, Fla. 101, 195
Jamaica 93, 96, 100, 121, 143
James Chapman and Company (Factorage House) 87
Jay, William 126
Jefferson County, Fla. 88
Jekyll Island 158, 168, 200, 223–24
Johnson, Guy B. 172
Johnson and Wylly (Factorage House) 96
Johnston, James 59
Johnston and Robertson (Factorage House) 100
Johnstone, Mckewn 21
Jones, Charles B. 138
Jones, Charles Colcock 57–58, 70, 73–75, 154, 156, 158–59, 163
Jones, George Noble 103–104
Jones, Noble Wimberly 29
Joseph Habersham (Factorage House) 86
Jubilee Singers 148

Kemble, Fanny 126, 157, 163, 181
Kennedy and Parker (Factorage House) 100
Kennerly, S.W. 153
Kew Plantation 31
Kincaid, George 30
King, Anna Matilda 109, 136
King, Henry 111

King, Mallory P. 224
King, Mitchell 110–11, 220, 222
King, Roswell Jr. 69, 117
King, Stephen 226
King, Thomas Butler 57, 116, 133, 224
Kingsley, George 195
Kingsley, Zephaniah 101, 195
Knight, Franklin W. 179
Kollock, George 42
Kollock, P.M. 139
Kollock Plantation 65

Lambert, John 115
Land Tenure 19–20, 29; Bounty Grant System 30; By Women 24; Family Right System 24–25; Head Right System 30; Restrictions 18
Lang, George 226
Lange, John Peter 58
Laurel Grove Cemetery (Savannah, Ga.) 148, 153
Laurens, Edward R. 158
Laurens, Henry 27, 97, 99
Lazarus (Biblical Character) 181
Le Conte, John R. 138, 171, 223
Le Conte, Joseph 159, 223
Lee, Thelma 145
Legare, John D. 71, 225–26
Le Havre, France 78, 88
Leigh, Francis Butler 107–108
Leigh, James Wentworth 157
Leon County, Fla. 88
Lewis, George 68, 149, 153
Liberia 204–205
Liberty County Association 158
Liberty County, Ga. 23, 28, 32, 37, 55, 70, 73–74, 85, 103–105, 138, 148, 156–57, 205, 222–23
Liele, George 143
Liquor 18
Little Ogeechee River 26
Little Warsaw Island 195
Liverpool, England 78, 101
Livestock 24
Livestock Fodder 6
Lizard (Racing Boat) 168
Locke, John 17
Louisiana 104, 132, 137, 193; Camps of Runaway Slaves 188
Lovell, Caroline Couper 4
Lumber 23
Lutheran Church 164
Lyell, Charles 61, 167

McAllister, Joseph L. 222
McAlpin, Henry 57, 122, 126, 136, 222
McGillivray, William 30
McIntosh, County Ga. 28, 32, 36–37, 55, 77, 86, 101–103, 105, 118, 121, 156, 171, 178, 180, 223–224
Mackay, Eliza 110
Mackay, Isabella 203
Mackay, William 139
McLean, Andrew 29
McLeod, Donald 40
McLeod, Elizabeth Harris 40
McLeod, Francis Henry 37, 40, 57, 85, 219
Macon, Ga. 205
McQueen, Margaret 109
Madison County, Fla. 88
Maitland, John 189
Malaria 7, 136–37
Mallard, Mary S. 58
Mallard, R.Q. 65
Mallard, Thomas 223
Mallard, Thomas S. 223
Manigault, Charles 34, 50, 65, 67–69, 72, 220
Manigault, Louis 34, 36, 42–43, 220
Mariners and Overseers Medical Companion, The 132
Market Square (Savannah, Ga.) 107
Marseilles, France 88
Marshall, Andrew 149, 153, 178, 195–96
Maryland 98, 104, 194
Maryland State Colonization Society 205
Mason, Lowel 154
Massachusetts 203
Maybank, Sandy 57–58, 73

Maybank Plantation 73
Measles 136, 139
Memphis, Tenn. 104
Mendel, E. 107
Methodist Church 164
Methodist Episcopal Church (St. Marys, Ga.) 157
Mexican War 104
Middleton, James M. 222
Midway Cemetery 157
Midway, Ga. 156
Midway Presbyterian Church 157
Milledgeville, Ga. 36, 205
Mirault, Louis 196
Mississippi 104, 132, 137, 193, 204; Camps of Runaway Slaves 188
Mitchell, Robert 106
Mobile, Ala. 78
Molasses 86, 113, 116–19, 220, 224
Mongin, William H. 140
Monteith Plantation 25
Montevideo Plantation 73
Montgomery River 220
Moor, Francis 100
Moore, Matthew 143
Morel, Andrew 196
Morel, John 20, 31–32, 203
Morris, Charles W. 223
Morris, R.L. 223
Mulberry Grove Plantation 25, 30–31
Mules 48–49, 174
Mullryne, John 30
Mumps 139
Mutton 113, 115
Myers, Jim 102
Myrick, Shelby Jr. 37

Natchez, Miss. 104
National Association for the Advancement of Colored People 148
Naval Stores 23
Neely, Annie 103–104
New Bedford, Conn. 78
New Hampshire 29
New London, Conn. 200
New Orleans, La. 74–75, 88, 104
New Purchase Tract 23
New Settlement Plantation 25
New York 29, 94, 203
New York, N.Y. 76–78, 88
Newport, Conn. 78
Neyle, Sampson 110
Nightingale, P.M. 223–24
North Carolina 4, 9, 22, 110, 137; Camps of Runaway Slaves 188
Northup, Solomon 70
Norton, Elizabeth A. 174

Oakland Plantation 105
Oats 6, 40
Odingsells, Anthony 195, 205
Odingsells, Charles 195, 205
Odingsells, Hannah 195
Odingsells, Mary Ann 195
Ogeechee Baptist Church 148
Ogeechee River 5, 15, 21, 25, 34–35, 37, 55, 85, 126, 132, 153, 220, 222, 226
Ogeechee River Canal 85
Ogeechee River District 34, 37, 219
Oglethorpe, James 17, 20, 23; as Slaveholder 19
Ohio 175
Okra 117
Olmsted, Frederick Law 61, 126, 181
Olympia (Boat) 174
Onesimus (Biblical Character) 154
Onslow Plantation 54
Oranges 84
Orphanages 197
Othello (Sloop) 35
Ottolenghe, Joseph 141–42
Owens, George 226

Padelford and Company (Factorage House) 78
Panic of 1837 60, 77, 87, 221
Parrish, Lydia 166
Patterson, William 222
Paul (Biblical Character) 154
Pearl (Slave Ship) 96
Peas 6, 24, 40, 113, 115, 117–18, 220

Penman, Edward 31
Penman, James 31
Perteet, Solomon 195
Petersburg, Va. 199
Philadelphia, Pa. 27, 88, 205, 224
Phillips, Ulrich B. 3
Physicians 133, 136, 139–40, 208, 221; Dental Services 139; Interest in Health of Slaves 130, 132; Medical Licenses 139
Pickering, Thomas 189
Pimentos 46
Pinckney, Charles Cotesworth 158
Pinckney, Robert 102
Pleasant Grove Church (Hinesville, Ga.) 156
Poerier and Matthiesen (Factorage House) 78
Pope, Alexander 6
Population 8, 18, 22, 32, 34, 36; *see also* Census of 1790, Census of 1850, Census of 1860
Pork 24, 113–15, 117–19
Port Royal, S.C. 162
Porter, James 196
Potatoes 117
Potter, James F. 34, 54, 57, 67, 109, 220, 222
Potter, John 34
Potter, Thomas N. 34, 222
Presbyterian Church 73, 149, 154, 156–57, 164
Price, Eugenia 4

Quarterman, Thomas 223

R. Carnochan (Factorage House) 86
R.M. King (Factorage House) 86
Railroads 60, 192, 221
Read, Jacob 34
Reconstruction 164, 197
Retreat Plantation 110, 133
Rhett, R.B. 223
Rhode Island 94, 203
Rice 3–5, 20, 22–23, 76–78, 81, 97, 99, 105, 113, 224
Rice Birds: *See* Bobolinks
Rice Cultivation; Animal Pests 50; Construction of Drainage System 48; Floodgates 48; Harvest 49–50, 55, 57; Land Clearing 46; Preparation for Planting 48–49, 54; Tidal Flow Method 4–5, 10, 15, 21–22, 37, 46, 48–49, 207, 225; Type of Land Required 5, 10
Rice Flour 84–85, 113, 220
Rice Mills 30, 35, 37, 55, 57–58, 66, 85, 220–21, 224–25
Rice Plantations 8, 21, 30–31, 34–35, 45, 61–62, 64–65, 68, 73, 98, 114, 116–17, 126, 130, 132–33, 137, 143, 156–58, 162, 167, 178, 181, 193, 205, 207, 219, 222–26; Absentee Ownership 7, 27, 104, 208; Attitude of Landowners 44; Average Size 36; Capital Investment 9, 27, 41, 57, 224; Cash Flow Problems 76; Contract System for Medical Care 139; Estate Executors 81, 84, 86, 88–89, 105; Estate Inventories 40, 105; Fee Bill System for Medical Care 139; Higher Quality of Life 5, 7, 11, 111, 126, 140, 182, 193, 206, 208–209; Journals of Owners 41–42, 54; Journals of Travelers 4, 35, 61, 71, 89, 100, 115, 122, 126, 225; Land Value 5, 31, 36, 40–41; Livestock 40; Miscellaneous Produce 84; Overview of Operation 37; Popular Literature 4; Requirements for Skilled Labor 43, 57, 61–62; Return on Capital 3–4, 26–27, 43, 77, 220–21,224; Self Sufficiency 119, 126; Tax Records 42; Wills of Owners 142, 195, 199, 208
Rice Production 32, 93; Annual Yield 9–10, 22, 26–27, 34,

Rice Production *(cont.)* 36–37, 40–42, 66, 219–224; Compared to Cotton Production 57; Crop Prices 27–28, 31, 34, 40, 84, 87, 220–21, 223, 226; Exported 22–23, 88; In Africa 97, 100–101; Local Manufacture of Shipping Barrels 85; Marketing Costs 86–87; Marketing Months 86; Preparation for Market 55, 57, 85; Seed Prices 31; Storm Damage 221; Total Investment Required 27; Transportation to Market 37, 57, 84–86; Transportation to Mill 35; Yield Linked to Irrigation 21
Richmond, Va. 109, 199
Richmond Hill, Ga. 103
Richmond Plantation 31
Riley, E.A. 226
River Street (Savannah, Ga.) 95
Robert Habersham and Son (Factorage House) 78, 84
Robert Mure and Company (Factorage House) 87
Rogers, Charles W. 5, 222
Rogers, William M. 222
Roman Catholic Church 158, 164, 197, 200
Ross, Daniel 199
Royal African Company 19
Royal Council 25
Royal Governors 22, 25
Rum 18, 23, 116, 118–19, 121
Rutledge, John 189
Ryals, J.J. 226

St. Andrews Episcopal Church (Darien, Ga.) 157
St. Augustine, Fla. 18
St. Bartholomews Episcopal Church (Burroughs, Ga.) 153
St. Catherines Island 102, 223
St. Croix 93
St. Cyprians Episcopal Church (Darien, Ga.) 157
St. Johns River 9
St. Kitts 93
St. Marks, Fla. 88
St. Martin 93
St. Marys, Ga. 40, 78, 101, 106, 157–58, 168, 194, 226
St. Marys River 15, 23, 98
St. Matthews Episcopal Church (Savannah, Ga.) 145, 153
St. Petersburg, Russia 88
St. Simons Island 26, 40, 133, 166–67, 204, 223–24
St. Stephens Episcopal Church (Savannah, Ga.) 145, 153
Salt 116, 119, 220
Salzburgers 24; Resisting Slavery 19
Santee River 72
Santo Domingo 189, 193, 196
Sapelo Island 36, 57, 110, 122, 171, 179, 203, 223
Sapelo River 121
Satilla River 15, 21, 26, 35, 43, 98, 167, 223, 226
Savannah, Ga. 19–20, 22–23, 25, 32, 34–35, 40, 57, 69, 73–75, 84–85, 87, 97, 105–107, 122, 126, 132–133, 136, 139, 141, 153–54, 158, 168, 173–74, 178, 188–89, 191–93, 196–97, 204, 221; As Residence of Absentee Plantation Owners 7; Black and Immigrant Population 8, 60; British Occupation in 1779 68; Commercial Growth during 1850s 88; Cotton Merchants 36; Factor's Walk 78; Factorage Houses 78, 95; Founding of Georgia Medical Society 130; Free Negroes 194–95, 205; Negro Orphanage 197; Seaport Activity 23, 78, 86, 88; Slave Port of Entry 24, 94–95, 99–100
Savannah African School 196
Savannah and Atlanta Railroad Company 60
Savannah River 3, 15, 19, 21–23, 25–26, 30–31, 37, 43, 55, 67,

Savannah River *(cont.)*
69, 72, 78, 86, 115, 139, 142–43, 145, 149, 168, 183, 188, 220–21, 226
Savannah River Association (Baptist Church) 148–49
Savannah River District 220
Savannah Steam Rice Mill 221
Savory, George Reeves 200
Savory, Samuel 200
Scotch Highlanders 19, 156
Scotland 25, 149, 187
Screven, George B. 220
Screven, James P. 43, 220–21
Screven, John 81
Screven, Thomas P. 220
Sea Gull (Boat) 174
Seabrook, Whitemarsh B. 158
Second African Baptist Church (Savannah, Ga.) 145–46, 148–49, 154
Second Continental Congress 27
Seminole Indians 29, 187
Senegal 94
Seven Years War 23, 95, 98; Effect on Slave Prices 97
Sharpe, Henry 143
Shepard, Thomas J. 73
Sherman, William Tecumseh 37
Shingles 22–23
Sickle Cell Anemia 136–37
Sierra Leone 94
Silk 17–18, 141
Silk Hope Plantation 26
Simpson, Edward 190–91
Simpson, Jack 191
Simpson, Rosa 191
Singleton, Paul 102
Skidaway Island 110, 195
Skinner, Thomas 65
Slave Drivers 49, 65–67, 69, 75, 208; Cruelty 68–70; Demotions 70; Desirable Traits 67; Duties 69, 71–72; Number Required 67; Relationship with Owners 73–75
Slave Labor 98; Acclimation of New Arrivals 101–102, 130; Classification by Strength 54;
Slave Labor *(cont.)*
Digging Canals 60; Discipline 74; Factory System 8; Gang System 8, 45–46, 61–62, 71, 118, 208; Hiring System 8, 57–61; Law Requiring Presence of White Overseer 71, 73; Number Required 5, 8–10, 25, 93, 207; Summer Heat Hazards 59–60; Task System 8, 45–46, 54, 61–62, 71, 116, 207–208; Women Preferred for Rice Harvest 50; Work Assignments 54–55; Work Clothing 49–50
Slave Overseers 50, 54, 64, 67–69, 71, 81, 84, 117, 122, 133, 143, 208, 221; Desirable Traits 65–66; Manual for Slave Care 132; Relationship With Owners 65–66, 75
Slave Ownership 5–6, 11, 19, 25, 32, 34, 42, 122, 219–26; By Free Negroes 195–96, 199
Slave Population 32, 95, 98, 104–105, 141
Slave Rebellions 18, 99, 183, 192; Denmark Vesey Slave Conspiracy of 1822 193; Encouragement by Spain 18; Linked to Literacy 142; Stono Rebellion of 1739 183
Slave Religion 8, 74, 141–43, 153, 173–74, 177–78, 182, 193, 209–210; African Heritage 159, 162–63; Baptisms 143, 145, 149, 156–58; Brush Arbors 162–63; Church Associations 148–49, 158; Churches 145, 148, 179, 210; Excommunication 148, 156–57; Form of Social Control 74, 154, 157–59, 164, 175, 205; Holy Communion 157; Hymns 145–46, 148, 162, 166; Membership Totals 165; Missionaries and Evangelists 141–43, 156–59, 163–64; Missionary

Slave Religion *(cont.)*
movement of 1830s 158; Participation in White Churches 141, 148, 156, 158–59, 163–65; Praise Houses 159; Religious Freedom 165; Respect from White Community 148–49, 156; Ring Shout Dance 162; Secret Meetings 162; Sermons 163–64; Sunday Schools 154
Slave Trade 19, 43, 69, 148; Action by Plantation Executors 109–11; Advertisements 96, 106–107; African Homelands 62, 94, 96–97, 100, 186–87; Attitude of Owners 111, 156; Buyer Preference for Certain African Homelands 97, 100; Enticing African Natives 101–102; Family Groups 74–75, 102, 105–106, 108–12, 154, 156; Grooming for Market 108; Importation of Slaves Prohibited 99, 101, 103, 189; Imports from West Indian Islands 93, 99; Mortality during Passage 96–97, 102; Mortgage Collateral 106, 112; Physical Examinations of Slaves 108; Regulation of Slave Ship Conditions 96; Reputations of Slave Traders 99; Resale of Slaves 74, 105–107, 176; Slave Prisons 102; Slave Ships 24, 99, 101–102, 167; Smuggling 101–103; Sources of Slaves 94; Use of Merchant Ships 93–94; Value of Slaves 5–6, 40–42, 74, 105–109, 220, 221, 226
Slavery 3–4, 15, 17, 44, 76, 93, 99, 106, 112, 141, 159, 164, 207, 209; Attitude of Owners 206; Changes in Legal Codes 193, 206; Cohabitation 200, 203; Death Penalty for Slaves 184;
Slavery *(cont.)*
Georgia Slave Code of 1755 183; Introduction in Georgia 19–20, 95; Legal Codes 183; Legal Obligations of Owners and Hunting 188; Friendship with White Children 168; Gardening 8, 62, 113, 115–16, 118, 122, 126, 185; Legal Status of Slaves in Court 184; Manumission 9, 143, 176, 184, 188, 192–94, 199–200, 203–204, 206, 208; Moral Obligations of Owners 154; Mutilation of Slaves 184, 187, 190; Negro Act of 1735 (prohibiting Slavery) 17, 19; Patrol System 185; Plantation Laws 192; Prohibitions Against Secret Meetings of Slaves 183; Public Opinion in Georgia, 1735 19; Punishments 184, 206; Resistance of Slaves 191–93; Rights of Slaves to Adequate Food and Clothing 185; Wills of Owners 109–111, 203–204
Slaves: African Heritage 9, 46, 57, 62, 97, 145, 166–67, 172–75, 177–79, 182, 209; African Languages 142, 172–73; Animal Stories 174–75, 179; Artistic Talent 179–80; Assistance of Colonization Societies 204–205; Assistance to British Forces during Revolution 188–89; Attitude of Owners 9, 208–209; Attitude Toward Drivers 71; Burials 58, 180–81; Care of Aged 119; Care of Pregnant Women 133; Care of Slave Children 117, 122; Clothing 81, 118–19, 208, 220; Creolization 181–82, 194, 209; Dancing 159, 166–67, 179; Desire for Freedom 175–77, 190–91; Diet 8, 113–19, 130, 137, 140, 208;

Slaves *(cont.)*
Diseases 136–40; Family Concept 177; Fertility 42, 103–104, 111, 177; Festivities 167–68; Fishing 208–209; Geophagy 117, 138; Gullah Dialect 172–74, 179; Hospitals 133, 136, 138; Housing 8, 119, 121–22, 126, 130, 133, 140, 208; Hunting and Fishing 8, 62, 113, 118, 168, 171, 184, 208–209; Infant Mortality 42, 136–38, 140; Kidnapped by Indians 171; Leisure Activities 61–62, 208; Life Expectancy 132; Literacy 142–43, 146, 153, 163, 172, 183, 185, 190–91, 195–97, 204; Maroon Communities 188; Marriages 177–78; Medical Care 8, 59, 61, 119, 122, 126, 130, 132–33, 136–40, 208, 220; Midwives 136; Mortality 130, 132, 137, 140, 221; Mulattoes 104, 158, 187, 194, 199–200, 209; Runaways 18, 84, 98, 119, 149, 154, 175, 184–92; Schools 196–97; Skirmishes with Indians 171; Slave Narratives 70, 101–103, 175, 197; Songs 70–71, 114, 118, 143, 159, 166–67, 174, 176–77, 179, 182; Suicide 68–69; Travel Passes 143, 145; Travel Restrictions 183–84; Use of Boats and Canoes 8, 118, 143, 166–68, 174, 209; Use of Ponies 168; Vaccination for Smallpox 138; Voodoo Practices 178
Small and McNish (Factorage House) 81
Smallpox 138, 187
Smith, Reed 172
Society for the Propagation of the Gospel 141
Soil Types 17
South America 50
South Carolina 3, 18–22, 25, 27, 34–35, 41, 61–62, 66, 71–72, 93–95, 97–101, 107, 137, 148, 172, 182, 192–93, 207, 219; Camps of Runaway Slaves 188; Fertility of Rice Lands 9–10; Indigo Production 28; Land Available for Rice Industry 44; Rice Industry 4–5, 7; Slave Codes 183; Slave Population 98; Slave Rebellions 183
Southern Agriculturalist 226
Spain 17; Encouraging Slave Revolts 18; Encouraging Slave Runaways 186; Spanish Governor at St. Augustine 18
Spalding, Charles 110, 121
Spalding, Elizabeth 110
Spalding, Isham 200
Spalding, Thomas 36, 57, 110, 116, 121, 171–72, 179, 223
Spaulding, Patience 101
Stafford, Robert 122
Stafford, Thomas 168, 200
Star (Racing Boat) 168
Starobin, Robert S. 3
State Bank of Georgia 81, 110
Stephens, Thomas 19
Stephens, William 19–20, 97
Stevens, Henry 223
Stevens, John P. 103, 223
Stevens, John S. 73
Stevens, William 223
Stewart, William A. 172–73, 179
Stick Daddy 179
Stirk, John W. 106
Stoddard, Albert H. 173–74
Stono Rebellion of 1739 18
Sudden Infant Death Syndrome 138
Sugar 23, 57, 76–77, 86, 116, 207, 224
Sugar Cane 57, 223, 225
Sugar Mills 57, 121, 225
Sugar Plantations 8–9, 132
Sullivan, J.S. 139
Sunbury, Ga. 24, 104; Church Associations 148; Imports of Slaves 94; Seaport Activity

Sunbury, Ga. *(cont.)* 23; Settlements by Carolinians 98
Sunbury Baptist Association 148–49, 157, 165
Sunbury Baptist Church 148
Swan, Dale Evans 3
Sweet Potatoes 6, 113, 115, 117–18
Syphilis 140
Syrup 86
Szwed, John F. 172, 178–79

Tabby Construction 57, 119, 121, 133
Tattnall, Josiah 30, 105–106, 203
Taylor, Susie King 196–97
Tecumseh (Boat) 174
Telfair, Edward 29
Telfair Academy of Arts and Sciences (Savannah, Ga.) 180
Terrill County, Ga. 6
Tetanus 137
Tetany 137
Texas 104
Thickets, The 86, 121
Thomas, Edward J. 114, 159, 167–68
Thomas, John 178
Thomas Plantation 118
Thorpe, Ed 102
Tides 15, 46, 48
Timber 22–23
Tobacco 62, 76–77, 99–100, 103, 116, 119, 207
Tobacco Plantations 9
Tompkins, Lawrence 203
Tompkins, Matilda 203
Trees 15, 17
Trieste, Italy 88
Troumontaine, Julian: *See* Fromotin, Julien
Troup, Daniel H.B. 224
Troup, James R. 224
Troup Square (Savannah, Ga.) 153
Trustees of The Colony of Georgia 17–20, 37
Tubman, Emily 205
Tubman, William Vaccanarat Shadrack 205
Tucker, John F. 220
Turnbull, Nichol 57, 59
Turner, C.T. 6
Turner, Lewis 139
Turner, Lorenzo D. 172
Turnips 113, 115–17
Turtles 116
Tuscaloosa County, Ala. 195
Tweedside Plantation 31, 34, 109

Uncle Remus Stories: *See* Slaves-Animal Stories
Underwood, Katie 179
Unitarian Church 153
University of South Carolina 179

Vallambrosa Plantation 34–35
Vanstory, Burnette 4
Varnedoe, Nathanial 222
Virginia 22, 94, 109, 137, 143, 203; As Slave Exporter 103–104; Camps of Runaway Slaves 188; Slave Population 98

W.M. Tunno (Factorage House) 78
Wacamaw River 62
Waldburg, George W. 223
Waldburg, Jacob 121, 223
Walnut Hill Plantation 26
Walthour, George W. 223
War of 1812 27, 35, 171, 204
Waring, William R. 110
Warsaw Island 195, 205
Waters, George M. 204
Watt, Alexander 100
Wayne, Anthony 30–31
Wesley, John 141
West Indies 21, 23, 46, 68, 71, 93, 96, 99, 156, 190, 207; Absentee Plantation Ownership 7; Indigo Production 28; Rice Industry 7
Weston, P.C. 66
Wheat 6
Wheeler, Richard 6

Whipple, Henry Benjamin 35, 167
White, Joshua E. 130, 132
White Bluff Congregation 106
White Hall Plantation 66
White Laborers 59–60
Whitefield, George 19–20
Whitehead, John 88
Whitmarsh Island 81
Whitney, Eli 29
Whooping Cough 139
Wightman, William 34
Wilcox County, Ga. 171
Wild Heron Plantation 37, 40, 55, 85
Wilkes County, Ga. 6, 23
William and Mary College 103
William H. Smith and Company (Factorage House) 78
William Moore and Company (Factorage House) 78
Williams, Joseph 156–57
Williams, Rosanna 101
Williamson, Sarah 110
Wilmington Island 102, 221
Wine 17–18
Winkler, Zachariah M. 220
Winn, Effie Wilson 103–104
Winter, Cornelius 143
Winyah Bay Region, S.C. 21
Woodbine, Ga. 102
Woodhouse, Mary 196
Woodmanston Plantation 119
Works Projects Administration 103, 175
World War I 203
Wright, Alexander 21, 25
Wright, Elizabeth Izard 25
Wright, James 20–23, 25, 28, 30–31
Wright, Sarah 109–110
Wylly, Alexander 30

Yamacraw Village, Ga. 143
Young, Clara 163
Young, Francis 106

Zouberbuhler, Bartholomew 141–43

Slavery and Rice Culture in Low Country Georgia, 1750–1860 has been set into type on the Linotron 202 digital phototypesetter in ten point Caledonia with two points of spacing between the lines. The book was designed by Judy Ruehmann, composed by Williams of Chattanooga, printed offset by Thomson-Shore, and bound by John H. Dekker & Sons. The acid-free paper on which the book is printed is designed for an effective life of at least three hundred years.

THE UNIVERSITY OF TENNESSEE PRESS : KNOXVILLE